THE RELIGIOUS LIFE OF INDIA

KABIR AND HIS FOLLOWERS

THE RELIGIOUS LIFE OF INDIA

KABIR AND HIS FOLLOWERS

BY THE

REV. F. E. KEAY, D. Litt. (Lond.)

AUTHOR OF 'HINDI LITERATURE'
ANCIENT INDIAN EDUCATION.' ETC.

GYAN

Published by

GYAN

Gyan Publishing House
5, Ansari Road
Daryaganj, New Delhi-110002
Phone: 011-47034999, 9811692060
E-mail: books@gyanbooks.com

Distribution Network
gyanbooks.com
India, USA, Canada, UK, Australia, France

ISBN : 978-81-212-2368-3 (PB)
First Published, 1931

2nd Impression 2021

Printed at: Gyan Press, Delhi.

The Religious Life of India
Kabir and His Followers
Author: Rev. F. E. Keay

THE RELIGIOUS LIFE OF INDIA

KABĪR AND HIS FOLLOWERS

BY THE

REV. F. E. KEAY, D.Litt. (Lond.)

AUTHOR OF 'HINDI LITERATURE,'
'ANCIENT INDIAN EDUCATION,' ETC.

ASSOCIATION PRESS
(Y.M.C.A.)
5 RUSSELL STREET, CALCUTTA

HUMPHREY MILFORD
OXFORD UNIVERSITY PRESS
LONDON, NEW YORK, TORONTO, MELBOURNE, BOMBAY
MADRAS AND CALCUTTA

1931

KABÎR, WORKING AS A WEAVER AT HIS LOOM, WITH TWO DISCIPLES

Mughal School. Eighteenth Century.

Reproduced by permission from an Oxford University Press illustration of the picture in the British Museum.

EDITORIAL PREFACE

The purpose of this series of small volumes on the leading forms which religious life has taken in India is to produce really reliable information for the use of all who are seeking the welfare of India. Editors and writers alike desire to work in the spirit of the best modern science, looking only for the truth. But, while doing so and seeking to bring to the interpretation of the systems under review such imagination and sympathy as characterize the best study in the domain of religion to-day, they believe they are able to shed on their work fresh light drawn from the close religious intercourse which they have each had with the people who live by the faith herein described; and their study of the relevant literature has in every instance been largely supplemented by persistent questioning of those likely to be able to give information. In each case the religion described is brought into relation with Christianity. It is believed that all readers, in India at least, will recognize the value of this practical method of bringing out the salient features of Indian religious life.

PREFACE

In sending out this book for publication I have to express my thanks to very many persons who have helped me in obtaining information about various matters connected with Kabīr and the Kabīr Panth. This has been gathered from many places. There are other points on which I should have liked to have obtained information, but the Kabīr-panthī centres are widely scattered and not always in accessible places; and it has not been possible to visit more than a few of them.

There are many matters in connection with the literature which still need elucidation; and if some day a competent Hindi scholar with sufficient leisure to make a critical study of the texts should be forthcoming, he may be able to throw light on some of these problems.

In spelling Hindi words and names, it is not easy to be consistent. If one keeps strictly to the transliteration of them as they are spelt and pronounced in Hindi, the form may sometimes appear strange to those who are accustomed to see them in the Sanskritized form which is generally adopted in books on Indian subjects. I have, therefore, had to use my discretion even at the risk of some inconsistency. In the case of place names and Indian words that are familiar in their Anglicized form, e.g. 'Sanskrit,' 'Hindi,' the diacritical marks have been omitted.

The sources from which the extracts from Kabīr's teaching in the following pages have generally been taken are:

(1) The *Kabīr Kasauti* (a Hindi Life of Kabīr).

(2) *Śrī Kabīr Sāhib ka Jīwan Charitra* (a Hindi Life of

Kabīr) often referred to briefly as *Kabīr Charitra* or *Jīwan Charitra.* Narsinghpur: Sarasvati Vilas Press. 1905.

(3) Ahmad Shah's translation of the *Bījak.* 1917.

(4) Macauliffe's translation of the *Ādi-Granth* (in Vol. VI of his *Sikh Religion.* 1909).

The matter contained in this book was originally presented as a Thesis in connection with the University of London; but it has since been considerably revised, and in parts re-written.

TABLE OF CONTENTS

LIST OF ILLUSTRATIONS

CHAPTER I

THE ENVIRONMENT OF KABĪR

EVERY man is, to a greater or less extent, the product of the times in which he lives, and in order to understand the life of Kabīr it is useful to take a glance at his environment.

Kabīr lived in the fifteenth century after Christ. Politically, this was a time of great disorder in North India. The Sultanate of Delhi had once been a strong government, and had exercised great power, but it was now in a state of decline. It is usual to date this decline as beginning from the disastrous reign of Muhammad bin Tughlak, who ruled from A.D. 1325 to 1351. His reign was a time of rebellion, famine, cruelty and misery. His successor, Firoz Shāh Tughlak (1351–88), was a better ruler than Muhammad, but did little to stem the tide of disaster; and then, after a few insignificant rulers had occupied the throne, came the invasion of Tīmūr in 1398. The few months of his stay in India were a terrible time for the inhabitants of the places through which he passed. Delhi was sacked, and its inhabitants put to the sword, and wherever he went there was massacre and pillage. When Tīmūr returned to his own land, he left behind him famine, pestilence, and anarchy. The year of his invasion (A.D. 1398) is the traditional date of the birth of Kabīr; and though he was probably born somewhat later, there must have been many persons living during his boyhood who had witnessed and survived that time of sickening horrors.

After the departure of Tīmūr, the Sayyids became rulers of Delhi; but their power only extended over the city and a very small territory adjoining. Then in 1450, Bahlol Khān, an Afghan of the Lodī tribe, who had been Governor of the Panjab, seized the throne. He was a rough soldier who cared little for pomp. He conquered the kingdom of Jaunpur, and also recovered a certain amount of control over other territory formerly belonging to the rulers of Delhi. But his power was very limited and depended on his keeping on good terms with his Afghan nobles, who were very turbulent and unruly. On his death his son, Nizām Khān, was chosen by the nobles to succeed his father. He took the royal title of Sultan Sikandar Ghāzī, but is generally known as Sikandar Lodī. He reigned from 1489 to 1517. This was the sovereign who came in contact with Kabīr, and who is said to have banished him from Benares. Many legends are told as to what happened at their meeting. Sikandar Lodī was, like his father, dependent on his Afghan nobles. Though often lax himself in his religious observances, he was a bigoted Muhammadan, and very hostile to Hinduism. He destroyed many Hindu temples, and in other ways also troubled the followers of the Hindu religion. But though he and his father did something to hinder the decay of the power of the Sultanate of Delhi, they could only delay the impending disaster. The Mogul invaders were already at the door; Sikandar's son and successor, Ibrāhīm Lodī, was in 1526 defeated and slain at Panipat by Bābur, and the empire passed into the hands of abler and stronger rulers.

During the period of the Sultanate of Delhi, the Hindu religion had been exposed to constant danger. The more ruthless sovereigns, or governors of provinces, often carried out wholesale massacres and destroyed Hindu shrines, while even milder rulers often used force to bring about conversions to Islam. The *Jizya*, a tax on non-Muhammadans, was generally enforced, and many at least of the poorer and less educated Hindus could not resist the temptation to become Muhammadans in order to avoid the imposition. Yet in spite of persecution, Hinduism flourished, and this was a period marked by the growth of the teaching of *bhakti*, one of the greatest conceptions of the Hindu faith.

Bhakti, which means devotion or loving faith, involves the idea of God as a personal Being; and it has its beginnings far back in the history of Hinduism. For a time indeed it was overshadowed by the 'monism' of Śaṅkara (often called Śaṅkarāchārya) whose exposition of the Vedānta left no real place for a personal God, except as a creation of the empiric mind. But at a later period, bhakti ideas were revived. Leaving aside such theistic movements as were associated with the worship of Siva, like that connected with Mānikka Vāchakar (about A.D. 1100) we may say that the great leader of the revival of theism was Rāmānuja, a worshipper of Vishṇu, who lived about A.D. 1100. Like Śaṅkara he wrote a commentary on the *Vedānta-sūtras*, which is known as the *Śrī-bhāshya*. In this he opposed the teaching of Śaṅkara, and claimed that his system of *Viśishṭādvaita*, or modified monism, was the true teaching of the Upanishads. The Supreme God is called Vishṇu and is personal; man's spirit is an *aṁśa*, or portion of God; but even when finally re-united to God, it retains its own individuality and consciousness. He held very strongly the doctrines of incarnation and of bhakti.

The teaching of Rāmānuja gave a great impulse to the Vaishṇava form of Hinduism; and in the centuries before Kabīr the Bhakti Movement developed greatly in North India. Hindus recognize two principal incarnations of Vishṇu, namely, Kṛishṇa and Rāma. Some regard Kṛishṇa as the Supreme God and pay their devotions to him, while others choose Rāma for their deity. Both divisions, however, have much in common. They both believe in one personal God who is full of love and pity towards his devotees, accept the doctrine of incarnation, and worship idols. Both hold that the human soul is a portion of the divine, but that it will nevertheless eternally retain its individuality, and that men of all castes can be saved through bhakti towards the Lord. Both make large use of the vernaculars, and exalt the *guru*, or religious teacher, to a place of great authority. Both use a *mantra*, a secret phrase or password which, on initiation, is whispered to the novice by the guru: both partake of a sacramental meal, and have orders of ascetics.

With regard to worshippers of Kṛishṇa, we may notice certain leaders who were contemporary with Kabīr. Between 1450 and 1480, there flourished a Gujarati poet, named Narasiṁha Mehta, who wrote in that language, and possibly also in Hindi, lyrics in praise of Kṛishṇa and his consort, Rādhā. Vidyāpati and Umāpati, about the middle of the fifteenth century, wrote Krishnaite lyrics in the Maithili dialect of Bihari. Mīrā Bāī, a Hindī poetess, who was a devotee of Kṛishṇa, flourished about 1470. Her guru is said to have been Rai Dās, of the *chamār* or leather-workers' caste, who was a disciple of Rāmānanda and a friend of Kabīr. Vallabhāchārya, who was born in 1479 and taught the Krishnaite form of Hinduism at Gobardhan, near Muttra, must have begun his work as a teacher during the latter part of the life of Kabīr. His son, Viṭṭhal Nāth, succeeded him in 1515, shortly before Kabīr's death. It is evident, therefore, that Kabīr's lifetime was a period of great activity, so far as the Krishnaite form of Vaishnavite teaching is concerned.

Amongst those who worshipped Rāma, it was Rāmānanda who gave the greatest impulse to the movement in North India in the period in which Kabīr lived. Rāmānanda lived probably from about 1400 to 1470. He was an ascetic who about the year 1430 began to preach at Benares that the eternal God should be worshipped under the name of Rāma, that Rāma alone is the source of release from the evils of transmigration, and that release should be sought by fervent devotion (*bhakti*) towards him. Rāmānanda was less strict in matters of social usage than the followers of Rāmānuja, though he did not in any way interfere with the privileges of Brahmans. The bhakti sects had long recognized that not only persons belonging to the high castes, but even those reckoned as outcastes, could by means of bhakti obtain salvation, but Rāmānanda seems to have gone one step in advance of this in admitting such persons as *bairāgīs*, or ascetics. Among his personal disciples are said to have been Sena, a barber, Dhanā, a simple peasant who was a Jāt, Rai Dās, the Chamār (a leather-worker and therefore an outcaste) and even a woman; while of special interest to us is the mention, among Rāmānanda's disciples, of Kabīr, the Muhammadan weaver.

Though Rāmānanda may have criticised idolatry, there is no trace of his having given up the worship of idols. Nor was any break made with the Hindu pantheon, or the old mythology. It was left for Kabīr to preach a doctrine of theism which would not tolerate polytheism, incarnations, idols or myths. Rāmānanda's great contribution to the religious life of India was to insist with great vehemence on the absolute value of bhakti, or loving faith in a personal God, as the means of obtaining salvation and all spiritual blessings. It was a religion which appealed to men's hearts, and was therefore more popular than the cold intellectualism of many of the Brahman teachers.

It was possibly Muhammadan influence which made Rāmānanda less strict in social usage than other Hindu teachers before him. Certainly it was this Muhammadan influence which we find to a much greater extent in the teaching of Kabīr. Hindus and Muhammadans had lived side by side for centuries in India, and the Muhammadan population had now greatly increased. Though at first the Muhammadans kept aloof from those they despised as idolaters, it was impossible for the people of the two religions to be kept always apart; and contact with one another meant mutual influence. Even as early as the Tughlak period, the Muhammadans in India were looked upon by their co-religionists elsewhere as little better than heathen, and Tīmūr regarded his invasion as a holy war to rectify this state of affairs. Living side by side, and having often to face the same dangers, Hindus and Muhammadans had learnt to co-operate with, and tolerate, each other. Firoz Shāh Tughlak, who was a zealous Muhammadan, did his best to stem the tide of declension; and when he found Muhammadans who seemed to have adopted the vile rites of Tantric Hinduism, he punished them ruthlessly. Many Muhammadan women, perhaps only recent converts to Islam, were attracted by idolatrous practices. But it was not only amongst the lower orders that Hindu influence was felt. *Sūfīism*[1] is full of Vedantic ideas, and many Muhammadan scholars studied Sanskrit literature and philosophy. During the reign of Sikandar Lodī, a Muhammadan noble, Ahmad Khān, son of the Governor of Lucknow, was accused, though it seems

[1] The Sūfīs are Muhammadan mystics. See below, pp. 90 ff.

unjustly, of becoming a convert to Hindu doctrines. Many Muhammadans in high position in those days were converts from Hinduism, and naturally carried over many of their old ideas with them to the new faith. Hinduism had long held the idea of God as a unity which lies behind all the seeming differences of the universe. But the Muhammadan insistence on the unity of God as a cardinal doctrine, and their view of Him as a Divine Person came to have its influence on some Hindu thinkers. On the other hand the pantheistic thought of Hinduism found many points of contact with the teaching of Sūfiism. In seeking union with God by ascetic practices, and in other ways, the Sūfīs were teaching doctrines which were very similar to those of some Hindu teachers. Two orders of Sūfīs, at least, were probably established in India earlier than the time of Kabīr, and it is possible that he himself in some way came under their influence; even if he was not, as some have thought, himself a Sūfī. It is certain at least that long before the time of Kabīr, Muhammadan and Hindu ideas had been brought into contact and that there was mutual influence. It was his work to develop and extend the movement.

In the days in which Kabīr lived, a development of vernacular literature had already begun. This was helped by the Vaishṇava revival in its various forms, as all the bhakti sects came to use the vernacular. The destruction of Hindu schools and monasteries and the scattering of their scholars by Muhammadan rulers must have given a serious set-back to Sanskrit scholarship. It was perhaps partly on this account that the vernaculars came more into use for religious literature. The followers of Rāmānuja, as well as the other chief sects, largely used Sanskrit for their literature, though they used the vernacular also. Rāmānanda and his successors practically gave up the use of Sanskrit and used the vernacular instead.

Kabīr has sometimes been called the 'Father of Hindi Literature,' though he scarcely deserves the title. Yet it is true to say that he was one of the first great writers of Hindi religious verse, and has an important place in the history of Hindi literature. The first great Hindi work which has come down to us is the *Prithī Rāj Rās* of Chand Bardāī (1191); but till the end of the fourteenth century there was little in the way of Hindi literature that we know of except bardic chronicles. The *Ādi-Granth* (the religious book of the Sikhs) has preserved a few specimens of Hindi religious literature which may be older than Kabīr; for example, the verses of Sadnā and Nāmdev, and also verses of some who were Kabīr's contemporaries, like Rai Dās. Another contemporary was Mīrā Bāī, the Hindu poetess. Vidyāpati and Umāpati in Bihar also belong to this time. This was the period of the youth of Hindi literature; and, in using the vernacular for their religious verses, writers were venturing on new paths. The classical period of Hindi literature did not come till a century later.

Kabīr thus lived in a century when there was much political chaos on account of the weakness of the Sultanate of Delhi. But it was nevertheless a period of great literary and religious activity. The Bhakti Movement in its various forms was making great headway, and was inspiring many to write devotional verse. Perhaps the very uncertainty of life in those days may have helped to popularize a religious movement which appealed to the hearts of men, and offered them consolation amidst the troubles of life in the favour of a God who cared for them, and could be approached in personal devotion by all, whether learned or unlearned. And there were also other influences, as we have seen, leading men to a conception of God as a personal Being, and to a new religious outlook.

According to tradition, Kabīr was brought up and lived in Benares, a town where he could feel all these influences in the fullest degree. This picturesque and venerable city, sacred to all Hindus, with its labyrinths of narrow streets, its numerous shrines with their minarets and balconies and carved oriels, its broad and stately flights of steps leading down to the river Ganges, its temples and schools, its throngs of mendicants and devotees, could not but make a deep impression on a thoughtful boy like Kabīr. Here he would come in contact with, or hear of, religious teachers expounding their various doctrines. Here he would meet pilgrims from all parts of India, bringing (in those days without telegraphs and newspapers) news from other lands and provinces, and telling what others did and thought. Here he would see human life at its best and at its worst. His residence in Benares and his contact there with men of various types cannot but have been a formative influence in the life of Kabīr.

CHAPTER II

THE LIFE OF KABĪR IN LEGEND

NUMEROUS legends are in existence with regard to the birth, life and death of Kabīr. In this chapter we shall see what the legends have to say about him, and in the next try to come to some conclusions as to the real facts of his life.

Seeing that the legends are so unreliable, one might be disposed to pass them over altogether; but apart from the fact that in many cases they probably contain some grains of historical truth, it is important for a true understanding of the Kabīr Panth to know how the followers of Kabīr regard him. The books in which these legends are related seem to be of quite modern origin, though no doubt in many cases they pass on stories which have been current for a long time in the Panth.

THE BIRTH OF KABĪR.—According to the simplest story of the birth of Kabīr, it happened in this way. A certain Brahman attended on the great ascetic teacher, Rāmānanda. One day he took his daughter, who was a virgin-widow, to see the holy man. Not knowing of her widowhood, Rāmānanda wished her the blessing of a son. His words could not be recalled, and when a child was born, the mother placed it on a lotus-flower in the Lahar Talāo,[1] where it was found by a Muhammadan weaver, Nīrū, and his wife, Nīmā. A variation of this story makes Rāmānanda, when he had discovered his mistake, promise that the birth of the child should be miraculous; that he would issue from the palm of his mother's hand, and when he grew up, would reform religion and save the world. The traditional date of Kabīr's birth is A.D. 1398, on a Monday in the bright half of the month of *Jyeshth* (May–June).

[1] *Talāo*, a pond or lake.

A more elaborate setting of the story of Kabīr's birth relates how Gosain Ashṭānanda, a disciple of Rāmānanda, saw a wonderful light descending on the Lahar Talāo and other portents. When he related this to Rāmānanda, the latter replied that the light which he had seen had come in the form of a child who had descended on a lotus-flower, and that its complete brightness would soon be manifest amongst men.

Now Nīrū, the Muhammadan weaver, lived at Benares, and one day he was bringing home his newly-wedded wife, Nīmā. As they passed along the side of the Lahar Talāo, Nīmā, being thirsty, went to drink water, and saw resting on a lotus-plant a large and beautiful child, which she brought out of the tank to Nīrū. There was much discussion as to what they should do with the child; but eventually they decided to take it home and adopt it. According to some the question was decided by the child himself uttering a verse in Hindi, saying that, on account of Nīmā's kindness to him in a previous birth, he had come to their house, and would deliver them from transmigration. This account says also that in a previous birth Nīrū and Nīmā had been Brahmans, but had been born again as Muhammadan weavers on account of their carelessness with regard to religion.

When the time came to name the child, Nīrū called the Qāzī,[1] who came and opened his Quran to find a name. He found there four names—Kabīr, Akbar, Kibra, and Kibariya. All these have the same meaning, coming from a root meaning 'great,' and are used of God. The Qāzī was astonished, and looked again, but could find no other name. The whole Quran seemed to be filled with these four names. Other Qāzīs came, but the result was the same. Then, it is said, the Qāzī advised Nīrū to destroy the child; but, though he plunged a knife into him, there was not a drop of blood, and the child was unharmed. Nīrū, seeing this, was terrified, but the child uttered a verse saying he was not born of flesh, but was light alone. So the name of Kabīr was given to him.

[1] *Qāzī*, a Muhammadan religious functionary.

LEGENDS OF KABĪR'S CHILDHOOD.—One legend says he grew without taking any food. The weaver and his wife however were anxious; and so Kabīr consented to take milk, which was given miraculously day by day by a calf.

Kabīr in his childhood performed many miracles, and to the astonishment of all began to teach other boys about God and to have learned discussions with *sādhus*.

One day a cow was to be sacrificed according to the Muhammadan custom. Kabīr reproached the Qāzī for his sin in killing a cow, and having raised it to life again, disappeared. Only after Nīrū and Nīmā had fasted for three days did Kabīr return home. The Brahmans were very much pleased with Kabīr's protest, but on this occasion it is said Kabīr uttered the following verse, in which he spared neither Hindus nor Muhammadans (called 'Turks'):

> O *Sants* (i.e. holy men)! I have seen the way of both.
> Hindus and Turks heed no warning; to all the taste of their desires is sweet.
> Hindus keep fast on *Ekādaśī*,[1] they eat only *singhārās*[2] and milk.
> They abstain from grain, but do not check the mind's desire: next day they eat the flesh of beasts.
> Turks keep fast and hours of prayer: they cry aloud on the name of God.
> How will they find Paradise? When evening comes they slaughter fowls.
> Hindu and Turk, each has renounced his mercy in his heart.
> One kills by *halāl*,[3] one kills by *jhatkā*[4]; but fire is kindled in both their houses.
> For Hindu and for Turk there is one path; so the *Sat Guru*[5] has taught;
> Says Kabīr, Listen, O Sants: cry 'Rāma'; cry 'Khudā'—it is all one!
> (*Or perhaps*, 'Do not call Rāma God.')[6]

KABĪR ADOPTS HINDU PRACTICES.—When Kabīr began to repeat the names of Rāma or Govinda or Hari, the Muhammadans accused him of being an infidel. And when after some days he put on his neck a Hindu sacred thread

[1] The eleventh day of the half-month, observed as a fast.
[2] *Singhārās*, water chestnuts.
[3] The orthodox Muhammadan formula when an animal is killed.
[4] The orthodox Hindu method of killing an animal.
[5] *Sat Guru*, true teacher; a title of Kabīr.
[6] *Bījak*, *Śabda* 10. For the *Bījak* and its sections, see pp. 51 ff.

and on his forehead a sect-mark, the Brahmans also were angry, and told him these were not the signs of his religion but of theirs. They also reproached him with having no *guru* (religious teacher) and told him that no one could obtain salvation without a guru. To remedy this defect Kabīr decided to try and become a disciple of Rāmānanda; and knowing that this great teacher probably would not accept a Muhammadan weaver as his disciple, Kabīr resorted to a stratagem. It was the custom of Rāmānanda to go out at four o'clock in the morning to bathe in the Ganges. One day when he was going to bathe, Kabīr went and lay in his path. Rāmānanda came along wearing wooden sandals, which struck against Kabīr's head. When Kabīr began to cry, Rāmānanda stood still and placing his hand on the boy's head said, 'Don't cry: say "Rām, Rām!"' Kabīr stopped crying and said 'Gurujī, can *I* say "Rām, Rām!?"' Rāmānanda replied, 'Yes, say, "Rām, Rām!"' and Kabīr repeated the words. Going to his own house Kabīr put on the garb of a Vaishṇava ascetic and claimed that he had become a disciple of Rāmānanda. The Hindus were angry and went to ask Rāmānanda if he had made a Muhammadan weaver his disciple. This he denied; but, when the boy was brought before him and related what had happened, Rāmānanda acknowledged Kabīr as his disciple. Some versions of this story add many marvels; saying for example, that Kabīr miraculously assumed the form of a little child, and so on.

KABĪR REFUSES CIRCUMCISION.—At this point in the story many place the attempt to circumcise Kabīr, though in some accounts it is placed earlier. It is said that when Kabīr's foster-parents found they could not restrain his Hindu proclivities, they determined to have him circumcised; and, on an appointed day, the weavers assembled together and the Qāzī was called. Kabīr however exhibited such strange portents that the Qāzī was terrified, and on this occasion Kabīr is said to have uttered the following verses:

> Vain-glorious of authority, you make me to be circumcised; never will I endure it, brother!
>
> If it is God that makes thee to be circumcised, why came not this cutting of itself?

If by circumcision one becomes Turk, what then will be said of your women?
'Half the body,' so the wife is styled; then you still remain Hindu!
By putting on the sacred thread, does one become a Brahman?
What hast thou given to women to wear?
She from birth is but a Śūdra! Why dost thou eat the food she brings, O Pāṇḍe?[1]

KABĪR AND RĀMĀNANDA.—According to some accounts, Kabīr lived with Rāmānanda as his disciple and was respected by all the other disciples as foremost. He is said to have shown miracles to Rāmānanda on several occasions, and to have given instruction to his guru. One story of this period must suffice. On one occasion when Rāmānanda wanted to perform the *Śrāddha* ceremony for his departed guru, he sent his disciples to get the milk which was required. While the other disciples went to those who sold milk, Kabīr went to a place where the bones of dead cows were lying, and there asked for milk. When he was asked to explain to the guru this strange conduct, he replied that he thought the milk of dead cows to be most suited to the dead guru.

KABĪR'S HOME-LIFE.—Most accounts of his life, however, imply that Kabīr continued to live with his foster-parents, and followed his trade as a weaver, while at the same time receiving and serving sādhus and mendicants. He often seemed to his family to be neglecting his trade. The complaints of Nīmā are described in the following verse:

Thou art always rising early and bringing fresh utensils; thy life hath gone in plastering cooking-squares;
Thou payest no attention to thy weaving; thou art engrossed in the pleasure of saying 'Rām, Rām!'
Who in our family hath ever uttered the name of Rāma? Since this worthless son of ours began to wear a rosary, we have had no peace.
Hear, wife of my eldest brother-in-law! Hear, wife of my youngest brother-in-law! a wonderful thing hath occurred;
This boy hath ruined our weaving business; why is he not dead?

Kabīr replied to his mother as follows:

The one God is the Lord of all happiness; the guru hath granted me His name.

[1] *Bījak*, *Śabda* 84.

He preserved the honour of the saint, Prahlād, and destroyed Harnakhas with Narsiṅha's claws.
Prahlād abandoned the gods and ancestors of his house and embraced the instruction of his guru, Nārada.
Saith Kabīr: God is the destroyer of all sin; He saveth his saints.

Many of Kabīr's poems are connected with his work as a weaver. To a sādhu, who urged him to give up this mean employment, he is said to have replied as follows:

Weaver, weave the name of Hari, on which gods, men and *munis* (sages) are meditating.
He stretched the warp and took the shuttle. The four Vedas are the wheel.
One beam is Rāma Nārāyaṇa, fulfilling the purposed work.
He made the ocean of the world a trough; therein he kneads the starch.
The body of that starch is stiffened: few know that it is starch.
Moon and Sun, they are two treadles; in mid-ocean the warp is made.
As the Lord of the *tribhuvana* (three worlds) brushed on the starch, Syāma joined the broken ends.
He set the pegs, and when he took the reed, then Rāma was bound.
As the reed beats up the warp, the three *lokas*[1] were bound: none he left free.
The three lokas were made one loom; the warp worked up and down.
The Eternal Purusha bade me to sit beside him; Kabīr entered into Light.[2]

One day, it is said, Kabīr was sitting in the market, selling the cloth he had woven. He asked for a price of five *takas*,[3] but no one would offer more than three. Then a broker came along and offered to help Kabīr. He at once put up the price and asked for twelve takas, and eventually sold the cloth for seven takas out of which he paid Kabīr five, retaining the balance. Kabīr then said:

I speak the truth, and no one heeds; but lies the world believes.
Witness this cloth, worth takas five; but seven *he* receives.[4]

THE LEGEND OF LOI, KABĪR'S WIFE.—According to Muhammadan tradition, the wife of Kabīr was named Loi. Hindus however are very careful to explain that she was

[1] *Loka*, world. [2] *Bījak*, *Śabda* 64.
[3] A *taka* was a coin of those days.
[4] *Śrī Kabīr kā Jīwan Charitra*, 1905 edition, Narsinghpur, p. 14.

not his wife, but only his disciple, while some accounts of Kabīr omit mention of her altogether.

When Kabīr was about thirty years of age, it is said he was once wandering in the forest and reached the hut of a certain sādhu, where he rested. He found there a girl of about twenty years of age who asked him who he was. He replied, 'Kabīr.' She then asked his caste, to which question again he replied, 'Kabīr.' She asked his order, and again received the answer, 'Kabīr.' She then asked his name, and was told it was 'Kabīr.' The girl was much surprised and said she had seen many sādhus but never one who answered in this fashion. Kabīr replied that all others had name and caste and order, but he had none. Meanwhile six sādhus had arrived, and the girl brought seven cups of milk and set one before each. Kabīr did not drink his milk, but said he was keeping it for another sādhu who was on the further bank of the Ganges. Before long, to the astonishment of all, this sādhu appeared. In further conversation, it came out that once a sādhu had lived in this hut, who one day saw something in the middle of the Ganges wrapped in a woollen cloth and carried along by the stream. On getting hold of it he found a girl-child, whom he brought to his hut and reared with milk. Because he had found her wrapped in woollen cloth (loi) he named her Loi. On his death-bed he had told her that one day a saint would come and be her guide. The end of it was that Loi became a disciple of Kabīr and followed him to Benares. Loi, it is said, learned Kabīr's trade, and also worked as a weaver, though the accounts generally try to make it clear that she was not his wife, but his disciple. Sikh traditions, preserved by Macauliffe, say that Loi, no less than Nīmā, was alarmed at his neglect of his weaving and also at his constant entertainment of holy men. On one occasion Loi refused to prepare a meal for a sādhu and was sharply rebuked by Kabīr. Loi afterwards pleaded for forgiveness; and the verses spoken on these occasions are given in the legend.

Kabīr's Children.—Two children, Kamāl and Kamālī, who lived in Kabīr's house, were not, it is said, his offspring, but adopted by him. One day, when Kabīr was walking on the banks of the Ganges with a certain Shaikh Taqqi,[1] the corpse of a child was seen floating by. Shaikh Taqqi challenged Kabīr to raise it to life. This he did, and taking it home he adopted it as his own son. The Shaikh said, 'You have indeed shown great perfection (*kamāl*). So the boy was named Kamāl. The story of the coming of Kamālī is similar. According to some accounts she was a child who had died in the house of a neighbour and Kabīr raised her to life; according to others, the daughter of Shaikh Taqqi, who had already been eight days in the grave.

Of the after life of Kamāl, little is recorded. A couplet which is preserved in the *Ādi-Granth* is as follows:

> Kabīr's family was ruined when his son Kamāl was born.
> Ceasing to remember Hari, he brought home wealth.

Some say that when Kamāl grew up, he opposed his father's teaching, and composed verses in refutation of it. Some, however, explain this verse in other ways. One tradition makes Kamāl not the son, but a disciple of Kabīr, who in his turn became the guru of Dādū, founder of the Dādūpanthī sect. Another story connects Kamāl with Shaikh Taqqi, and says that as he differed from his father, Kabīr, the Shaikh gave him permission to settle at Jalalpur, some ten miles from Jhuṣi.

With regard to Kamālī, the following story is told. When she was twenty years of age she was one day drawing water from a well. A Brahman, who was thirsty, asked for a drink, but was afterwards horrified to find he had taken water from a weaver's daughter. Kabīr was consulted, and the Brahman complained bitterly that the girl had broken his caste. But Kabīr replied as follows:

> O Paṇḍit, think, when thou drinkest water.
> In the mud-dwelling, wherein thou sittest, the universe is contained:
> Where fifty-six *kotis* of Yādavas[2] perished, eighty-eight thousand men and *munis*:
> At every step prophets are buried, they decayed to dust therein.
> Fish, tortoise, and crocodile there gave birth, the water is filled with blood.

[1] For Shaikh Taqqi, see below, p. 36 f.

[2] A *koti*, ten millions. The Yādavas were the tribesmen of Kṛishṇa.

The water of the river flows in through its channels; men and cattle dissolved in it.
The bones are dissolved and the marrow melted; how else comes the milk?
Thou, O paṇḍit, thou didst sit down to drink; yet the earthen pot thou accountest defiled.
Renounce the Vedas and the Book, O paṇḍit; all these are fictions of the mind.
Kabīr says, Hear, O paṇḍit; these are your pious deeds.[1]

The paṇḍit, whose name was Har Deva, then fell at the feet of Kabīr and begged him to receive him as his disciple. Kabīr accepted him, and Kamālī was given to him in marriage.

KABĪR'S TRAVELS.—According to the legends, Kabīr was a wide traveller; and even visited distant places such as Balakh and Bokhara.

On one occasion it is said that he went to Jhūsī to visit Shaikh Taqqi, who was then his *pīr*.[2] In response to a request for food, Kabīr was provided only with vegetables, cooked rice, and spiced milk. Feeling aggrieved at receiving this somewhat meagre fare, Kabīr exclaimed:

Greens, rice, and this spiced whey:
In my *pīr's* house, no more than they?

Shaikh Taqqi replied:

Clod, what more would your stomach get?
Before you six months' plague I set![3]

After which, Kabīr suffered for six months from dysentery, and the watercourses at Jhūsī where he dwelt during this time are still pointed out, one of them being known as Kabīr Nāla.[4] But most accounts of Kabīr's life only speak of Shaikh Taqqi as the rival and enemy of Kabīr.

Many stories are told of things which happened at places which Kabīr visited during his wanderings. These are generally embellished with the miraculous; in fact, Kabīr appears in them often as one endued with divine power. Many of the legends record the great opposition he received

[1] *Bījak*, *Śabda* 47.
[2] *Pīr*, a Muhammadan religious teacher.
[3] Ahmad Shah's *Bījak*, p. 8. [4] *Nāla*, a ditch or small stream.

and the attempts made to humiliate him, all successfully overcome through miraculous events which took place on his behalf. Other stories are told of his discussions with various opponents. One of these was Gorakhnātha, a celebrated *yogī*.[1] Another was Sarvānanda, a conceited young Brahman paṇḍit, who claimed the title of *Sarvajīta*[2] because no one could stand against him in argument. Both of these had, in the end, to acknowledge themselves defeated, because of the miraculous power which Kabīr displayed.

A Muhammadan *faqīr*[3] named Jahāngast, having heard of Kabīr, went to see him. Kabīr hearing of his coming tied up a pig at his door. The faqīr, seeing the pig, went away disgusted; but Kabīr called him back and said:

> I have tied up what is unclean at my door, but you have tied up what is unclean in your heart. Anger, pride, avarice, etc., are unclean; and these are inside you. What you think to be unclean is not unclean; but anger is unclean.

So the faqīr became a disciple of Kabīr.

KABĪR AND NĀNAK.—Nānak, the founder of the Sikh religion, is said to have met Kabīr, and to have treated him with great affection and respect. On one occasion when Kabīr was visiting Nānak and wanted milk, he caused it miraculously to flow from a five days' old calf, to the great astonishment of Nānak.

Once, when people began to flock in great numbers to Kabīr, so that his meditations were interrupted, and he had little time to spend in devotion to God, he resorted, it is said, to a strange plan to keep people away from himself. He pretended to be drunk, and went round the city with his arm round a courtesan's neck. The pious were scandalized and people ceased to come to him, thinking he must really be a wicked man.

RĀJĀ BIR SIṄHA.—Among Kabīr's disciples were some of high position. One of these is said to have been Rājā Bīr Siṅha. One story of his meeting with Kabīr is as follows: The rājā had built for himself a beautiful palace at Jaunpur, and when it was completed he invited many friends to a great feast. All admired the new building,

[1] *Yogī*, ascetic. [2] *Sarvajīta*, All-victorious. [3] *Faqīr*, holy man.

except a sādhu who was present, who said that it had two serious defects. When asked what these were, he said that the first was that the building would not last for ever, and the second was that its owner would pass away even before the building. The rājā at first was angry, but eventually recognizing the unknown sādhu as Kabīr, he fell at his feet and acknowledged him as his guru. On this occasion Kabīr expressed his thoughts in the following poem:

> You built a spacious palace, and called many together to make it famous:
> You crowned it with a dome of gold, but in a moment's space you will go and leave it all, says Kabīr.
> Though a house be built and decked with emeralds and diamonds worth millions.
> It cannot be seen but for four short days; death will come and destroy it.
> The houses where seven *Śabda's*[1] sounded, and rejoicing was made from door to door, are empty and crows abide there.
> Says Kabīr, for ten days only may your drum be heard; thereafter this city, quarter and street, you will see no more.
> Says Kabīr, after death none will remember your name; all will run to the inhabited city.
> Madman, thou hast forgotten death; this body will be mingled with the earth, as the salt in the flour.[2]

In Gujarat, a Solankhi Rājā and his consort asked for the blessing of a son; Kabīr granted this blessing, and when he was born promised that his race should rule for forty-two generations. Kabīr, it is said, established him at Bandhogarh,[3] and the present Rājā of Rewah is a descendant of this family.

DHARM DĀS.—With regard to Dharm Dās, a famous disciple of Kabīr, who became a leader of the Kabīr Panth in the Central Provinces, there are different accounts. All agree that he was a wealthy merchant of Bandhogarh, and by caste a *Baniyā*. According to one account he was, even in his childhood, very religious, and spent much time and wealth in the worship of images, and other pious works. He first met Kabīr when on a pilgrimage to Muttra, and

[1] *Śabda*, sound or word; also a section of the *Bījak*.
[2] Ahmad Shah's *Bījak*, p. 15.
[3] The old capital of what is now Rewah State. It was destroyed by the Emperor Akbar.

after some days he met him again at Benares. He heard Kabīr speaking against idolatry, pilgrimages, and other Hindu practices. The priests were very angry with him, but Dharm Dās checked their anger and conversed for a long time with Kabīr. After seeing a miracle which Kabīr worked for his benefit, Dharm Dās became a disciple. His wife, Āmīn, and his elder son, Chūrāmaṇi, also became disciples; but the younger son, Nārāyaṇ Dās, refused, and persisted in regarding Kabīr as a heretic and a magician.

Another account says that Dharm Dās was present when a great discussion was going on between the paṇḍits and Kabīr. He was very much impressed by the simplicity and directness of Kabīr, which contrasted very favourably with the hair-splitting of the paṇḍits and their pedantic quotations from the Vedas and other books. Being convinced of the truth of Kabīr's teaching, he requested Kabīr to accept him as his disciple, but was told to wait. Later on at Muttra he was one day cooking his food and saw that the wood for his fire was full of ants. While he was grieving that one meal must mean the destruction of so many living creatures: Kabīr came up and addressed him in the following *sākhī*:[1]

> Life cannot be sustained but at the cost of life; life preys on life;
> How can mercy be shown to all living? O man, consider![2]

Again Dharm Dās asked to be initiated as a disciple, but was again told to wait. A third time Kabīr met him in Bandhogarh, and the faith of Dharm Dās was still further strengthened. Kabīr now bade him sell all his possessions and keep only a blanket for his covering. His wife, Āmīn, also became a follower of Kabīr.

KABĪR AND SIKANDAR LODĪ.—The persecution of Kabīr by the Emperor Sikandar Lodī figures in all the accounts, but the stories of this vary greatly.[3] According to one account, the enemies of Kabīr, Hindu and Muhammadan, went to the emperor in full daylight with blazing torches to make complaint. They said that his realm was in darkness since Kabīr, who was a Muhammadan, had put on

[1] *Sākhī*, couplet. [2] Ahmad Shah, op. cit. p. 17.

[3] See e.g. Ahmad Shah, op. cit. pp. 24–26; *Jīwan Charitra*, pp. 27–30.

a sacred thread and cried everywhere, 'Rām Rām!' Shaikh Taqqi, who was the pīr of the emperor, and very jealous of Kabīr, supported their complaints. The emperor hearing of this was very angry, and sent for Kabīr, who did not however arrive till the evening. When he arrived, he did not make obeisance, and when told to do this he replied that he had not learnt to make obeisance except to God. The emperor asked him why he had delayed in obeying the royal summons. Kabīr replied that he had been engaged in watching a spectacle. When asked what this was he said that he had seen a passage smaller than a needle's eye through which thousands of camels and elephants were passing. The emperor accused him of being a liar, to which he replied:

> O Kabīr, speak not untruth.
> None knows what may be in the fourth part of a second.
> O Kabīr, a drop has entered into the sea, all know it.
> But the sea has entered into a drop; few can understand.
> The outward eyes are perished; the mind's eyes are perished.
> O Kabīr, he who has lost all four [eyes]—what can one find in him?

When asked by the emperor to explain his meaning Kabīr replied:

> O Shāh, see how far away from each other heaven and earth and the sun and moon are. In the vast spaces between how many camels and elephants and other beings go to and fro. All these are seen in the pupil of the eye. Is not the pupil of the eye like the eye of a needle?

The emperor was satisfied with the explanation of Kabīr, and dismissed him. But the enemies of Kabīr were very much displeased that he had been let off; and Shaikh Taqqi and the others again accused him to the emperor as being a disturber of the peace, hateful alike to Hindus and Muhammadans, one who habitually associated with low-caste reprobates and women of bad character. So the emperor again sent for Kabīr, and told him how the people had accused him. Kabīr replied:

> That I know all to be one, what cause of grief is that to others?
> If I am dishonoured, I have lost my own honour: others need pay no heed.

Mean I am, and with the mean I would be numbered; I have no hire with others.
For honour and dishonour I care not; he whose eyes are opened, he will understand.
Kabīr says, Honour is based on this. Renounce all else, sing only Rāma.
Till now I have fared well: this one case alone remains.
When this soul is seized by Yama,[1] will this honour stand or vanish?

The Qāzīs present then demanded that he should live as a true Muhammadan; but Kabīr answered that he knew not the difference between Hindu and Muhammadan, for in all hearts there was but one Master. Then they accused him of being only a low-caste weaver, and yet calling himself Kabīr, which was a name of God. The emperor then asked him what his real name was. To this Kabīr replied:

My name is Kabīr; all the world knows this.
In the three worlds is my name; and happiness is my abode.
Water, air, the seasons, thus I created the world.
The unstruck wave thunders in the heaven and Soham keeps time.[2]
I made manifest the seed of Brahma. From the bands of Yama I gave release and made the body clean.
Gods, men, and *munis*[3] do not find the end. Kabīr's saints alone can find it.
By Vedas and the Book none will reach the shore. So deep is the mysterious knowledge.
Hear, O Sikandar: I am a pīr of both religions.

The emperor told Kabīr that this was blasphemy, and that he would go to hell. Kabīr replied as follows:

Into Hell fall Turk and Hindu,
Qāzī, Brahman both deserve it![4]

This brought matters to a crisis; and the emperor gave orders for Kabīr to be bound with chains and put into a boat full of stones, which was then pushed out into the river Ganges and began to sink. Kabīr sank with the boat, and when he disappeared his enemies rejoiced and followers began to weep. But a moment later he was seen seated on

[1] The god of death.
[2] *Soham*, here a name of the Supreme God.
[3] *Munis*, sages.
[4] See Ahmad Shah, op. cit. p. 25; *Jīwan Charitra*, p. 28.

a deer-skin on the water and floating up against stream. Then people came to the emperor and requested that Kabīr should be cast into the fire. He was bound in a basket and the fire heaped round him, but when the fire had died down Kabīr walked out unharmed. Then the enemies of Kabīr cried out that he was an infidel and a magician, and demanded that he should be trodden under foot by an infuriated elephant. Kabīr was then bound hand and foot, but when the elephant was brought it would not go near Kabīr, and the driver called out that there was a lion in front of the elephant frightening it. The emperor being very angry, himself got on the elephant; but when he found the words of the driver were true, he prostrated himself at the feet of Kabīr, asked pardon for his fault, and requested Kabīr to punish him as he wished. Kabīr replied:

> For him who sows thorns for thee, do thou sow flowers:
> For thee the harvest will be flowers; but for him sharp pains.

There is also a much more elaborate account than this of Kabīr's meeting with the Emperor Sikandar Lodī. In this Rāmānanda also appears, whom the emperor kills and Kabīr raises to life. Kabīr cures the emperor's sickness, and performs various marvels, and after all kinds of attempts have been made to put him to death comes out triumphant.

THE LEGEND OF KABĪR'S DEATH.—According to tradition, Kabīr lived to be 119 years, 5 months, and 27 days old; and his passing took place in A.D. 1518 at Maghar, not far from Gorakhpur, in the Basti District. When he felt that the time of his departure was drawing near, he announced that he was going away to Maghar. According to popular superstition all who die at Maghar must be born again as asses; while death at the holy city of Benares is sufficient in itself to bring salvation. The people therefore urged him not to go to Maghar, and the whole city was overshadowed with gloom at the thought of his going away and was filled with lamentation. But Kabīr addressed them as follows:

> O people, you are simple of understanding.
> As water mingles with water, so Kabīr will mingle with the dust.
> If *Maithul* is your real abode, then your death will be at Maghar.
> One who dies at Maghar will not see death (i.e. will be free from the bondage of death).

If he dies elsewhere, he will bring shame on Rāma.
'One who dies at Maghar becomes an ass!' A fine thing, you have lost your confidence in Rāma!
What is Benares, what the waste land of Maghar, if Rāma dwells in my heart?
If Kabīr leaves his body in Benares, what credit will it be to Rāma?[1]

Rājā Bīr Siṅha, who was a disciple of Kabīr, when he heard that Kabīr would go in two days' time to Maghar and pass away there, gathered his army and marched to Maghar, and waited for his arrival. Kabīr himself was accompanied on his way by no less than ten thousand followers and disciples, all of whom were weeping. The ruler of the country in which Maghar is situated was then a Pathan named Bijlī Khān, who was also a disciple of Kabīr, and who was much pleased to think he would have the honour of performing the last rites for Kabīr. So he too was expecting his arrival.

When Kabīr reached Maghar, he came to the bank of the Ami river, where there was a sādhu's hut. Going into the hut he sat down. Kabīr asked for lotus-flowers and two sheets; and lying down told the people to close the door of the hut. Then Rājā Bīr Siṅha said: 'Gurujī, I will take your body and perform the rites according to the Hindu religion.' But Nawab Bijlī Khān said, 'I will never allow this to be done; I will bury you according to Muhummadan rites!' Kabīr saw that the two were ready to fight, and that blood would be uselessly shed, for their armies were prepared for battle. Then he admonished them both and said to them; 'Be careful, do not discuss this amongst yourselves, and do not use your weapons. He who acknowledges my words will be pleased.' Both armies obeyed, and fighting was averted. Then while all prostrated themselves before Kabīr, and all were filled with grief, Kabīr uttered the following verses:

Sing, O Bride, the bridal song of blessing, to my house has come Rājā Rām my husband.
My body, my soul, are transported with delight. The five elements form his bridal company.

[1] *Bījak, Śabda* 103.

KABĪRPANTHI SĀDHU AT MAGHAR

In the background is the little shrine (without any image) in the garden of the dwelling house which stands north of the maṭhs and has subterranean passages leading to the Hindu maṭh.

He called himself a 'Hindu sādhu,' but his appearance suggested a Sikh. He declined to talk much or to answer many questions.

Rāma Deva has come to be my guest; I am inebriated with the joy of youth.
My body delights in the lake of the Vedas: Brahma himself chants the Vedas.
With Rāma Deva I tread the sacred circle. Blessed, blessed is my lot!
The three and thirty millions of the gods are come; eighty-six thousand men and sages.
Kabīr says, I go hence, wedded with the Purusha, the One, the Immortal.[1]

After this, Kabīr lay down and spread the sheets over himself. He then told the people to close the door and leave him inside, which they did. When the door was closed, a sound came from the room; on hearing which all who were present were deeply moved, and shouted *Jayjaykar*![2] because their guru had gone to the *Satya Loka*.[3]

When the room was opened, nothing was to be seen except two sheets and some flowers in them. One sheet, and half the flowers, Rajā Bīr Siṅha took, and the other sheet and the remainder of the flowers, were taken by Nawāb Bijlī Khān. The body of Kabīr was not seen. In fact, his followers say he never had a body but was only a manifestation of glory. Rājā Bīr Siṅha took his portion to Benares, where he cremated it and buried the ashes at what is now the Kabīr Chauṛā. Nawāb Bijlī Khān buried his portion at Maghar. Both Hindus and Muhammadans afterwards built a shrine at Maghar.

Even after his passing away, Kabīr is said to have appeared sometimes to his disciples. Thus he manifested himself once at Muttra and gave teaching to one whose name was Ratna. He also appeared later to Dharm Dās at Bandhogarh, where he showed to him all the rules for the Panth and what religious duties are required. He told him all about the forty-two generations of his successors and warned him against the deceitfulness of Kāl.[4] Then he disappeared.

[1] Ahmad Shah, op cit., 27; *Jīwan Charitra*, p. 48.
[2] A cry of rejoicing and victory. [3] *Satya Loka*, heaven.
[4] A personification of Time, or the World.

CHAPTER III

THE HISTORICAL KABĪR

THE traditional accounts of Kabīr are so mixed up with legends that it is by no means easy to disentangle from them the true story of his life. Yet if we are to understand the man and his significance, we must make the attempt.

SOURCES OF HISTORICAL KNOWLEDGE OF KABĪR.—As materials for our task, we have first of all the legends themselves, which, in spite of all accretions, do probably contain some germ of historical truth. In interpreting them we must be guided by the known historical facts of the period in which Kabīr lived, and by the likelihood of his circumstances under such conditions.

But we may also get help from the verses of Kabīr, which, especially those in the *Ādi-Granth*,[1] contain many allusions to the events of his life, and tell us much both of his inward struggles, and of his outward difficulties. The verses were composed from time to time, as the occasion suggested, and reflect Kabīr's circumstances, and the feelings and thoughts of the moment. But in using them to reconstruct the details of Kabīr's life, we are met by certain difficulties. First of all, we cannot be absolutely sure of the genuineness of any particular verse which is ascribed to Kabīr, and therefore it would be rash to place too much reliance on details which are recorded only once or very seldom. Where, however, circumstances are frequently referred to in the verses, there seems little reason to doubt that they preserve authentic details of Kabīr's life. Another difficulty is that we do not know the order in which the verses were composed. If it were possible to arrange them in any kind of chronological order, they

[1] See below, pp. 57 ff.

would be of more help in showing the development of Kabīr's inner life and his search after God. Then there is also the obscurity of meaning which is so often found in Kabīr's verses, and we may run the risk of interpreting literally what Kabīr only intended as an allegory. The Sikh paṇḍits reported by Macauliffe give a traditional or invented explanation of the circumstances under which most of the verses of Kabīr in the *Ādi-Granth* were composed. It is obvious, however, that very little reliance can be placed upon such explanations. Sometimes indeed the traditional circumstances seem to fit the verse very well, but very often they do not. Some of the explanations have probably been invented, in order to explain a difficult verse.

With regard to the legendary material, there are many traces of its gradual growth; and the reasons for its enlargement are often not far to seek. Whatever were the circumstances of the birth of Kabīr, he was undoubtedly brought up as a Muhammadan weaver, and had a Muhammadan name. Most of his followers, being Hindus, were anxious to get rid of, or explain away, any circumstances of his life which seemed to be out of keeping with his position as a great religious teacher. Later on, when he had come to be regarded as a Divine Being by his followers, the tendency was to add marvel upon marvel in order to magnify his fame and glory. It is just possible also that some of the more recent enlargements of the legends may have been due to a desire to assimilate the life of Kabīr to that of Christ.

KABĪR'S BIRTH: DATE AND PLACE.—The traditional date of Kabīr's birth is A.D. 1398, and he is said to have lived till A.D. 1518. The latter date is probably correct, and fits well into the facts; but the date of his birth seems placed too early. It may have been with a desire to connect him with Rāmānanda that the date of his birth was placed so early; for Rāmānanda is often said to have died about the year 1410, when Kabīr would have been twelve years old. There is, however, good reason for thinking that Rāmānanda was born about 1400 and flourished as a religious leader from about 1430 to 1470. If, therefore, Kabīr were born about 1440, as has been suggested, and became the disciple of Rāmānanda about 1455, when fifteen years of age, this would fit in well with the circumstances and make Kabīr still an old man of 78 years of age when he died. Nānak lived from 1469 to 1538, and would thus be 29 years younger than Kabīr, which also fits in well. The Emperor Sikandar Lodī reigned between 1488 and 1512 and visited Jaunpur in 1495. These dates also fit in with the probable dates of Kabīr's life.

With regard to Kabīr's birth-place, the *Benares Gazetteer* says he was born at Belhara, a village in the district of Azamgarh; but the tradition is very strong which places his birth at Benares.

Kabīr's Upbringing and Ancestry.—All Kabīrpanthīs admit that Kabīr was brought up in the house of Nīrū (or Nūr Ālī) the weaver, whose wife was named Nīmā. But if he were really their son, he would have two defects in the eyes of Hindus—firstly, because he would be a Muhammadan, and secondly, because weavers are regarded as low-caste. It may therefore have been with a desire to get rid of these defects that his real mother was said to have been a Brahman virgin-widow, and later that a still more miraculous origin was ascribed to him. On the other hand, there is nothing inherently improbable in Muhammadans adopting a waif and bringing him up. Mr. Ahmad Shah suggests that if Kabīr were a Hindu widow's son of illegitimate birth, Gosain Ashṭānanda, who is mentioned in the story, may have been the real father; but there is nothing to corroborate this.

The name Kabīr is undoubtedly Muhammadan. Some Hindus say it is really *Kar-bīr*, or 'Hero (*bīr*) of the Hand (*kar*)' and explain this as referring to his having sprung from the palm of his mother's hand as one version of his birth relates. But this etymology may be dismissed at once as fanciful.

The name Kabīr is not so unusual as the legends seem to indicate. Reference to other persons named Kabīr have been found in history.

Hindu Influence on Kabīr.—There has been a good deal of speculation as to how Kabīr, if he were of Muhammadan origin, could have grown up with such a background of Hindu ideas in his mind. But, in any case, he was brought up in the household of a Muhammadan; and, unless we are to give undue weight to heredity, we must seek other reasons than his having Hindu parents to account for his acquaintance with Hindu thought. It has been suggested that Gosain Ashṭānanda, knowing the boy's real Hindu origin, took care surreptitiously to teach him Hindu ideas. But it seems probable that the explanation is to be found elsewhere. The poorer Muhammadans often take little interest in the education of their children; and here was a clever boy with a strong religious instinct, cast on his own resources, to pick up what information and ideas he could from those with whom he came into contact. There was a spiritual hunger in his heart which was unsatisfied, and if he came in contact with the Muhammadan teachers or *mullas*, their pedantry and punctiliousness as to petty details may have repelled him. But in Benares, with all its temples and pilgrims, there were other influences at work. The religious glamour of this wonderful city cast its spell over him. At that time, Rāmānanda, at the height of his fame, was teaching with earnestness a way of union with God, and of obtaining salvation, which formed a great contrast to the mere ceremonial of many Hindus and Muhammadans. Can we wonder if the boy was captivated, and that he longed to become a disciple? Can we regard it as impossible, under such circumstances, when he was in daily contact with Hindus of all classes, and heard the teaching of the great Rāmānanda himself, that he should have assimilated a vast amount of Hindu thought? Later, indeed, there came a reaction. The teaching he had received was not all he had hoped it would be; and he could see defects in the ideas even of his own guru. Then it was that he struck out a line for himself. But, for the present, he was under the spell of the great teacher, and, in his anxiety to join him as a disciple, was ready to find what means he could to become initiated. This need not mean that to begin with he heard the teaching from Rāmānanda's own lips. At first he would hear of it from those around him; and it seemed to this thoughtful and religious boy to meet his spiritual needs. There is however a probability that he did actually become a disciple of Rāmānanda; for the tradition with regard to this is very strong. Rāmānanda is mentioned in one place in the *Bījak*,[1] namely in *Śabda* 77: 'Rāmānanda drank deep of the juice of Rāma; says Kabīr: I am weary with repeating this.'

In Rabindranath Tagore's *Poems of Kabīr*, p. 36, there is a verse in which Kabīr says: 'I became suddenly revealed in Benares, and Rāmānanda illumined me.'

Kabīr's Domestic Life.—Naturally, the unusual circumstances of a Muhammadan boy becoming the disciple of a Hindu teacher in a conservative society like that which exists in India caused a great flutter. There are many verses in the writings ascribed to Kabīr which corroborate the tradition that Kabīr was misunderstood by his own family, and that his domestic life was not altogether easy. Leaving aside the question as to whether Kabīr was the son, or only the adopted son, of Muhammadan parents, his unusual religious views, which led him to think more of his attitude towards God and the things of God, than of the ordinary affairs of life, seemed to have caused them no little concern. When Kabīr says: 'Kabīr has died by the faults of the world, walking in obsequiousness to the family'[2] (or, as it may be translated, 'Kabīr, man acts out of regard for his family, and thus dieth from worldly troubles') he is no doubt speaking from his own experience. He knew how hard it is for anyone to shake himself free from the influence of his family, and act contrary to their wishes, even when he feels conscience urging him to do so. His mother seems often to have reproached him with neglecting his work and urged him to give up his strange fancies. It would seem not impossible that Kabīr's father (or foster-father) died while he was still a young man, leaving him largely responsible for the support of the family. The following may have been composed when he was reproached by his mother, after his father's death, and urged to give up the ideas which she thought were deceiving him:

[1] For the *Bījak*, see below, pp. 51 ff.

[2] *Ādi-Granth*, *Slōk* 166. For the titles of the sections of the *Granth*, see p. 58.

Say, who is son? Who is father and paternal uncle?
Who dies, who causes agony?
Hari the deceiver has practised deceit on the world.
In separation from Hari how shall I live, O my mother?
Say, who is a man, or who is a woman? (*or*, 'who hath a husband, who hath a wife?')
Reflect on this truth in thy body.
Kabīr says, My mind is reconciled with the deceiver.
The deceit is gone, the deceiver is known [by me].[1]

Kabīr's interest in religious matters, and the time he spent in devotion and conversing with holy men, no doubt meant less application to his business; but Kabīr, believing he was acting in accordance with God's call, relied on him to supply the needs of himself and his family. He refers to this in a verse where he says:

O thou compassionate to the poor, I trust in thee!
All my family I have put into the boat.[2]

It seems however that the mother of Kabīr was greatly distressed at his conduct. She no doubt reminded him that he ought to stick to the work of his caste as a weaver and leave religious matters to Brahmans and Mullas. Her lament is thus versified by Kabīr:

Kabīr's mother sobbeth and weepeth, saying, O God, how shall these children live?
Kabīr hath given up all his weaving, and hath inscribed God's name on his body.[3]

To which Kabīr replied:

While the thread was passing through the bobbin, I forgot my beloved God.
My understanding is mean, my caste is that of a weaver;
But I have gained the name of God as my profit.
Saith Kabīr, Hear, O mother!
The one God will provide for us and them.

The following verse may refer to Kabīr being bereaved of his father and mother, It is true that the phrase, 'My mother has died' is traditionally explained as referring to Kabīr's release from *Māyā* (or illusion). But even then there is no reason why Kabīr may not have found a

[1] *Ādi-Granth, Gaurī* 39. [2] *Ādi-Granth, Gaurī* 61.
[3] *Ādi-Granth, Gūjarī* 2.

spiritual significance in his domestic troubles. In his sorrow Kabīr finds comfort in God as his Father:

> By my Father I have been comforted.
> [My] bed is pleasant, nectar is put into my mouth.
> How shall I forget that Father from [my] mind?
> Having gone onwards [to the next world] the play is not lost.
> My mother has died. I am quite happy.
> [Though] I do not put on a quilted garment, I feel no cold.
> (I am) a sacrifice to that Father by whom I was begotten.
> My fellowship with the Five[1] is dissolved.
> The Five are beaten and put under my feet.
> By remembering Hari my body and mind have become happy.
> My Father is the great Lord.
> How shall I go to that Father?
> When the True Guru meets with [me], the way is shown.
> The Father of the world is pleasing to my mind.
> I am thy son, thou art my Father.
> In one place is the dwelling of [us] both.
> Kabīr says, By me the one is comprehended.
> By the favour of the guru all has become known to me.[2]

WAS KABĪR A MARRIED MAN?—This question cannot be answered with certainty, but the evidence seems to show that he was. For Muhammadans there is no difficulty in regarding him as a married man; for their *sūfīs* are married; but Hindus, convinced that a celibate and ascetic life is of greater sanctity, have taken great pains to explain the circumstances in such a way as to show that Kabīr was unmarried, and insist that Loi, as well as Kamāl and Kamālī, were really disciples. Even so, some of the legends say that Loi went to live at Kabīr's house and learned his trade of weaving, which would not be very likely in the case of a female disciple. There are two poems which certainly seem to imply, if they do not state, that Loi was the wife of Kabīr.

In the first of these, Loi, being alarmed, like the mother of Kabīr, at the neglect of his weaving and also at his constant entertainment of holy men, addresses him thus:

> Thy threads are broken, thy size is at an end,
> Thy reeds shine over the door,
> Thy poor brush hath gone to pieces,

[1] 'Fellowship with the Five' elements means entanglement in the deceits of Māyā (illusion).

[2] *Ādi-Granth*, *Āsā* 3.

May death light on this shaven fellow's head!
This shaven fellow hath lost all his property.
I am persecuted by those [sādhus] coming and going.
Kabīr now never speaketh of his beam or shuttle;
His mind is only concerned with the name of God.
His daughter and sons have nothing to eat;
Men with shaven heads are crammed in, night and day;
One or two are in the house, and one or two are on the way.
We have only a pallet [on the ground]; *they* get a bed [to sleep on].
They rub their heads [with satisfaction] and [carry] books in their waist-bands;
We get parched pulse, they bread [to eat].
The shaven-heads and my shaven-headed [husband] have become all one.

To this complaint Kabīr replied:

These shaven-heads are the support of the drowning.
Hear, O blind misguided Loi!
Kabīr hath taken the protection of these shaven-heads.[1]

Another interesting verse is given below; of which the traditional explanation, given by the Sikh paṇḍits, is that on one occasion Loi refused to prepare a meal for a holy visitor. Kabīr expressed his displeasure. Afterwards Loi in these lines pleads for forgiveness, and the last two lines are Kabīr's reply. It is, however, not impossible to regard the verse as being addressed by Kabīr to God, and that in the verse Kabīr regards himself as a wife wedded to God as husband. This is supported by the use of similar language elsewhere. In this case, the lines would show that Kabīr turned from the sorrows of domestic life to find his consolation in God. He had now no more confidence in Loi, but there was no one between himself and God.

Better is a saw [put on my neck], than that thou turn away [from me].
Cling to my neck, hear my entreaty!
I am a sacrifice [to thee]; turn thy face [to me], O beloved!
Why dost thou turn away from me? (Why) dost thou beset me?
When thou splittest [my] body [in two], I do not move back my limbs.
Though my body fall [to the ground], I do not break my love.
Between me and thee there is no other.
Thou art [my] dear husband, I am [thy] wife.

[1] *Ādi-Granth*, *Gauṇḍ* 6.

Kabīr says, Hear, O Loi!
Now no confidence is put in thee.[1]

Another verse, given below, which may be connected with Kabīr's domestic life, hints that he was actually married a second time. It seems best, however, to interpret it as an allegory; for it would seem improbable that Kabīr married a second time, and there is certainly no tradition to support this. The traditional explanation is that Kabīr's natural understanding was his 'first wife' and his spiritual enlightenment the second; on the other hand, the first wife may be Loi, and the joy of his spiritual enlightenment contrasted with the unhappiness of his married life.

The first (wife was) ugly, of low caste, of ill-boding features; wicked in the house of her father-in-law (and) in her father's house.
The present [wife] is beautiful, intelligent, of auspicious features, easily child-bearing.
It was lucky that my first wife died; may she whom I keep now live through all ages!
Kabīr says, When the younger one came, the good fortune of the elder one ceased.
Now that the younger one is with me, another (husband) is taken by the elder one.[2]

The following verse may refer to Kabīr's domestic circumstances:

The name of my daughter-in-law [was] Dhania (mistress).
Now the name of Rām-janiā is given [to her].
By these shaven-heads my house is made gloomy.
They have put [my] son to the uttering of Rām!
Kabīr says, Hear, O my mother!
By these shaven-heads my (low) caste is done away.[3]

According to the traditional explanation of the above, by the Sikh paṇḍits, as given by Macauliffe, Kabīr's mother addresses him in the first four lines. Dhania was Kabīr's wife, but the holy men who frequented the house called her Rām-janiā, or worshipper of Rām. But as the name is also applied to courtesans dedicated to an idol, Kabīr's mother was greatly offended by it. She also complains of Kabīr devoting himself to religion and neglecting his business. If this is the correct explanation of the circumstances of the verse, the question still remains whether Dhania is to be identified with Loi.

In another verse of the *Rāg Āsā* section of the *Granth*,

[1] *Ādi-Granth*, *Āsā* 35. [2] *Ādi-Granth*, *Āsā* 32.
[3] *Ādi-Granth*, *Āsā* 33.

Kabīr seems to be speaking against the veiling of women. According to Macauliffe it was addressed by Kabīr to the second wife of his son Kamāl. Trumpp, however, translates it as referring to a wife rather than to a daughter-in-law. Macauliffe's translation is as follows:

> Stay, stay, my daughter-in-law, veil not thy face,
> At the last moment it will not avail thee the eighth of a *paisa*.[1]
> She who preceded thee used to veil her face;
> Follow not thou in her footsteps.
> The only advantage of veiling thy face is
> That for five or ten days [people will say]: 'A good daughter-in-law hath come!'
> Thy veil will [only] be real,
> If thou sing God's (i.e. Hari's) praises and skip and dance [in his service].
> Saith Kabīr, O daughter-in-law, thou shalt be victorious (i.e. obtain salvation)
> When thou passest thy life in singing God's (i.e. Hari's) praises.[2]

KABĪR AND HIS CHILDREN.—With regard to Kamāl and Kamālī, the same ideas of Hindu asceticism have probably led his followers to try and show that their coming to Kabīr's house was in an unusual way; but there seems no reason to doubt that they were his children. About twelve miles from Jhūsī, the tomb of a certain Shaikh Kamāl is shown; but it cannot be certainly identified as being that of Kabīr's son.

KABĪR AND THE WEAVER-CASTE.—Kabīr refers to his caste as that of a weaver again and again, and there can be no doubt on this point, whatever other uncertainties are connected with his life-story. Here is one passage:

> By caste a weaver and patient of mind
> Utters Kabīr with natural ease the excellencies [of Rām].[3]

And so in other passages. Many of his metaphors, too, are drawn from weaving.

We have seen in the account of Kabīr's home-life, how he was reproached by his mother and his wife for giving up his weaving. Whether Kabīr did forsake it altogether, or whether he only paid less attention to it than formerly,

[1] *Paisa*, a quarter of an anna, about a farthing.
[2] *Ādi-Granth*, *Āsā* 34. [3] *Ādi-Granth*, *Gauṛī* 26.

and spent more time in religious meditation and teaching, does not seem quite clear. One or two passages might be taken to indicate that he did give up his work:

> The weaver knows his own house; Rāma is known (as being) in his very heart.
> Kabīr says, The workshop is broken up,
> (When) the threads are joined with the threads on the border.[1]

> Turning away [from the world] I have forgotten both caste and lineage.
> My weaving is [now] in the infinite silence.[2]

It does not seem however that Kabīr ever became a wandering sādhu. Indeed he deprecates the practice:

> He who hath obtained God.
> Wandereth not from door to door.[3]

In spite of Hindu prejudices, we must, therefore, regard him as a householder. He may of course have journeyed occasionally to other places. In fact, in *Ramaiṇī* 48 of the *Bījak*, we are told of certain visits he made:

> Through Manikpur Kabīr passed;
> There he heard of the fame of Shaikh Taqqi.
> At the place which is called Jaunpur,
> And at Jhūsī I heard the names of many pīrs.
> There are written twenty-one pīrs.
> They all were giving discourses in the name of the prophet.
> When I heard the talk, I could not refrain myself:
> Seeing these graves, ye are gone astray.
> The works of the friend of God and of his prophet,
> Followed by you in practice only, are become unlawful.
> O Shaikh Akardi and Shaikh Sakardi, listen to my words.
> See the beginning and the end from age to age with open eyes.

KABĪR AND SHAIKH TAQQI.—The above verse is also interesting because of its reference to Shaikh Taqqi. He is mentioned again in *Ramaiṇī* 63 of the *Bījak*, which is addressed to him. His relation to Kabīr is very obscure. In the legends he generally appears as the enemy and persecutor of Kabīr. Some of the stories make him the pīr, or spiritual preceptor, of the Emperor Sikandar Lodī, and jealous of Kabīr, because he thought the latter was replacing himself in the favour of the emperor.[4] On the other hand,

[1] *Ādi-Granth, Āsā* 36.
[2] *Ādi-Granth, Bhairau* 7.
[3] *Ādi-Granth, Mārū* 3.
[4] See above, p. 20 f.

Muhammadan tradition claims that Shaikh Taqqi was the pīr of Kabīr. Bishop Westcott thinks he has found traces of *two* Shaikh Taqqis, either or both of whom may be referred to in the verse last quoted. Shaikh Taqqi of Manikpur Kara in the Fatehpur district was a cotton cleaner by profession and belonged to the *Chistia* Order of Sūfīs, and his descendants are still to be found in that district. He died in 1545, and is apparently the same Shaikh Taqqi who is referred to in the *Khazinat-ul-Astia* (Treasury of Saints) a book published at Lahore in 1868. According to this book Shaikh Taqqi was a weaver and died in 1574, when he was succeeded by Shaikh Kabīr the weaver. The latter is described as being a great spiritual leader and the author of many Hindi writings. It is said that though he taught the Sūfī doctrine of *Wisāl*, or union with God, he was silent with regard to the contrary doctrine of *Firāq*, or separation. On account of his tolerant views he was accepted as a leader by Hindus as well as by Muhammadans, and died in 1594. Kara Māṇikpur was for a short time the military headquarters of the Emperor Sikandar Lodī. It is now the headquarters of the sect of Malūk Dāsīs, or followers of Malūk Dās, who is said to have been born in 1574. The indebtedness of Malūk Dās to Kabīr is apparent. His followers recognize certain Kabīrpanthī works, and when on pilgrimage to Jagannath visit the *maṭh* (or monastery) of the Kabīrpanthīs.

There was however a Shaikh Taqqi of Jhūsī, who belonged to the Soharwardia Order of Sūfīs, and died in 1429. His tomb at Jhūsī is still a place of pilgrimage. If Kabīr met a pīr at Jhūsī, it must have been one of the successors in office of this Shaikh Taqqi; otherwise the dates will not fit. Kabīr is said to have been a young man of thirty years when he first met the Shaikh. It was this Shaikh who is said to have provided the meal for Kabīr mentioned above (page 17). Kabīr is said to have sought from him such a blessing that he might be able to remove the differences which separated Hindus and Muhammadans. The Shaikh however could only promise that both Hindus and Muhammadans should reverence Kabīr. Kamāl was angry when he heard his father's request, and asked the Shaikh to release him from his obligation to his father, for he could not look upon Hindus with favour. The Shaikh allowed Kamāl to settle at Jalalpur, about ten miles from Jhūsī. According to this tradition it was on this account that Kabīr uttered the words (which appear in slightly different versions): 'The family of Kabīr became extinct when his son Kamāl was born.' Previous to the Mutiny of 1857, there was a large mosque at Jhūsī associated with the memory of Shaikh Taqqi. Bishop Westcott thinks there may have been some confusion between the 'twenty one pīrs' ('*ikkīs pīr*') and the 'solitary tree' (*akelā peṛ*) a large tree which is still shown under which a Muhammadan saint used to dwell. Shaikh Akardi and Shaikh Sakardi are said to have been the caretakers of the tomb of Shaikh Taqqi.

We have thus two traditions, one of which makes Kabīr the disciple of Rāmānanda, while another connects him with Shaikh Taqqi. It may have been that Kabīr as a youth came for a time under the spell of the great Rāmānanda, but that later on he also received instruction from Shaikh Taqqi (whether at Manikpur or at Jhūsī, or at both) and that after this, he struck out a line for himself? The relation of Kabīr to the Sūfīs will be discussed in a later chapter.

KABĪR'S SIMPLICITY OF LIFE.—Kabīr seems to have lived a life of poverty. This was due not merely to his neglect of his occupation for religious concerns, but because he seems to have regarded the possession of wealth as a great hindrance to spiritual progress.

> Kabīr says, I have neither a thatched roof, nor hut, neither have I a house or a village.
> I think Hari will ask, 'Who art thou?' I have neither caste nor name.[1]

That he was hard-pressed sometimes for the necessities of life appears from the following verse, in which he asks God to supply his simple needs:

> A hungry man cannot perform service;
> Take back this rosary of thine:
> I only ask for the dust of the saints' feet.
> Since I owe not any man.

[1] *Ādi-Granth, Ślok* 60.

O God, how shall I fare if I am shamed before thee ?
If thou give me not [of thine own accord], I will beg for it.
I beg for two seers of flour, a quarter of a seer of clarified butter and salt ;
I beg for half a seer of *dāl*[1] which will feed me twice a day.
I beg for a bed with four legs to it, a pillow and a mattress ;
I beg for a quilt over me ; and then thy slave will cheerfully serve thee.
I have never been covetous ; Thy name alone becometh me.
Saith Kabīr, My soul is happy : and when my soul is happy then I recognize God.[2]

WAS KABĪR LITERATE ?—Kabīr was most likely an unlettered man. He tells us distinctly :

I am not skilled in book knowledge, nor do I understand controversy.[3]

or again :

I touch not ink nor paper, nor take pen in my hand ; of the greatness of the four ages Kabīr has given instruction with his lips.[4]

The circumstances of Kabīr's caste and upbringing make it very probable that he was unable to read or write. In one place he refers to his provincial dialect as unintelligible to many :

My speech is of the East ; no one can understand me, only he can understand me, who is from the furthest East.[5]

He did not however altogether despise learning. He says :

I know that reading is good, [but] better than reading is meditation (*jog*).[6]

Or, as it has also been translated :

I [first] thought that learning was good, [then] that the jog was better than learning.

It was the knowledge of God, and of the things of God, which Kabīr sought after with all his heart and mind, rather than the learning of the schools.

KABĪR'S UNPOPULARITY.—It was not only in the family circle of Kabīr that he was misunderstood. By many others also he was criticized and despised for what seemed to

[1] *Dāl*, lentil.
[2] *Ādi-Granth, Soraṭhī* 11.
[3] *Ādi-Granth, Bilāvalu* 2.
[4] *Bījak, Sākhī* 188.
[5] *Bījak, Sākhī* 194.
[6] *Ādi-Granth, Ślok* 45.

them his strange ideas. Kabīr evidently felt this keenly, though he held himself up against it, and sought consolation and refuge in God.

> Why do the helpless people censure [me], in whose mind there is no divine knowledge? Kabīr delights in Rāma; all other concerns are given up by me.
>
> I gather no leaves [to offer to idols] and I worship no idols.
>
> . . . .
>
> People say Kabīr is mad:
> But [only] God knoweth Kabīr's secret.[1]

Sometimes Kabīr was the victim of slander, which he takes, however, in good part, realizing that it would in the long run do him good rather than harm, and that evil would recoil on the slanderer's head:

> Slander me, slander me, O people, slander me!
> Slander is very pleasant to the people.
> Slander [is my] father, slander [is my] mother,
> If one is slandered he goes to Paradise,
> The blessing of the Name is settled in [his] mind
> When he, who is of a pure heart, is slandered,
> The slanderer washes then my clothes.
> Who slanders me, he is my friend.
> My thought is in the slanderer.
> He is a slanderer who stops the slander.
> The slanderer seeks my life.
> Slander against me I like and love.
> Slander effects my salvation.
> To humble Kabīr, slander is the best.
> The slanderer is drowned; I cross over![2]

Kabīr was sometimes compelled even to meet with the vilest abuse. He was called pander, dancer, street-walker and thief. Kabīr however defended himself against these attacks, and preserved a quiet dignity amidst it all.

> Now I say, O Rāma, I trust in thee!
> What need have I then to bow to any one![3]
>
> When He (the Supreme) is considered by me as the only one,
> Then why are the people annoyed by it?
> I am without honour, my honour is lost.
> May not any one fall into my track!
> We are tardy, tardy in the mind.

[1] *Ādi-Granth, Ślok* 46. [2] *Ādi-Granth, Gauṛī* 71.
[3] *Ādi-Granth, Gauṛī* 22.

We have no partnership nor fellowship with any one.
Honour or dishonour, we do not care for it.
Then you will know, when the plaiting[1] is laid open.
Kabīr says, The honour of Hari is real (i.e. the honour that Hari bestows).
Give up all and adore only Rāma![2]

KABĪR'S CONDEMNATION OF THE BRAHMANS.—It was the Brahmans especially who opposed Kabīr: and even the legends support this. In rejecting the ceremonial practices of Hinduism and teaching his own doctrines, he was running counter to their prestige and influence, and naturally incurred their displeasure. There are many references to this in Kabīr's verses. They seem constantly to have taunted him with his low caste; but Kabīr reproaches them on the other hand with their ignorance of spiritual truth and failure to show the path of salvation. Thus he speaks:

Thou art a Brahman, I am a weaver of Benares; how can I be a match for thee?
By repeating the name of God I have been saved; while thou, O paṇḍit, shalt be lost by trusting to the Vedas.[3]

Or again:

Paṇḍits have gone astray reading and studying the Vedas; they do not know the secret of their own selves.
Their evening and morning prayers, their six modes of worship,
And many things like these they consider virtuous deeds.
They made the *gāyatri*,[4] to be recited in all four ages;
Go and ask them who has thus found salvation;
If touched by another you wash your body;
But tell me, who is meaner than you?
These are your good deeds, yet you are consumed with pride;
From such pride no one will derive any benefit.
He whose Name 'is the breaker of pride';
How can he tolerate your pride?
They who give up pride of race and attachment and search for the Word[5] alone.
Renouncing the shoot and seed of all desire, these men become freed from body and from space.[6]

KABĪR'S ATTITUDE TO ISLAM.—Kabīr's attitude towards

[1] 'Plaiting' here denotes false show, or imposition.
[2] *Ādi-Granth*, *Gauṛī* 3.
[3] *Ādi-Granth*, *Rāmkalī* 5.
[4] The *Gāyatri* is a Sanskrit verse which is daily repeated by Brahmans.
[5] The Śabda or Divine Utterance.
[6] *Bījak*, *Ramaiṇī* 35.

Hinduism is dealt with in a later chapter, as well as his attitude towards Islam. But we may note in passing that he came into conflict with the Muhammadan maulvis no less than with the Brahman paṇḍits.

> I have seen many pīrs and *auliyas*[1]; they read the Book, the Qurān;
> They initiate disciples and give instruction in such knowledge as they have.
> They sit them down[2] full of vanity, and in their mind is vain glory.[3]

At one time Kabīr seems to have contemplated a pilgrimage to Mecca; but if so, he was led to abandon the idea.

> I was going on a pilgrimage to the Ka'abah, onwards the Lord met with me.
> The Lord began to quarrel with me: 'By whom has [this] ever been ordered?'[4]

There is no indication, however, in what period of his life, or in what stage of his religious experience, this occurred.

KABĪR AND THE GORAKHNĀTHIS.—Gorakhnāth, a famous yogī, figures in the legends as an opponent of Kabīr; but this could not have been the Gorakhnāth who was the founder of the Kanphata Yogīs; for if he is a historical person, he lived much earlier than Kabīr. But a Gorakhnāth is frequently referred to in the verses of Kabīr:

> If the mango and the *maulsi* tree be cut, they bear no fruit; the slit ear will not heal.[5] (The slit ear is a mark of the Goraknāthis)
> O Gorakh, whose renown remains, if he understands not the songs?

This opponent of Kabīr, if the contest has any historical basis, may have been a leader, though not the founder, of the Kanphata Yogīs, who seem to have been very active at that period, for Kabīr frequently ridicules their practices. In those days, many of these yogīs bore arms. It is this practice which is alluded to in the following verse:

> O brother, never have I seen Yogī like this!
> Puffed up with pride he walks, caring for nothing;

[1] *Auliya*, a holy man or saint.
[2] Sit them down; in Hindī, *āsan māri*, sitting like ascetics.
[3] *Bījak, Śabda* 4. [4] *Ādi-Granth, Ślok* 197. [5] *Bījak, Sākhī* 56.

He teaches the religion of Mahādeva;
And therefore is called a 'great *mahant*.'[1]
In market and street he sits in the posture of a yogī;
He is an imperfect *siddha*,[2] a lover of *Māyā*.
When did Dattatreya attack his enemies?
When did Sukdeva lay a cannon?
Or Vāsudeva wind a horn?
They who fight are of little wisdom;
Shall I call such ascetics or bowmen?
They have renounced the world, yet coveting rules their mind;
They wear gold and disgrace their order,
They gather horses and mares.
They acquire villages and go like millionaires.
A beautiful maiden is not fitting in the company of Sanaka and his kind.
He who carries a blackened vessel will one day be fouled.[3]

We can hardly wonder that the outspoken rebukes of Kabīr stirred up many enemies against him. According to the legends, Hindus and Muhammadans joined together to persecute him; and there is nothing improbable in this. It seems that having failed in other ways to silence him they at last appealed to the Emperor Sikandar Lodī, taking advantage of his visit to Jaunpur, which took place in 1495. Jaunpur is not very far from Benares, and Kabīr was summoned to answer the charges against him. He was accused of being a turbulent, quarrelsome person, was always abusing others and causing them offence, and the emperor was urged to take action against him. What transpired is so wrapped up in legend that it is impossible to say exactly what happened. There is a verse in the *Ādi-Granth*, which, if genuine, would at least seem to corroborate the account of his escape from being drowned:

The Ganges is a deity deep and profound; I, Kabīr, was made to stand in it with chains on my feet.
My spirits fell not; why should my body fear?
My mind was absorbed in God's lotus-feet.
My chains were broken by the ripple of the Ganges;
[And I found myself] seated on a deer-skin,
Saith Kabīr, I had no friend or companion
[But] God the Protector both by water and land.[4]

[1] *Mahant*, devotee.
[2] *Siddha*, one who has obtained spiritual perfection; *Māyā*, Illusion.
[3] *Bījak*, *Ramaiṇī* 69.
[4] *Ādi-Granth*, *Bhairau* 18.

KABĪR'S DEPARTURE FROM BENARES TO MAGHAR.—Quite likely it was due to a decree of the emperor that Kabīr left Benares for Maghar; and this is probably the substratum of truth behind the story of his punishment by him. At all events it is certain that Kabīr in his later years left Benares and went to live at Maghar, where he died. Some of the accounts place the removal just before his death. This great crisis in his life is referred to in several verses. Whether Kabīr was driven from Benares on account of persecution, or left it of his own accord, to find a place which would give him more peace from controversy in his declining years, it is certain that the place was regarded as most unpropitious by Hindus.[1] But Kabīr realized that it was not the place where a man dwells, but the relationship which he has to God, which is the all important thing.

> Say, O Rāma, what is now my state?
> People tell me I had little sense to leave Benares.
> [My] whole life is lost in Śivpuri (Benares).
> At the time of death I have risen and come to Maghar.
> Many years I have practised austerities at Kāsi (Benares)
> Death has come on in the dwelling of Maghar.
> Kasi and Maghar I consider as the same.
> How shall I come across by slight devotion?
> Saith Kabīr, My guru Rāmānanda, Ganesha, Śiva, and all men, know
> That Kabīr when dying uttered God's holy name.[2]

> If the hard-hearted one die at Benares, he is not saved from hell.
> If the saint of Hari die at Haramba,[3] he saves his whole relationship.'[4]

> If Kabīr leave his body at Benares, what obligation is he under to God?
> Saith Kabīr; Hear, O people, let no one make a mistake;
> What [difference is there between] Benares and the barren Maghar, if God be in the heart?[5]

KABĪR'S DISCIPLES.—How many disciples Kabīr made during his lifetime cannot be said; but many persons must have been attracted by his earnest and vigorous message.

[1] See above, p. 23. [2] *Ādi-Granth, Gauṛī* 15.
[3] According to Macauliffe, 'Haramba' in the above verse is a synonym for Maghar. [4] *Ādi-Granth, Āsā* 32.
[5] *Ādi-Granth, Dhanāsarī* 3.

THE HINDU SHRINE AT MAGHAR WITH THE *PŪJARĪ*

On the right is a sādhu's shrine (known as 'Kamāl's shrine').

THE MUHAMMADAN SHRINE AT MAGHAR

The legends have many stories of converts being won, but it does not seem that Kabīr organized a sect, or formally admitted disciples. The foundation of the panth[1] seems to have come later.

In one passage in the *Ādi-Granth*, his disciples are alluded to. Trumpp translates the verse thus:

> By Kabīr many disciples and friends were made, but no friend of Keśava.
> They were gone to join Hari, [but their] mind stopped in the midst [of the way].[2]

There are many stories in the legends which speak of Kabīr sitting with other devotees. He seems to have loved the company of those who were really earnest seekers after God. But he had no patience with hypocrisy or mere outward religion. He must often have been a somewhat lonely man, and he spared none in his plain-speaking. There is a reference by Kabīr in one place in the *Ādi-Granth* to two contemporary religious teachers. He says:

> When the body is dissolved, where is the mind absorbed?
> By the favour of the guru, Jayadeva and Nāma (or Nāmdeva)
> Have by love of devotion known [it].[3]

One or two verses of Nāmdeva and Rai Dās are included along with those of Kabīr in the *Ādi-Granth*. Trumpp regards them as quotations by Kabīr of these writers, and if this is so, it would show his acquaintance with their teaching. In the legends, Ravidās, or Rai Dās, the Chamār disciple of Rāmānanda, appears as the friend of Kabīr, though he is also mentioned as holding discussion with him.

THE DEATH OF KABĪR.—With regard to the circumstances of the death of Kabīr at Maghar, little can be said

[1] *Panth*, literally a way, or path, here means a sect.

[2] *Ādi-Granth*, *Ślok* 96. Macauliffe makes this verse to be one of self-reproach on the part of Kabīr; but in either case the fact of his making disciples is referred to. The difference in meaning of the two renderings may serve to show the obscurity of much of Kabīr's verse; for Macauliffe's runs thus:

> Kabīr hath made many disciples and followers, but hath not made God his friend.
> He set out to meet God, but his heart failed him half-way.

[3] *Ādi-Granth*, *Gauṛī* 36.

that rests on reliable historical evidence; but that he did die there seems quite certain, and to-day his reputed tomb there is in the keeping of a family of Muhammadan weavers, while side by side is a monastery occupied by Hindu members of the Kabīr Panth.[1]

KABĪR'S SPIRITUAL LIFE.—What can be said of the inward struggles and spiritual development of Kabīr? Much of this aspect of his life will be dealt with more fully when we come to consider his teaching in Chapter V. But at the risk of some repetition, we must, in order to complete this sketch of his life, give here at least some account of his spiritual development.

We find him then as a man who is face to face with the great mysteries of life, one who thinks deeply with regard to the problems of death and the life beyond:

> Where is thy speaking [soul] absorbed?
> This doubt seizes me daily, and no one clears it up for me.[2]

The answers given by the Brahman teachers and Muhammadan maulvis bring him no peace. They seem to him to be too insistent on the externals of religion and the weary round of ritual and ceremony, which he despises as a hollow sham. But he finds rest for his mind by meditation on God:

> Saith Kabīr, My attention is directed to that place where God dwelleth night and day,
> His secret he himself fully knoweth; he is ever imperishable.[3]

His spiritual awakening is described in two of his verses:

> Kabīr being beaten cried much; in pain he cries [even] more.
> [After] a blow has hit the vital part.
> Kabīr remained dead on the spot.
> Kabīr says: The blow of the spear is easy, in being applied it takes away the breath.
> [But he who] undergoes the blow of the Śabda—of that guru I am the slave.[4]

The meaning seems to be that the Word (Śabda) of the guru which brought to him enlightenment seemed like a heavy blow. All his former ideas were brought to the

[1] For the legend of Maghar, see above, pp. 23 ff.
[2] *Ādi-Granth, Gauṛī* 52. [3] *Ādi-Granth, Gauṛī* 52.
[4] *Ādi-Granth, Ślok* 182, 183.

ground, as with a heavy blow, under which he fainted away. The old Kabīr was dead, but a new Kabīr arose.

In many verses Kabīr shows a deep self-abasement: and whether these were composed before his spiritual awakening, or (as it seems more likely) were dictated by the passing mood of the moment, they are very striking. They show us Kabīr with a deep consciousness of sin within him, and a profound sense of his unworthiness before God:

> How shall I cross the sea, O master? How shall I cross the sea? I am full of many sins.
> How shall I serve and worship thee, how meditate on thee? Only without am I white, just like a heron.
> My nature is a snake's, and I am a great sinner.
> The conscience is foul, and like a cat.
> I see it to be contrary and crazed, wrapt in the cloak of the six *Darśanas*.[1]
> Kabīr says, Listen, O men that are mine: all are caught in the noose of a scheming witch.[2]

The following seems to have been written at a late period of his life:

> Though man leave his home for the forest-region, and gather tubers to live on,
> His sinful and evil mind even then abandoneth not misdeeds.
> How shall I be saved? How cross over the great terrible ocean?
> Preserve me, preserve me, O God! I, thy slave [have come to] thine asylum.
> The desire to gratify my evil passions forsaketh me not;
> Though I make many efforts to guard myself against them,
> I am entangled in them again and again.
> My life hath passed—youth and old age—no good have I done;
> This priceless human life attached itself to a *kauṛi*,[3] and became like it.
> Saith Kabīr, O my God, thou art contained in everything;
> There is none so merciful as thou; none so sinful as I.[4]

The two following occur in the same Rāg:

> Preserve me, O God, though I have offended thee.
> I have not practised humility, the duties of my religion, repetition of thy name, or worship; I am proud, I [wear] my turban on the side of my head.

[1] These are the six philosophical systems of Hinduism.
[2] *Bījak, Śabda* 104.
[3] *Kauṛi* is a small shell used sometimes in India as a coin of very small value.
[4] *Ādi-Granth, Bilāvalu* 3.

Believing this body immortal, I have pampered the frail and perishable vessel;
I have forgotten him who made and favoured me, and I have attached myself to strangers.
I am thy house-breaker and not thy saint; I fall at thy feet for protection.
Saith Kabīr, Hear this supplication, send me not intelligence of death![1]

O Sovereign of the world, Lord of the earth, Mammon hath caused me to forget thy feet.
Even a little affection for thee is not felt by thy slave; what shall thy poor slave do?
Curse on [this] body! Curse on [this] wealth! Curse on this perishable intellect and understanding![2]

The following from another Rāg expresses even deeper contrition:

O God, such sinners are we,
That we have never performed service for that Lord who gave us souls and bodies.
(The passion) to possess others' wealth, children, and wives, and to slander and calumniate others, hath not forsaken us.
We suffer transmigration again and again; this law is not broken.
I have not wandered even for a moment to where the conversation of the saints of God is held.
Libertines, thieves, panders and drunkards—with them have I ever consorted.
My possessions are lust, wrath, covetousness, pride and envy.
Mercy, honesty, and service to the guru (have) not (come to me even) in my dreams.[3]

Such passages, however, do not represent the constant mood of Kabīr. In others he is more hopeful, and he believes himself to have found the road to God which others have missed:

Kabīr (says), On the road which the paṇḍits have gone, on that the baggage-people follow after.
There is one difficult pass of Rāma; to that Kabīr is climbing up.[4]

He even believes that he has found God within himself and so is at rest:

What the paṇḍits and the mullas prescribed for me, I have received no [advantage] from, and have abandoned.

[1] *Ādi-Granth Bilāvalu* 6.
[2] *Ādi-Granth, Bilāvalu* 9.
[3] *Ādi-Granth, Rāmkalī* 8.
[4] *Ādi-Granth, Ślok* 165.

My heart being pure, I have seen the Lord; Kabīr having searched and searched himself, hath found God within him.[1]

Little as we know of the circumstances of the life of Kabīr, what has been written above may perhaps be sufficient to help us to form some picture of the man as he really was. We see a poor unlettered weaver in a humble home, having to struggle hard to earn his daily bread, but with a deeply religious and earnest nature, which longed for union with God. In his intense eagerness to find out the reality of things eternal, and his hatred of shams, he was contemptuous of all merely formal and outward piety, and regardless of conventions of caste or society. He is in many ways a man of humility and docility, and yet restrains not his language in denouncing that which seemed to be false and hypocritical. He has a deeply sensitive nature, and yet nothing will turn him aside from what he believes to be truth. Often misunderstood by his family, and brought into violent opposition with the society around him, because of his denunciation of its sins and exposure of its follies, he takes refuge in God and finds his solace in communion with Him. In a later chapter something will be said of the work of Kabīr as a thinker and an author, as well as of the vast influence he has had in India. Like other great men, he was in many things before his age, seeing things which the world around him would take centuries to learn; and yet, like other great men also, he never shook himself entirely free from his environment and the limitations which it involved. But whatever limitations he may have had, and whatever faults and failings, he must undoubtedly be given a high place amongst the great men of India.

Although he was universally despised and hated by both Hindus and Muhammadans, was persecuted by Brahmans, and even by the Muhammadan emperor, he nevertheless set himself with amazing boldness to attack the current opinions of his day. Like Socrates of old amongst the Greeks, he tried to penetrate behind the conventionalities of speech and popular ideas to the reality of things. He exposed with merciless severity the weak points of both

[1] *Ādi-Granth, Bhairau* 7.

Hinduism and Islam: and his influence was not only great in his own life-time, but has continued to the present day. It is to be found far outside the sect which acknowledges him as its founder, and even outside those sects which honour him as a teacher. There are few names in the religious history of India greater than that of Kabīr; and he holds an important place, too, in the history of Hindi literature.

We may fittingly close this chapter with a quotation from the *Bhakta Mālā* (Garland of Saints) a poetical work, which gives an account of many Indian devotees, and was written by Nabhā Dās, about the year 1600:[1]

> Kabīr refused to acknowledge caste distinctions, or to recognize the authority of the six Hindu schools of philosophy; nor did he set any store by the four divisions of life (*āśrams*) prescribed for Brahmans. He held that religion without bhakti was no religion at all, and that asceticism, fasting and almsgiving had no value if unaccompanied by worship (*bhajan*, hymn-singing). By means of *ramaiṇīs*, *śabdas* and *sākhīs* he imparted religious instruction to Hindus and Muhammadans alike. He had no preference for either religion, but gave teaching that was appreciated by the followers of both. He spoke out his mind fearlessly, and never made it his object merely to please his hearers.

[1] A commentary, also in verse, was added by Priya Dās in 1712. The commentary gives some of the legends about Kabīr which have already been noticed. But in the original text of Nabhā Dās, the notice of Kabīr, short as it is, gives a very fair and historical picture of Kabīr and his work.

CHAPTER IV

THE KABĪR LITERATURE

A. THE *BĪJAK*.—The most authoritative record of the teaching of Kabīr is found in the *Bījak*, a collection of poems which form the scriptures of the Kabīr Panth. These hymns are written in Hindi in various metres. According to the Rev. Ahmad Shah, the Hindi is the dialect spoken in the neighbourhood of Benares, Mirzapur, and Gorakhpur. Sir George Grierson, however, challenges this statement. He says that the language of Benares, Gorakhpur, and East Mirzapur is one form or another of the Bhojpuri dialect of Bihari, and that there is not a single form typical of this language in the *Bījak*. The language is really old Avadhi, a dialect of Eastern Hindi used in West Mirzapur, Allahabad and Oudh, and similar to that used by Tulsi Dās in his famous Rāmāyana. Kabīr himself says: 'My speech is of the East; no one can understand me. Only he can understand me, who is from the furthest East.'[1]

The language used in the poems is obscure and nearly always difficult. Colloquialisms, idiomatic and elliptical structure of sentences, and frequent play on words increase the difficulty. Many words used by Kabīr have now become obsolete; and he does not always keep to grammatical accuracy. Over two hundred words of Persian, Arabic, or Turkish origin are found in his verses in the *Bījak*—words which had found their way into the language through intercourse between Hindus and Muhammadans. Kabīr wrote in the popular speech of his day, so his language is uncouth and his style unpolished. In making use of the

[1] *Bījak*, *Sākhī* 194.

vernacular at all, instead of Sanskrit, for religious purposes, he was guilty of an innovation which met with strong opposition from orthodox Brahman scholars. At a much later period Tulsi Dās had to meet similar objections. The Rev. Ahmad Shah quotes a saying of Kabīr that Sanskrit is like the water of a well, while the *bhāshā* (the vernacular) is like the flowing waters of a river. The use of the vernacular instead of Sanskrit for religious teaching made it possible to popularize religion in a way which before had been unknown; and in doing this Kabīr, if not the first, was certainly one of the pioneers.

The word *Bījak* means (1) essence or seed, (2) an invoice, and (3) a document by which a hidden treasure can be located. It is the third meaning which is probable here. In the 37th *Ramaiṇī* there is a verse which says:

> The *Bījak* tells the secret of that treasure which is hidden; the word tells of *jīva*[1]; few are they who understand.

It is said that in the neighbourhood of Benares there is a race of people who are in the habit of burying treasure for safety, and the place of concealment is remembered by the secret sign of a chart which is carefully preserved. This chart is called a *bījak*. The custom may have been in use elsewhere, and Kabīr was no doubt familiar with it. The compiler of the collection probably chose this word as a suitable title for verses which were considered to reveal the hidden treasures of religious knowledge.

The *Bījak* consists of a collection of verses which are arranged according to the various metres in which they were written. Apart from this there seems to be little or no arrangement in the work. As usually published to-day, the *Bījak* consists of the following:

1. *The Ādi-Maṅgal.* A short introductory poem.
2. *Ramaiṇīs*, which are short doctrinal poems consisting of an indefinite number of *chaupāīs*,[2] followed by a *dohā*,[3] called the *sākhī*.

[1] *Jīva*, soul, or life.
[2] *Chaupāī*, a verse of four lines in a particular metre.
[3] *Dohā*, a couplet in a particular metre.

3. *Sabdas*, which are of a similar character but in the *lalita* metre, and without any *sākhī*.

4. *The Chauntīsī*, or the 34 consonants (including *ksha*) of the Nāgari alphabet, with their religious significations.

5. *The Vipramatīsī*, which is an attack, in thirty short verses, on the orthodox religious system of the Brahmans.

6. *Kaharās*, *Basantas*, *Chānchārīs*, *Belīs*, *Birhūlīs*, and *Hiṇḍolās*; all religious songs in various metres.

7. *Sākhīs*, which are short apophthegms consisting of a single couplet (*doha*) like the *sākhīs* of the *Ramaiṇīs*.

8. The *Sāyar Bījak ko Pad*, 'summing up of the whole *Bījak*,' which ends with the verse:

> Kabīr said, Within the Creator is all, and the Creator permeates all:
> Without the secret all are sunk in error; only the holy man, the wise, can comprehend.

The *Ramaiṇīs* and *Śabdas* form the bulk of the work, and the *Sākhīs* come next in length.

The *Bījak* has come down in various editions which differ considerably one from the other; and for the present we are very far from being able to say what the true text of the *Bījak* is.

1. An edition of the *Bījak* was printed at Benares in 1868, which contains the commentary of Viśvanāth Siṅha, Rājā of Rewah.

2. In 1890, the Rev. Prem Chand of the Baptist Mission, Monghyr, printed an edition at Calcutta. The order of the verses is different from that of other editions, and does not agree with any of the editions published by Kabīrpanthīs themselves.

3. An edition issued at Allahabad in 1905 contains the commentary of Pūran Dās of Burhanpur.

4. In 1911 the Rev. Ahmad Shah of Cawnpore published a text which follows the order of the edition of the Rājā of Rewah, but the verses not found in this but found in other editions have been added at the end, thus making up the number of *Sabdas* to 115 and the number of *Sākhīs* to 445.

The variations in the number of verses included may be seen at a glance in the following table:

RĀJĀ OF REWAH 1868	PREM CHAND 1890	PŪRAN DĀS 1905	ĀHMAD SHAH 1911
Ādi Mañgal			Adi Mañgal
		Pritham Anusār	
84 Ramaiṇīs	84 Ramaiṇīs	84 Ramaiṇīs	
	113 Śabdas	115 Śabdas	115 Śabdas
	Chauntīsī	Chauntīsī	Chauntīsī
	Vipramatīsī	Vipramatīsī	Vipramatīsī
12 Kaharās	2 Chānchārīs	12 Kaharās	12 Kaharās
12 Basants	Birhūlī	12 Basants	12 Basants
Chauntīsī	2 Belīs	2 Chānchārīs	2 Chānchārīs
2 Belīs	3 Hiṇḍolās	2 Belīs	2 Belīs
2 Chānchārīs	12 Kaharās	Birhūlī	Birhūlī
3 Hiṇḍolās	12 Basants	3 Hiṇḍolās	3 Hiṇḍolās
Birhūlī	364 Sākhīs	353 Sākhīs	445 Sākhīs
383 Sākhīs	60 Supplementary Sākhīs		Sāyar Bījak ko Pad.

There are also other editions in existence, and many manuscripts mostly modern. If there are any ancient manuscripts, they are carefully guarded by members of the Panth, and are not available for examination.

It may be said at once that the *Ādi Mañgal* and *Sāyar Bījak ko Pad*, which appear in the Rājā's edition, and the *Pritham Anusār*, which appears in the edition of Purān Dās, are quite obviously not part of the original text. They were probably added by the editors themselves. The *Ādi Mañgal* contains in twenty-five couplets an account of creation. Its tone differs greatly from that of the genuine poems of Kabīr. In it Kabīr asserts himself in an unexpected manner:

> After this came I for the sake of the True Word: the origin of the beginning and the end I now proclaim to you.
> I have come to bring this message, to wake the world from its sleep;
> Thus says Kabīr, the awakened Guru, by the orders of the Almighty.

The *Sāyar Bījak ko Pad* contains the following:

> O *Sants*,[1] the teaching of the *Bījak* is with authority;
>
> . . . .
>
> The teaching of the *Bījak* is known to few.

Such passages as these show on the face of them that they could not have been part of the original work of Kabīr. And the same is true of the *Pritham Anusār*.

Apart from this, it is in the *Sākhīs* that the greatest amount of variation seems to occur. This is not perhaps surprising, for a very large number of *Sākhīs* have been collected which are ascribed to Kabīr and are not in the *Bījak*, and copyists may often have been tempted to add those which were familiar to them.

The text of Pūran Dās seems to be that which is recognized by the section of the Kabīr Panth which has its headquarters at Benares; while the Chhattisgarh section[2] recognizes that of the Rājā of Rewah. In these two recensions the first two *Ramaiṇīs* are differently placed. According to a certain tradition there were two devoted disciples of Kabīr named Jaggo Dās and Bhaggo Dās. When Kabīr was about to depart from this world, he wrote his *Bījak* and gave it to their mother to be preserved. After Kabīr's death the brothers quarrelled about it, and each wanted to have the *Bījak* to himself. In order to reconcile them, their mother said that each should have the *Bījak*, with this difference; one should begin with the words: *Jīva rup* (*Ramaiṇī* 1 in Ahmad Shah's edition) and the other with *Antar Jyoti* (*Ramaiṇī* 2).

Another tradition says that the contents of the *Bījak* were originally dictated by Kabīr to one Bhaggo Jī or Bhagwān Dās. Bhaggo Jī took it to Dhanauti,[3] where it long remained in the keeping of the Dhanauti *mahants*, and was afterwards published in manuscript form. It is said by some that the *Bījak* was given to the royal family of Rewah by Kabīr himself, and that they have a manuscript written out by Dharm Dās in 1464; but on enquiry

[1] *Sant*, a holy man.

[2] See below, pp. 97 ff. Chhattisgarh is a district in the Central Provinces. [3] See below, pp. 105 ff.

being made from the officials of that State, no information could be obtained about this.

It seems most unlikely that Kabīr could read and write; but his admirers and followers treasured up his poems and repeated them to one another, and perhaps in some cases wrote them down. Then when the Kabīr Panth was definitely organized, the need for an authoritative scripture was probably felt, and steps taken to collect the various verses of Kabīr together.

This is the probable account of the origin of the *Bījak*. The compiler may have been Bhagwān Dās, and the compilation perhaps was not made till somewhere about 1600.

Even if we had an accurate and reliable text of the *Bījak*, as it existed when first compiled, we could not of course be sure that all was the genuine work of Kabīr; and it is very doubtful if it is so. But on the whole it seems likely that the bulk of it is his work. There is, generally speaking, a consistency about the style and ideas which seems to show it to be the work of one man.

In trying to distinguish the genuine work of Kabīr from later poetry, there are certain points which we may keep in mind. These are based on the idea that while we should not expect Kabīr always to be consistent in every detail, it is likely that there are certain lines of thought which we may expect to be fairly consistent in his teaching.

1. There are a number of Hindu ideas which the influence of Islam led him to condemn distinctly, such as idolatry, polytheism, mythology, divine incarnation, asceticism and severe austerities; so we should not accept any poem which contains a commendation of these. In the first *Kaharā*, for instance, there is a command: 'Make perfect your body by the practice of Yoga.' This raises doubts about its being the work of Kabīr. So also in the first and third *Hiṇḍolās*, there are references to 'incarnation,' which make the genuineness of these poems doubtful.

2. Kabīr laid great stress on the need of an enlightened guru, but he never suggested that any guru was divine, or that any guru should be worshipped. This would rule out, apart from other considerations, a large number of later Kabīrpanthī verses in which Kabīr himself is regarded not

merely as a guru, but as actually divine; although these verses are often ascribed to Kabīr.

3. While Kabīr might not condemn the observance of caste distinctions socially, he would never speak of the Brahmans as having special religious functions, or as being specially holy.

4. While he recognized both Hinduism and Islam as revelations of God, he would not naturally speak of the Vedas or the Qurān as inspired or authoritative literature.

5. It may also be added that any poem which contains an elaborate and advanced cosmogony is probably not by Kabīr. This would rule out not only the first two *Ramaiṇīs*, which there is reason to doubt on other grounds, but also a few other verses.

But even if tested by these strict standards, the bulk of the *Bījak* certainly seems to be the work of Kabīr.

B. THE *ĀDI-GRANTH*.—Another collection of Kabīr's poems has come down to us in the *Ādi-Granth*, which is the sacred book of the Sikhs. This work was compiled in 1604 by the orders of Guru Arjun, who was the sixth guru of the Sikhs. It is called the *Ādi-Granth*, ('Original Granth') to distinguish it from the *Granth* of the tenth guru, which was compiled by Guru Govind Singh at a later date. The compilation of the *Granth* may have been suggested by the *Bījak*. It contains the compositions of Guru Nānak, Guru Angad, Guru Amar Dās, Guru Rām Dās, Guru Arjun, Guru Tej Bahādūr (the ninth guru) and a couplet of Guru Govind Singh (the tenth guru). The compositions of these last two gurus were added after the first compilation. Besides the writings of these gurus, the *Granth* also contains panegyrics of the various gurus, and hymns of several *bhagats*, or devotees, such as Nāmdev, Kabīr and others, whose teaching was supposed to corroborate that of the gurus. Of these, the hymns of Kabīr are the greatest in bulk.

The *Ādi-Granth* is in three parts, the first of which is liturgical, while the second contains the general body of the hymns, and the third part is supplementary. It is in the last two portions that the verses of Kabīr are found. In the middle portion the hymns are arranged under thirty-one Rāgs, or musical modes, to which they are to be sung, each rāg being considered suitable to some season of the year, or time of the day.

The poems of the *bhagats*, or saints, are placed after the verses of the gurus at the end of each rāg, and it is here that we find the hymns of Kabīr. They are found in 16 out of the 31 rāgs, and are given as follows by Mr. Pincott[1]:

Rāg	No of Verses of Kabīr
Śrī	2
Gauṛī	76
Āsā	37
Gūjarī	2
Soraṭhī	11
Dhanāsarī	5
Sūhī	5
Bilāvalu	12
Gauṇḍ	11
Rāmkalī	12
Mārū	1[illegible]
Kedārā	6
Bhairau	20
Basantu	8
Sārang	2
Prabhātī	5
Total	225

In the last part of the *Granth*, which is called the *Bhog*, there are 244 couplets (or sākhīs) of Kabīr amongst the other matter. Altogether, according to Mr. Pincott, there and 1,146 stanzas of Kabīr to be found in the *Granth*. The number of stanzas is about two-thirds of the number to be found in the *Bījak*.

Leaving aside till a later chapter a consideration of the relation of Kabīr to the Sikh religion, it is important to consider what connection there is between these two collections of the poems of Kabīr. The verses in the *Granth* are not considered so authoritative as those in the *Bījak* by the members of the Kabīr Panth; and it is said that the Kabīrpanthī who sits at the Kabīr Gate of the Sikh Golden

[1] In an article in the *Journal of the Royal Asiatic Society*, 1886, pp. 437 ff.

Temple at Amritsar, only recites the *Bījak*. Some time ago the Rev. Ahmad Shah expressed the opinion that these poems in the *Granth* were 'in the spirit of Kabīr,' rather than by Kabīr himself. More recently however, he has reversed his opinion, and considers that they have the same marks of genuineness as the poems of the *Bījak*. It is interesting to notice that, on the whole, they probably contain more references to the personal life of Kabīr than the poems of the *Bījak* and contain fewer poems with an advanced cosmogony.

The translation of the *Ādi-Granth* by Macauliffe, who often uses the first person where Trumpp translates by the third, and the explanations of the occasions of the verses which Macauliffe gives, may tend to over-emphasize the personal element. But this is found even in Trumpp's more literal translation, and it does seem as if in the *Granth* there are to be found more poems which speak of personal experiences.

It is noteworthy that in the 'Kabīr portions' of the *Granth* (apart from a few brief sayings and couplets) there are only about two verses which do not contain the name of Kabīr, whereas in the *Bījak* we find about fifty-one such verses.

There are very few verses of Kabīr which are found both in the *Bījak* and the *Ādi-Granth*; but the following verses of the *Bījak* and *Ādi-Granth* may be compared. Even these are not quite identical, but differ in some details.

Bījak		Ādi-Granth
(1) Ramaiṇī 33	with	Gauṛī 30
(2) Śabda 73	,,	Soraṭha 2
(3) Śabda 112	,,	Gauṛī 42
(4) Śabda 97	,,	Prabhātī 2
(5) Chāñchārī 2	,,	Gauṛī 57
(6) Chauntīsī	,,	Gauṛī Pūrbī-Bāvanakhrī

The ślokas of the *Granth* are of the same form as the sākhīs of the *Bījak*, but there are only a few which are common to both.

It is indeed very surprising to find so few poems which occur in both collections. Yet the language and spirit of the two collections are the same, and there seems no reason to doubt that they both contain a large majority of poems which are the genuine work of Kabīr, though both in the *Bījak* and in the *Granth* many verses have probably been included which are by others. In some cases Macauliffe, in his translation of the Kabīr portions of the *Granth*, passes on a tradition that a poem here and there was composed by one of the Sikh gurus on a theme of Kabīr's (e.g. *Bhairau* 2); and this may have been the case with other verses where such a tradition has not been preserved. Other poems are said to be the utterances of other persons who addressed them to Kabīr, (e.g. *Gauṛī* 18, *Gūjarī* 2, *Bilāvalu* 4, *Gauṇḍ* 1 and 5). *Mārū* 9 is said to be by Kṛishṇa. *Āsā* 33, which refers to Kabīr's wife, is said to be partly by his mother, and so with one or two other verses. *Āsā* 13 appears to be an eulogium on Kṛishṇa, the opening lines being:

> My pilgrimage is to the bank of the Gomti,
> Where dwelleth the yellow-robed priest.

This poem, with such words in it as 'with my rosary on my neck,' would be strange if coming from Kabīr, and is evidently not his. For instance, *Gauṇḍ* 4 and *Bhairau* 8 refer to the miraculous escapes of Kabīr from drowning in the Ganges, and from being trodden down by an elephant when he was punished by Sikandar Lodī. They are probably not genuine poems of his. Again, *Basantu* 4 is full of mythology, and the Supreme Being is spoken of as becoming incarnate. This poem is therefore probably not genuine.

How are we to account for the two different collections of the *Bījak* and the *Granth*? It seems likely that Kabīr did not write down his poems, but recited them when teaching in Benares, and that certain of his disciples carried them away in their memories; so that it was not till a later date that they were written down. The many published versions of his poetry show certain similarities of style and diction and teaching; but also very large variations. Each collection has a large amount of matter peculiar to itself, and even when two collections contain the same poem, the text often varies seriously. Kabīr's own poems, as he recited them in Benares, were most likely, in the main, expositions of his monotheistic faith and way of life, and reasoned appeals to Hindus and others to think and decide for themselves. Now when his followers came to be organized as a sect, the leaders formed a collection of his teachings which would serve both as a 'Service Book' and a 'Bible.' But though a considerable portion of Kabīr's poetry would in all probability be well suited to those needs, the editors would soon discover that the poems did not by any means supply all the types of hymn, prayer, exhortation, praise, meditation and theological thought which they required. They would thus be compelled to supplement Kabīr's work by poems of other authorship—poems either already in existence, or specially composed for the collection. There were probably two principal oral traditions; one in the east, which became the nucleus of the *Bījak*, and the other in the north-west, which was the nucleus of the collection incorporated into the *Granth*.

Besides these two collections, there are current in India innumerable sākhīs, or couplets, which are attributed to Kabīr. The rhythm is often very striking and we can understand how easily remembered they are. No less than five thousand are said to be extant; whereas the *Bījak* only contains about four hundred. These sākhīs are short apophthegms containing some truth strikingly put, and are used like proverbs. It is not at all likely that all of them are really the work of Kabīr. Most of them are however in his spirit, and in substance consistent with the teaching to be met with in the *Bījak* and the *Granth*.

C. Rabindranath Tagore's *One Hundred Poems of Kabīr*.—In addition to these works of Kabīr, there has recently appeared in English a translation of a hundred poems of Kabīr by the great Bengali poet, Rabindranath Tagore, assisted by Miss Underhill.[1] This translation is supposed to be based upon the Hindi text (in Bengali characters) with a Bengali translation by Mr. Kshiti Mohan Sen, who has gathered from many sources a large collection of poems and

[1] Published by Macmillan, 1915.

hymns to which the name of Kabīr is attached. The Rev. Ahmad Shah has made a careful examination of this translation, and finds that it is really based not on the Hindi text but upon the Bengali translation, which is far from accurate. Mr. Kshiti Mohan Sen's collection is in four volumes and contains 341 poems. The hundred poems translated are taken from the first three volumes, which contain only 264. Of these hundred there are, according to Mr. Ahmad Shah, only five which in a mutilated form can be safely attributed to Kabīr. Poem 69 of the translation is the only one which occurs in both the *Bījak* and the *Granth*, and even this is only an extract from the poem as it is in those collections. Mr. Ahmad Shah considers that in the whole collection of Mr. Kshiti Mohan Sen there are only 18 poems and 39 sākhīs which bear any resemblance to the poems in the *Bījak*. In some of the poems there are lines or phrases here and there which come from the *Bījak*, but the remainder of the collection is, he thinks, by some author or authors unknown, of times more modern than Kabīr. The poems indeed are very beautiful, and as we might expect from the skilled hand of Rabindranath Tagore, are very fine also in their English dress; but he maintains that they cannot be regarded, except in fragments here and there, as the genuine work of Kabīr. With regard to the use of the name of Kabīr in these poems, we have to remember that the name of Nānak was used in all the compositions of the gurus in the Sikh *Granth* down to Guru Arjun. The use of the name of a great teacher in this way is not to be taken as forgery, but rather as showing respect; it is as much as to say, 'This is what the guru taught.' Mr. Ahmad Shah brings forward other considerations also, which suggest that these poems are not the work of Kabīr himself. Some Persian words are used which are not found in Kabīr's poems; some of the poems are in Panjabi and others contain Panjabi words. Moreover the Hindi is comparatively smooth and clear, as compared with the obscurity of much of Kabīr's verse, and seems to belong to a later period. Apart from linguistic considerations, the ideas are often different from those which we generally find in Kabīr. Consider for example the following (Kabīr is the speaker):

When He whose forms are manifold had not begun His play: when there was no Guru, and no disciple: when the world was not spread out: when the Supreme One was alone;—
Then I became an ascetic: then, O Gorakh, my love was drawn to Brahmā.
Brahmā did not hold the crown on his head: the god Vishṇu was not anointed as king; the power of Śiva was still unborn; when I was instructed in Yoga.
I became suddenly revealed in Benares, and Rāmānanda illumined me.[1]

Would Kabīr have written this?

Again, in Poem 42, Kabīr is represented as saying that he has bathed at the holy bathing-places, and cried aloud to the images. And in another poem we read:

Then I left off all rites and ceremonies, I bathed no more in the holy water.
From that time forth I knew no more how to roll in the dust in obeisance.[2]

Such experiences as these seem to be quite contrary to what we know of Kabīr's habits, as indicated in his recognized poems.

In Poem 47, the poet says, 'I sing the glory of forms'; which again is contrary to the known ideas of Kabīr.

In Poem 91, the author tells us he has learned the Sanskrit language; but even the legends which glorify Kabīr admit that this was not one of his accomplishments.

Mr. Ahmad Shah concludes, then, that while these poems are the work of a poet, or poets, of a distinguished order, they are not the work of Kabīr. Some passages indeed are true to his teaching, and contain genuine quotations from him; but the collection as a whole is the work of others. Some of them may have been composed by Sikh gurus. Some may have been the work of a Sūfī, for Sūfī ideas are to be found in them. The origin and development of this collection may have been similar to that suggested above for the *Bījak* and the *Granth*.

D. Kabīr's Place in Hindi Literature.—Kabīr undoubtedly holds a high place in the history of Hindi literature. In a previous chapter something has been said

[1] Poem 29. [2] Poem 65.

about the state of Hindi literature at the time of Kabīr, and his relation to it; and in an earlier part of this chapter we have considered the characteristics of his language. Leaving aside for the present his teaching, some further consideration must be given to his literary merits. It must be remembered that Kabīr composed no long treatise. His work consists of many short didactic poems, often expressed in terse and vigorous language.

As an example of the virility of his language consider the following:

> You believe those who are false: listen, O Sants and wise ones!
> The robber's den is within the heart: go not astray through folly.
> There is a roof of falsehood, it spreads over earth and sky.
> In all ten regions its noose is set: it has beset the soul.
> Devotion, sacrifice and rosary, piety, pilgrimage, fasting and alms,
> Nine bhaktis, Vedas, the Book—all these are cloaks of falsehood.
> One goes about with Śabdas, another boasts his doings.
> Ever they claim respect and renown—both sects, Hindus and Turks.
> In prating about the heavens, their hour of death has drawn near.
> Cherishing great conceit of heart, they are drowned where there is no water.
> Kabīr says, To whom shall I speak? All the world is blind.
> They keep away from one who speaks truth, and are the bond-slaves of liars.[1]

Kabīr, however, is often obscure, and his meaning can only be understood with the help of certain traditional explanations which have come down to us. Here is an example:

> The bees have flown, the cranes have settled: night is gone, day also will pass.
> The maiden Jīva shivers and shudders with fear; she knows not how her lover will receive her.
> An unbaked pot retains not water. When the swan departed, the body withered.
> My arms are aching with scaring the crows. Kabīr says, Now this tale is ended.[2]

According to the tradition, in this poem 'bees' and 'night' both mean 'youth'; 'cranes' and 'day' both mean

[1] *Bījak*, *Śabda* 113. [2] *Bījak*, *Śabda* 106.

'old age'; the 'lover' is God; the 'swan' is the soul and 'scaring the crows' means opposing ceremonial rules. This makes quite good sense; but it is doubtful whether apart from this traditional explanation the verse could have been easily understood.

In spite of the occasional difficulty of the Hindi, there is often a wonderful rhythm about the verse of Kabīr. This of course can only be felt in the original; and the Hindi text of the two following *sākhīs*, which illustrate also Kabīr's fondness for play on words, may give some little illustration of it:

Mālā pherata yuga gayā; pāyā na mana kā pher.
Kara kā mankā chhāṇrike; mana kā mankā pher.

'As he resolves his rosary, life passes away, and he knows not the secret of his heart. Throw away the rosary of the hand and revolve the rosary of the heart.'[1]

(*There is here a double play on words*: Mana, *heart;* mana ka, *of the heart;* manaka, *rosary;* pher, *secrets*, and also *revolve*.)

Here is another quotation:

Jā ghaṭa prema nā base; tā ghaṭ jānu masān:
Jaise khāla luhār ke; sāns letā binu prān.

'The ghat in which love dwells not, know that ghat to be a burning-ghat (*masān*); that heart is as the blacksmith's bellows, which breathe but have no life.'[2]

(Ghaṭa, *which means a vessel, is also used of the human heart; and also of a place where dead bodies are burned—a burning-ghat.*)

In some of his verses there is a tendency to coarseness, and this rugged prophet was not sparing in his invective:

If union with God be obtained by going about naked
All the beasts of the forest shall be saved!
What mattereth it whether man goeth naked or weareth a deerskin,
If he recognize not God in his heart?
If perfection be obtained by shaving the head,
Why should not sheep obtain salvation?
If, O brethren, the continent man is saved,
Why should not a eunuch obtain the supreme reward?

[1] Westcott, *Kabīr*, p. 80. [2] Westcott, op. cit. p. 84.

Saith Kabīr, Hear, O my brethren.
Who hath obtained salvation without Rāma's name?[1]

What shall one say to such people
As neither hear God's praises nor sing His attributes,
But who knock down the heavens by their boasting?
They whom God hath excluded from His service should always be feared.
They who give not a handful of water [to the thirsty]
Slander him who brought down the Ganges.
Sitting or standing, crooked are their ways;
They have ruined themselves and ruined others;
They know nothing save evil converse;
They obey not even Brahmā's bidding;
They have gone astray themselves and are leading others astray.[2]

Kabīr was quick to find illustrations of moral and spiritual truth in the incidents of common life; and many of his similies and comparisons are very striking:

Upside down the pitcher does not fill with water;
But upright the vessel fills.
For one object, men have tried this way and that:
Only by the Guru's gift will they cross safely.[3]

(*Here 'the pitcher' means the human soul.*)

Or again:

You yourself are self-deceived.
Like a dog in a house of looking-glasses, that died barking at illusion;
Like a lion, who looking in the water of a well sees his reflection and jumps straight in;
Like an elephant on a shining marble floor, who drives with his tusk at that;
Like a monkey, whose greed will not let him loose his hand: he is caught and led from house to house,
Kabīr says, O thou parrot in the springe, who caught thee?[4]

Though we cannot call Kabīr a 'nature-poet,' he was certainly alive to the beauties of Nature around him. The following is taken from the *Basantu Rāg* of the *Ādi-Granth. Basant* means 'spring-time,' and the poem seems to have been written under the grateful influence of an Indian spring, different altogether from an English spring, and yet still very beautiful.

[1] *Ādi-Granth*, *Rāg Gauṛī* 4.
[2] *Ādi-Granth*, *Rāg Gauṛī* 44.
[3] *Bījak*, *Śabda* 2.
[4] *Bījak*, *Śabda* 76.

The earth bloometh, the firmament rejoiceth;
Every heart is gladdened by God's lights.
The Lord rejoiceth in endless ways;
Whithersoever I look, there is He contained.
The four Vedas rejoice in worldliness;
So do the *Smṛitis* with the books of the Mussalmans.
Śiva practising Yoga rejoiceth;
Kabīr's Lord bloometh equally in all things.[1]

Like other Indian poets, Kabīr uses many conventional similies which are untrue to nature, e.g.

Though the *chātrik* has water all around him;
If the cloud yields no rain, he goes unsatisfied.[2]

(*Here there is an allusion to the supposition that the* chātrik, (*the pied-cuckoo*) *drinks only rain-drops.*)

Two other extracts will illustrate the wonderful poetic feeling we often find in the verse of Kabīr:

No one knew the mystery of that weaver: who came into the world and spread the warp.
The earth and the sky are the two beams: the sun and moon are two filled shuttles.
Taking a thousand threads, he spreads them lengthways: to-day he weaveth still, but hard to reach is the far-off end.
Says Kabīr, Joining *karma* with *karma*, woven with unwoven threads, splendidly the weaver weaves.[3]

Who was the painter who painted
The stars which appear in the sky?
Say, O paṇḍit, to what is the sky attached?
Fortunate is the wise man who knoweth this.
The sun and moon diffuse light;
God hath extended Himself in everything,
Saith Kabīr, He shall know this.
In whose heart is God, and in whose mouth is God.[4]

There is probably no Indian author whose verses are more on the lips of the people of North India than those of Kabīr, unless it be Tulsī Dās. As Sir George Grierson truly says, 'The words of two men of the past can still be heard in every village of Hindustan. These are Tulsī Dās, the abandoned child of a beggar Brahman tribe, and Kabīr, the despised weaver of Benares.'

[1] *Ādi-Granth*, *Basantu* 1.
[2] *Bījak*, *Ramaiṇī* 65.
[3] *Bījak*, *Ramaiṇī* 28.
[4] *Ādi-Granth*, *Gauṛī* 29.

CHAPTER V

THE DOCTRINES OF KABĪR

WHETHER by his upbringing Kabīr was a Hindu or a Muhammadan, there can be little doubt that his theology was steeped in Hindu thought. Although he rejected the authority of the Vedas, Purāṇas and other sacred books, he could not fail to be influenced by the environment in which he lived. Hindu thinkers for many centuries had been debating such questions as the method of creation, the nature of God, the relation between God and man, and the means by which salvation can be obtained; and various answers had been given. The answers which Kabīr gave to these questions were not entirely original, but were characterized by boldness and independence, for he ruthlessly cleared the ground of much useless superstition, and developed certain lines of thought which seemed to him to need more emphasis.

It is not easy to get a clear picture of the teaching of Kabīr in every detail. Apart from the uncertainty as to the genuineness of all the verses ascribed to him, he is often very obscure; and it is not difficult to find passages in which he appears to contradict himself. But while there may be uncertainty as to details, there are certain well-marked lines in his teaching which are often repeated; and with regard to these there can be little doubt. Kabīr was a practical religious teacher rather than a religious philosopher; and we must not, therefore, always expect absolute consistency in his thought. Moreover, while he was not without a constructive programme of teaching, and his doctrine by no means consists only of negations, yet he was undoubtedly greater as a critic of the weaknesses of the systems around him, than as the creator of a new system. It is this probably which has opened the way for so much of the later teaching of his followers to be foisted on to him, for they tried to supply the defects of his system.

KABĪR'S MONOTHEISM.—In the first place, Kabīr taught and emphasized the unity of God:

> He is one : there is no second.[1]
> Rāma, Khudā, Saktī, Śiva, are one : tell me, pray, how will you distinguish them ?[2]
> By the One name I hold fast : this Kabīr proclaims aloud.[3]
> In heaven, the realms below, in earth and waters, one alone, Rāma, watches over all.[4]
> Saith Kabīr, I have searched in heaven,[5]
> And have seen none equal to God.[6]
> The one Name, like the tree of life, saveth [mankind].[7]
> [Then shall man know] that one God is everywhere contained, and that there is no second.[8]

But though Kabīr believes in the unity of God, he makes use of many names in speaking of Him. He specially uses the name Rāma, but others occur such as Hari, Govinda, Nārāyaṇa, the Bow-Holder, Brahmā, Allāh, Khudā, and others. But if he uses many names for God, it is not to countenance polytheism, but rather to lead people to realize that, though they might use different names, there is only One God. He sometimes speaks of the Hindu deities; and he may use the stories connected with them to point some moral or religious truth, but never to recognize their separate existence:

> [O God], whether Allāh or Rāma, I live by thy Name; . . .
> Hari dwelleth in the south, Allāh hath his place in the west.
> Search in thy heart, search in thy heart of hearts; there is his place and abode.[8]
> Kabīr is a child of Rāma and Allāh, and accepteth all gurus and pīrs.
> Saith Kabīr, Hear, O men and women, seek the sanctuary of the One God.[9]

[1] *Bījak*, *Śabda* 43.
[2] *Bījak*, *Śabda* 48.
[3] *Bījak*, *Śabda* 62.
[4] *Bījak*, *Ramaiṇī* 59.
[5] *Ādi-Granth*, *Gauṛī* 34.
[6] *Ādi-Granth*, *Gauṛī* 37.
[7] *Ādi-Granth*, *Āsā* 11.
[8] *Ādi-Granth*, *Prabhātī* 2.
[9] *Ādi-Granth*, *Prabhātī* 2.

Who of men did not die? O paṇḍit, speak and make this plain to me.
Dead is Brahmā, Vishṇu, Maheśa; dead is Ganeśa, the son of Parvatī.
Dead is the Moon, the Sun, the Serpent-god:
Hanumān is dead who built the bridge.
Dead is Kṛishṇa, dead is the Maker. One only did not die—the Creator.
Kabīr says, He alone dies not who is not held in coming and going.[1]
You waver and know not the Supreme God, [wherefore] you worship gods and goddesses.[2]
Beings like Brahmā's [four] sons, Śiva, and Śeshnāga, know not thy secret. . . .
Beings like Hanumān and Garuḍa.
Indra and Brahmā, know not, O God, thine attributes.
The four Vedas, the Smṛitis, and the Purāṇas.
Vishṇu and Lakshmī know them not.[3]

KABĪR'S DOCTRINE OF CREATION.—In later Kabīrpanthī works there is a most elaborate cosmology, but it does not seem that Kabīr was responsible for this: and it is likely that the few verses, like the first and second *Ramaiṇīs* of the *Bījak*, which show an approach to a developed system, are later additions. Cosmology seems much less developed in the *Granth* than in the *Bījak*, and this is significant. It is doubtful if Kabīr had a clearly conceived system in his mind: and it is certainly next to impossible to reconstruct his system from his verses if he had one.

Verses from each of these works may be quoted which, if genuine, will give some idea of the thoughts of Kabīr about creation:

In the first beginning there was thought:
The second that appeared was a resting-place therefor.
Brahmā, Vishṇu, Śiva and Saktī then appeared:
From the first moment the soul sought to find the method of devotion.
Then appeared the Anda, Pinda and Brahamandā;[4]
Then the earth appeared and was divided into nine parts.
Then appeared air, water, and shade (i.e. trees);
Māyā appeared, diffused in many forms.
Then appeared Siddha, Sadhaka and Sannyāsī:[5]

[1] *Bījak*, *Śabda* 45. [2] *Ādi-Granth*, *Gauṛī* 45.
[3] *Ādi-Granth*, *Dhanāsarī* 3.
[4] Various primeval eggs from which creation issues forth.
[5] Various names for those who have attained to the knowledge of salvation.

They all engaged in the quest of the Immortal.
Then appeared gods, men, and sages and all else;
They all failed in the search.
Gods and souls appeared; the gods were lords, the rest their slaves:
Kabīr knows nothing more, his hope is in the name of Rāma alone.'[1]

God constructed an inaccessible fortress for His residence (the brain?)
Which He illumined with His light.

. . . .

He who fashioned continents and different countries,
The three worlds, the three [gods], and the three qualities,
[Though styled] inaccessible and invisible, dwelleth within the heart.
None can find the limit or the secret of the Sustainer of the earth;
He shineth in plantain-blossom and in the sunshine.
And hath His dwelling in the pollen of the lotus.
God's spell is within the twelve petals of the heart.
Where the holy Lord of Lakshmī reposeth.
The great (God) reacheth from the lower to the upper regions of the firmament;
He illumineth the silent realm,
Where there is neither sun nor moon.
He was in the beginning; He is without stain and happy.
Know that He pervadeth the body as well as the universe;
He batheth in Mansarowar (the lake of the heart);
His pass-word is 'Soham' ('*I am He*').[2]

KABĪR'S MONISM: ADVAITA OR VISISHṬĀDVAITA?—Was Kabīr's conception of God in accordance with Vedantic Monism (*Advaita*), or otherwise? Mr. Ahmad Shah is most emphatic in stating that his teaching *is* monistic. There are indeed many passages which seem to bear this out.

On the other hand there are passages (like that just quoted) which seems to agree with the *Visishṭādvaita* doctrine, or modified Monism, which regards the universe as the body or manifestation of God, and not as the creation of Māyā; and allows some kind of individuality to the soul after its absorption into the Supreme. Probably Kabīr was not logically consistent in his philosophical outlook; and he deprecated the mere discussion of religious truth which did not lead to anything.

[1] *Bījak*, *Ramaiṇī* 3. [2] *Ādi-Granth*, *Bhairau* 1.

Tat tvam asi[1] is the preaching of the Upanishads; that is their message.
Great is their reliance upon this; but how can they, however mighty, describe Him?[2]

Paṇḍit, your thoughts are all untrue; there is here no universe and no creator;
Nor subtle, nor gross, nor air, nor fire, nor sun, nor moon, nor earth, nor water;
Nor the form of light, nor *Kāl* are there: there is neither word nor body.
There is neither action nor virtue, no mantras and no worship at all.
Rites and ceremonies have no worth at all.
He is one, there is no second.[3]

Wherever, wherever one looks, there, there is He the same; He is found in every vessel.[4]

How can I explain His form or outline? there is no second who has seen Him.
How can I describe the condition of the unconditioned, who has neither village nor resting-place?
He who must be seen without qualities; by what name shall I call Him?[5]

When the fire of (avarice) is out, and the smoke (of desires) no longer issueth.
(Then shall man know) that one God is everywhere contained, and that there is no second.[6]

The joiner dwelleth ever separate (from the work).[7]

The Supreme Brahma of the Vedānta is an abstraction; for he is said to be *nirguṇa*, or without attributes. But man cannot worship a God who is without attributes; and wherever this doctrine is held, it has been found necessary to recognise God as being also *saguṇa*, or possessing attributes. This indeed is said to be due to *Māyā* (illusion), but at least it enables men to conceive of a personal God whom they can worship. In giving up the worship of Hindu gods, and making it clear that the Rāma whom he worshipped was not the incarnation of Vishṇu, but the

[1] 'Thou art That'; i.e. Thou (the human soul) art one with That (Divine Spirit).
[2] *Bījak, Ramaiṇī* 8.
[3] *Bījak, Śabda* 43.
[4] *Bījak, Śabda* 27.
[5] *Bījak, Ramaiṇī* 6, 7.
[6] *Ādi-Granth, Āsā* 11.
[7] *Ādi-Granth, Gauṛī* 52.

Supreme God, Kabīr was running the risk of losing hold on the personality of God. It is this difficulty that has probably led to his followers in later times deifying Kabīr himself, as it gave them a personal God who had appeared and lived amongst men. The God whom Kabīr worshipped was not however to him a mere abstraction. He used attributes to describe Him. He is the Saviour, is merciful, joyous, bountiful, happy, perfect, and may even be spoken of as Father.[1] God, if omnipresent and powerful, yet is one with whom man can have intercourse. Yet even in the same breath Kabīr speaks of Him as without qualities:

> O Kabīr, chide not the name of Him who is without qualities;
> Enjoy thyself in intercourse with that Lord.[2]

It must be confessed that the God of Kabīr, though real to him, is a very shadowy being; and, like other Hindu thinkers, Kabīr sometimes uses negatives in describing Him, and he speaks of Him as inaccessible and inapprehensible:

> He has neither caste, nor lineage, Kabīr says; He has neither day nor night.[3]

Kabīr and Idolatry.—If we compare Kabīr with the great Hindu philosopher, Śaṅkarāchārya, we note that although Śaṅkarāchārya was an uncompromising Monist, he nevertheless allowed a place in his scheme for the Hindu pantheon, and regarded idolatry as a help towards obtaining the knowledge and experience of the identity of the soul with God. But Kabīr had no place for idolatry; for it seemed to him that, if God is one, the whole basis of idolatry perishes. He was, therefore, unsparing in his denunciation of the practice:

> O mind, you make your gods and goddesses, and kill living creatures to make offerings to them;[4]
> But if your gods are true, why do they not take them when grazing in the fields?
> If God dwell only in the mosque, to whom belongeth the rest of the country?[5]
> They who are called Hindus say that God dwelleth in an idol: I see not the truth in either sect.

[1] e.g. *Rāg Āsā*, 3, quoted above, p. 32.
[2] *Ādi-Granth, Gauṛī* 9.
[3] *Bījak, Śabda* 98.
[4] *Bījak, Śabda* 70.
[5] *Ādi-Granth, Prabhātī* 2.

But Kabīr's condemnation did not stop short at idolatry. He denounced without compromise a large number of practices, both Hindu and Muhammadan, which seemed to him to be mere outward forms and superstitions and to have no value in leading men into real fellowship with God. His condemnation extended to pilgrimages, ceremonial purifications, fasting, sacred threads, circumcision, use of the rosary, and many other practices. Kabīr held very strongly the doctrine of *ahimsā*, or the sin of taking life in any form; and this makes him specially angry with the sacrifice of animals in worship by both Hindus and Muhammadans. He has no regard for the Vedas, the Quran, or other so-called sacred books. He may have respected in some ways their teaching, but not the superstitious and unmeaning regard for them held by paṇḍits, mullas and others:

> Devotion, sacrifice aud rosary, piety, pilgrimage, fasting and alms.
> Nine bhaktis, Vedas, the Book,[1] all these are cloaks of falsehood.
> One goes about with Śabdas, another boasts his doings.
> Ever they claim respect and renown—both sects, Hindus and Turks.[2]
>
> Qāzī, what is this book that you discourse on?
> You are jangling and wrangling always; nothing of wisdom do you know.
> Vain-glorious of authority, you make me to be circumcised: never will I endure it, brother!
> Leave these distractions, meditate on Rāma, O foolish mind![3]
>
> They who bathe in the evening and morning.
> Are like frogs in the water.
> When men have no love for God's name,
> They shall all go to the God of death.
>
> . . . .
>
> Saith Kabīr, Why perform so many ceremonies?
> Forsaking all other essences, quaff the great essence (of God's name).
> You [wear] *tilaks*[4] on your foreheads, [carry] rosaries in your hands, and [put on sectarian] dresses.
> People think that God is a plaything.[5]

[1] 'The Book'; i.e. the Quran. [2] *Bījak*, *Śabda* 113.
[3] *Bījak*, *Śabda* 84; cf. also *Śabda* 10, quoted on p. 11 above.
[4] *Tilak*, a sect-mark. [5] *Ādi-Granth*, *Bhairau* 6.

The Brahmans [yearly] observe twenty-four [fasts], on the eleventh (day of the dark and light halves of the lunar month); the Mussalmans fast in the month of Ramazān.
The latter put aside eleven months of the year, and say that the Treasure is in one alone.
What availeth it the Hindus to bathe [at Jagannāth] in Orissa; what [for the Mussalmans] to bow their heads in a mosque?
With deception in their hearts they repeat prayers; what availeth it them to go on a pilgrimage to Mecca?[1]

KABĪR AND ASCETICISM.—The Yogī ascetics, who seem to have been numerous in Kabīr's days, also come in for his condemnation:

Some shave men's locks and hang the black cord on their necks,
And pride themselves on the practice of Yoga.
What credit is there in causing your seat to fly?
Crow and kite also circle in the air.[2]

Sitting on the air, studying Yoga, Vedas, rites and astrology, they are demented. . . .
Kabīr says, The hope of the Yogī and the *Jaṅgama*[3] is withered.[4]

The Yogī says; Yoga is best of all: O brother, it has no rival:
Yogīs with plaited hair or shaven head, with sealed lips or matted locks—where did these find wisdom?[5]

The Yogī says that Yoga and nothing else is good and sweet;
They who shave their bodies, and the Ekśabdīs, say that they (alone) have obtained perfection.
Without God thou art lost in error, O blind one![6]

Thou dependest on a club, earrings, and patched coat,
In error thou wanderest in a [Yogī's] garb.
Put away thy devotional attitudes and thy suspension of breath:
Abandon deception, and ever worship God, O fool![7]

KABĪR AND CASTE.—In his crusade against everything that was unmeaning and unreal, we shall not be surprised to find that Kabīr disapproved of the caste system, just as he did of the division of his fellows into Hindus and Muhammadans. He rose above the divisions that separated men, and, believing as he did in one God, sought to make men realize they were all one family in Him.

[1] *Ādi-Granth, Prabhātī* 2.
[2] *Bījak, Ramaiṇī* 71.
[3] *Jaṅgama*, a kind of ascetic.
[4] *Bījak, Śabda* 26.
[5] *Bijak, Śabda* 38.
[6] *Ādi-Granth, Gauṛī* 51.
[7] *Ādi-Granth, Bilāvalu* 8.

Adam who was first, did not know
Whence came mother Eve.
Then there was not Turk nor Hindu; . . .
Then there was no race, no caste.
If thou thinkest the Maker distinguished castes:
Birth is according to these penalties for deeds.
Born a Śudra, you die a Śudra;
It is only in this world of illusion that you assume the sacred thread.

If birth from a Brahman mother makes you Brahman,
Why did you not come by another way?
If birth from a Turk makes you Turk,
Why were you not circumcised in the womb?
If you milk black and yellow cows together,
Will you be able to distinguish their milk?[1]

Saith Kabīr, renounce family, caste and lineage; become an ant, and thou canst pick up and eat [the sugar].[2]

KARMA, TRANSMIGRATION AND MĀYĀ.—But Kabīr held fast to the doctrines of Karma and Transmigration which are deeply woven in Hindu thought. A man (he believed) is bound by his actions, and every act is productive of future good or ill. Evil deeds destine a man to punishment by his being born in a lower state of life in his next birth, but good deeds also necessitate rebirth, only that in this case there is gain by securing a nobler position. But the weary round of births and rebirths goes on till the chain of transmigration is cut:

I was in immobile and mobile creatures, in worms and in moths;
I passed through many births of various kinds.
In this way I occupied many bodies,
But when, O God, I assumed [human] birth,
I was a Yogī, a Jāti, a penitent, a Brahmachāri,
Sometimes a king, an emperor, and sometimes a beggar.[3]

Through wanderings and error man comes again to his house (body).[4]

The soul plays in many forms—in various garbs;
Men like bees are swept away.
After birth and death, it comes again into a body.[5]

On account of Karma, one appeared in the womb.[6]

[1] *Bījak*, *Ramaiṇī* 62.
[2] *Ādi-Granth*, *Rāmkalī* 12.
[3] *Ādī-Granth*, *Gauṛī* 13.
[4] *Bījak*, *Ramaiṇī* 25.
[5] *Bījak*, *Ramaiṇī* 84.
[6] *Bījak*, *Ramaiṇī* 39.

All men bound by their acts transmigrate; attentively consider this.[1]

Though I have assumed many shapes, this is my last.[2]

Since my attention is fixed on God, I no longer suspect that I shall suffer transmigration.[3]

My dread of transmigration is at an end.[4]

It is because men are deluded by Māyā that they are not released from the toils of Karma. Kabīr also speaks of men being deceived by *Kāl.* In latter Kabīrpanthī theology, the relation of the two is definitely worked out, but in Kabīr they seem to have little difference, if any, in meaning:

After ten months you were brought from your mother's womb, and again were beset by Māyā.

. . . .

You have cherished hope of life; Kāl has choked your breath.[5]

Kabīr also took the term 'Māyā' from Hinduism, but with him, Māyā seems generally to have rather a different meaning from that in general use. It is amongst Hindus a philosophical concept to account for the apparent duality of the universe. This idea may be found in Kabīr, but it more often has rather an ethical content. Macauliffe uses the word 'mammon' to translate Māyā; because it stands in Kabīr-verse for what in Christian theology are called 'the deceits of the world and the flesh.' Māyā is generally spoken of as an evil woman, a witch, who entangles men with her deceit, and so is personified.

The woman hath conquered the three worlds;
She hath made the eighteen Purāṇas and the places of pilgrimage love her;
She hath pierced the heart of Brahmā, Vishṇu, and Śiva,
And infatuated great kings and sovereigns.
There are no bounds to the woman;
She is in collusion with the five evil passions.[6]

The fishes in the water are led by Māyā;
The moths round the lamp are influenced by Māyā;
Through Māyā the elephant feeleth lust;

[1] *Ādi-Granth, Gauṛī* 50.
[2] *Ādi-Granth, Āsā* 28.
[3] *Ādi-Granth, Bilāvalu* 11.
[4] *Ādi-Granth, Prabhātī* 1.
[5] *Bījāk, Sabda* 89.
[6] *Ādi-Granth, Gauṇḍ* 8.

Creeping things and bumble-bees perish through Māyā;
My brethren, Māyā is so bewitching that she deludes all living beings.

. . . .

The demigods are saturated with Māyā;
So are the ocean, the firmament, and the earth.[1]
Māyā and Desire are troubles of the world;
But no one thinks so of this.
Māyā and Desire are a troublesome noose;
He who escapes therefrom is a true worshipper.
O Sants, that which comes and goes, is Māyā.[2]

. . . .

In the form of a dwarf he did not tempt Bali; that which tempts is Māyā.
For lack of understanding the whole world is bewildered;
Māyā has deluded the world.[3]

God, according to the teaching of Kabīr, is one, and man can have intercourse with Him; but man is in the toils of Karma and Transmigration, and deluded by Māyā. The religious systems of the Hindus and Muhammadans, with their idolatry and ceremonial and vain learning, are of no avail to bring men into fellowship with God. How then can this be attained?

Kabīr and the Experience of God.[4]—Kabīr believed that man can approach God, but the great hindrance to this is moral. Only when sin is subdued can man arrive at a knowledge of God. But until this knowledge of God is acquired, men cannot rightly understand the things around them. Kabīr speaks of God as an illusionist; but when he recognized Him, the illusion vanished. God is all-pervading, and must not be regarded as dwelling in any confined locality. It is useless therefore to seek Him specially in temple or mosque. Everywhere He may be found, whatever name is given to Him. Kabīr taught men to look within their hearts to find God, but this can only be when the heart is purified from sin. Sin in the heart prevents men from recognizing God. Kabīr had nothing but condemnation for those who performed ceremonial ablutions and cleansings, and went through elaborate ritual to find

[1] *Ādi-Granth, Bhairau* 13. [2] *Bījak, Ramaiṇī* 76.
[3] *Bījak, Sabda* 8.
[4] See also above, pp. 46 ff.—'Kabīr's spiritual life.'

God, but paid no attention to the purification of the heart. What is the use of all this ceremonial and ritual, when men harbour deceit within, and practise fraud under the guise of holiness? The Hindu paṇḍits are proud of their learning and ceremonial, and despise those who are of lower caste than themselves. The Muhammadan mullas are equally puffed up with their vain knowledge of the Quran and traditions, and are punctilious about details; but unless these get rid of pride from their hearts, they cannot find God. The Yogī, too, is proud of his ascetic practices, and the hermit of his giving up all to dwell in the forest; but these things cannot in themselves expel evil, and wherever man is, his heart is full of wickedness. Birth as a human being gives to man a great opportunity to obtain release from the chains of transmigration, and that man is foolish indeed who does not seize his opportunity.

Kabīr himself greatly desires this knowledge of God, and therefore frequently confesses his sin to God and asks for cleansing. When God is known, man realizes his union with Him, a union which brings great joy and peace. Kabīr fully submits himself to God and believes that he has attained this union. Although men revile him and speak against him, he is therefore at peace. These points may be illustrated by some quotations:

> He is a mulla who struggleth with his heart,
> Who by the instruction of the guru contendeth with Death,
> And crusheth Death's pride.
> Salutation ever to that mulla!
> God is present; why describe Him as distant?
> Kabīr's God is the all-pervading.[1]
>
> . . . .
>
> Hari dwelleth in the south, Allāh hath his place in the west.
> Search in thy heart, search in thy heart of hearts; there is His place and abode.[2]
> God abideth in the heaven above, in the earth beneath and in every direction.
> The Supreme Being is ever the root of joy; the body may perish, but God shall not.
> I am anxious [to know]
> Whence the soul cometh and whither it goeth.

[1] *Ādi-Granth, Bhairau* 11. [2] *Ādi-Granth, Prabhātī* 2.

The body is contained in God, God in the body; He is uninterruptedly in all things.[1]

Unless you remove evil from your hearts, how shall you find [God] by dwelling in the forest?

They who deem their own homes equal to the forest are perfect [among] men.

. . . .

He who hath conquered his own heart hath conquered the world, because he is free from the deadly sins.

. . . .

I have met God who dwelleth in the heart.[2]

When a stream in lost in the Ganges,
It becometh as the Ganges itself;
Kabīr is similarly lost [in God] by invoking Him;
I have become as the True One and need not go elsewhere.[3]

What availeth devotion, what penance, what fasting and worship,
To him in whose heart there is worldly love?
O man, apply thy heart to God;
Thou shall not obtain Him by artifice.
Put away covetousness and the example of others;
Lay aside lust, wrath, and pride.
By the religious practices [of the superstitious] boasting is increased;
They join together and worship a stone.
Saith Kabīr, By devotion I have obtained [the Lord]
By becoming simple [in heart] I have met God.[4]

God is the Illusionist who hath illuded the world.

. . . .

Saith Kabīr, I have become reconciled with the Illusionist;
The illusion vanished when I recognized Him.[5]

O sovereign God, Thou art very fearless; Thou art a raft to save the world, O God.

When I was proud, Thou [wert] not [in me]; now that Thou art [in me] I am not proud.

Now Thou and I have become one; seeing that we are both one, my mind is satisfied.[6]

They who give up pride of race and attachment and search for the word alone.

Renouncing the shoot and seed of all desire these men become freed from body and from space.[7]

For him who knows not Rāma, the knot of doubt is not untied.

. . . .

[1] *Ādi-Granth*, *Gauṇd* 3.
[2] *Ādi-Granth*, *Mārū* 2.
[3] *Ādi-Granth*, *Bhairau* 5.
[4] *Ādi-Granth*, *Gauṛī* 6.
[5] *Ādi-Granth*, *Gauṛī* 39.
[6] *Ādi-Granth*, *Gauṛī* 72.
[7] *Bījak*, *Ramaiṇī* 35.

All read *Smṛiti* and *Vedas* and *Purāṇa*; none have vision of the Inward Light.

. . . .

Those who did not reach the shore when living, how can they cross when dead, who did not cross when living?
On whatsoever one fixes his faith when living, there he rests when dead.[1]

KABĪR AS A PREACHER OF RIGHTEOUSNESS.—As we have seen in the chapter on the life of Kabīr, he was himself a humble man. Unless he had been so, he could not so unflinchingly have denounced pride in others. He often confesses his own sin and failure, but he was undoubtedly a man of high moral ideals and attainment, and constantly appears as a preacher of righteousness. He condemns in no unsparing terms those who wilfully turn away from the light, though he does so without arrogance. But he does believe that his own sins have been blotted out and that he has found union with God:

These are your good deeds, yet you are consumed with pride:
From such pride no one will derive any benefit.
He whose name is 'the breaker of pride,'
How can He tolerate your pride?[2]

Renounce honour, renounce boasting;
Then the pride of your mind will be broken.
For those who steal and devour:
That plant will blossom again.
If one pursues riches and worldly honour:
That plant brings him again into the world.
Give up lies, know them to be lies; this world is all illusion.
For this cause do I speak, that you may find escape.[3]

They who crave for liquor and thirst for intoxication nowhere find content.
The drunken with lust and anger Māyā fills brimful, and gives them to drink.[4]

They give to thieves the seats of honour
And from the honest hide their face.
Kabīr says, Liars keep company with liars,
And robbers deal with robbers.
The three worlds are full of such: there is none to trust.[5]

[1] *Bījak, Śabda* 14.
[2] *Bījak, Ramaiṇī* 35.
[3] *Bījak, Ramaiṇī* 60.
[4] *Bījak, Śabda* 29.
[5] *Bījak, Śabda* 93.

I am the dust of the lotus feet
Of those whose hearts are filled with God.[1]

O God, I am thy child:
Why destroyest thou not my demerits?

. . . .

[O God] ever cleanse my mind and body,
And Kabīr will tranquilly sing thy praises.[2]

O God, such sinners are we,
That we have never performed service for that Lord who gave us our souls and bodies.

. . . .

O God, compassionate to the poor, merciful, dear to the saints, Remover of fear,
Prayeth Kabīr, preserve Thine afflicted slave, O God, and I will perform Thy service.[3]

Saith Kabīr, All my sins have been blotted out,
And my soul is absorbed in the Life of the World.[4]

'Be Prepared for Death.'—The transitoriness of the world, and the certainty of death for all, is a constant theme of Kabīr's. He earnestly calls all men to turn away from sin and seek God ere it is too late and the opportunity of life be gone. Men often bestow much thought on the body, but one day it will perish. No one can escape from death, which he often personifies as *Yama*. All the Yogīs, and those who prided themselves on their sanctity have come under the power of Yama. But for those whose minds have been filled with divine knowledge and have realized their union with God, death is not to be dreaded: for it is the gate which leads to happiness. Kabīr himself therefore has no fear of death.

I have seen the departure of all, cries Kabīr loudly.
If you would awake, awake; the robber is attacking in broad daylight.[5]

Dead is Brahmā, Śiva the lord of Kāsi:
With them lies dead the Immortal (i.e. Vishṇu);
In Mathura died Kṛishṇa, the cowherd:
One by one died the ten incarnations.
One after one died the founders of devotions:
Those who knew Him in qualities and without qualities.

[1] *Ādi-Granth, Gauṛī* 26.
[2] *Ādi-Granth, Āsā* 12.
[3] *Ādi-Granth, Rāmkalī* 8.
[4] *Ādi-Granth, Prabhātī* 1.
[5] *Bījak, Ramaiṇī* 44.

Nāth Muchandar escaped not, nor Gorakh, Dattātreya nor Vyāsa.
Kabīr cries aloud, All were caught in the noose of death.[1]

Such fools are men that they are ever collecting more:
Mortal themselves, they weep for the death of others.
Man does not think he will die himself:
His desire is to get ten half-pence more, and take and enjoy them.[2]

Dead, what will you do with your body?
The soul departs: at once it is cast forth.
When the corpse is thus forsaken, it meets varied usage: some burn it, some bury it in earth.

. . . .

Kabīr says, Hereafter you will curse your folly.
When from this house you must fare forth.[3]

You were still unsatisfied with the juice of Māyā, when Yama stalked you like a cat.
Kabīr says, Man has not yet awakened, though Yama's club strikes the crown of his head.[4]

The limbs [anointed with] ground aloe-wood, sandal, and fragrant soap
Shall be burnt with wood.
What is there to be proud of in this body and in wealth?
Both shall remain on earth and not go [with the soul] to the other world.
They who sleep at night and work by day,
Who utter not God's name for a moment,
Who eat betel and stretch out their hands [for more],
Shall at the hour of death be firmly bound as thieves.[5]

Thy stewardship being ended, thou must give thine account,
When the cruel messengers of Death come to take thee.[6]
Having beaten thy drums for four days thou shalt depart,
With all thine earnings, thy ready money and thy buried treasures, thou shalt take nothing with thee.
Saith Kabīr, Why remember not God? Thy life is passing in vain.[7]

KABĪR AND BHAKTI.—Kabīr is in the line of succession of those religious leaders who advocated Bhakti, or loving faith and devotion, for those who would find God. In connection with this, he speaks often of repeating the name of

[1] *Bījak, Ramaiṇī* 54.
[2] *Bījak, Ramaiṇī* 55.
[3] *Bījak, Śabda* 61.
[4] *Bījak, Śabda* 99.
[5] *Ādi-Granth, Gauṛī* 16.
[6] *Ādi-Granth, Sūhī* 16.
[7] *Ādi-Granth, Kedārā* 6.

God, especially the name of Rāma. To Kabīr, however, this was not a mere magic formula. The mere repetition of the name of God would not bring salvation any more than a man can taste sweetness by repeating the word 'sugar.' The repetition of the name of God with Kabīr, seems rather to be a means by which he reminds himself of God's reality and brings to recollection all that the name connotes, and so it helps him to realize his union with God.

In connection with bhakti, we find Kabīr using as an illustration the idea of husband and wife, God being the husband to whom the devotee owes loving trust and obedience, and with whom he is connected by the closest of ties. He also frequently speaks of 'drinking the elixir of Rāma,' which is another way of expressing the deep satisfaction that is obtained by estatic union with God.

> If by repeating Rāma's name the world is saved, then by repeating 'sugar' the mouth is sweetened.[1]
>
> Saith Kabīr, 'Utter two letters';[2]
> As sure as I have a master, He will save me.[3]
>
> The ambrosial name I repeat with my tongue.
> God hath made me His unbought slave.[4]
>
> . . . .
>
> My mind hath obtained resignation by the support of the Name.
> Deceitful Māyā hath led captive the whole world, but I have obtained immunity by repeating Rāma's name.[5]
>
> The Name of God saveth him who hath tasted its savour.
> Saith Kabīr, I have become gold; my doubts have fled; and I have crossed the ocean.[6]
>
> Repeat the name of Rāma, thou madman! the ocean of existence is hard to cross.[7]
>
> Such knowledge of the Supreme Being hath manifested itself: I am imbued with it (*literally*, I am steeped in His colour.)
> All the rest of the world is led astray in error, but my mind is intoxicated with the elixir of Rāma.[8]
>
> Saith Kabīr, By devotion I have obtained [the Lord.][9]

[1] *Bījak*, *Śabda* 40.
[2] i.e. R and M which with the long vowel Ā make RĀM.
[3] *Ādi-Granth*, *Gauṛī* 33.
[4] *Ādi-Granth*, *Gauṛī* 40
[5] *Ādi-Granth*, *Āsā* 25.
[6] *Ādi-Granth*, *Mārū* 3.
[7] *Bījak*, *Śabda* 15.
[8] *Ādi-Granth*, *Śrī* 2.
[9] *Ādi-Granth*, *Gauṛī* 6.

For gold He is not obtained;
Rāma is obtained for the price of the heart.
Now that Rāma is considered by me as my own,
My heart is comforted with natural ease.[1]

Kabīr, if I cast down mine eyes and take the Friend into my heart,
I enjoy every pleasure with my Belóved, and I disclose this to no one.[2]

All are wives of Rāma: unmovable Purusha[3] is the Husband.[4]

Man's love is toward woman and woman's love toward man.
But they who love the Purusha alone are few in all the world.[5]

Through blindness none has rest: not one considers;
Not knowing the bhakti of Hari, the whole world is drowned and dead.[6]

The Need for a Guru.—In order that man may gain bhakti and have union with God, Kabīr advocates guidance from a religious preceptor, or guru. This was another idea he took over from the general bhakti movement. Sometimes in his verses, Kabīr uses the word guru to mean God whom he also calls the Sat Guru, or True Teacher. God is himself the Great Teacher to whom Kabīr would resort for guidance. Still he also believes that the instruction of an earthly guru is valuable, one who himself has experienced enlightenment and union with God, and who wishes to pass on to others the blessings he has himself received. Great care must be taken in choosing a guru, so that a false teacher may be avoided; but when a true one is found, he must be treated with great reverence. In other sects, as well as in the later Kabīr Panth itself, the guru is regarded himself as divine, and worshipped with divine honours. But Kabīr always stops short of this, just as he rejected all divine incarnations.

Thou (i.e. God) art the True Guru; I am thy novice.[7]
Keep thy mind steadfast under the guru's instruction; in this way thou shalt quaff nectar.
The guru's arrow hath pierced this adamantine age, and let in the light of God's word.[8]

[1] *Ādi-Granth*, *Gauṛī* 19.
[2] *Ādi-Granth*, *Ślok* 234.
[3] Purusha, the Male, i.e. God.
[4] *Bījak*, *Ramaiṇī* 27.
[5] *Bījak*, *Ramaiṇī* 50.
[6] *Bījak*, *Ramaiṇī* 65.
[7] *Ādi-Granth*, *Gauṛī* 2.
[8] *Ādi-Granth*, *Gauṛī* 46.

The guru without putting an arrow on his bow hath pierced this world, my brethren.

By the favour of the guru thou shalt obtain the wealth of God.[1]

Can a man without feet ever leap?
Can a man without a mouth burst into laughter?
Without sleep can man repose?
Can one churn milk without a churn?
Can a cow without an udder give milk?
[Can one accomplish] a long journey without a road?
[So] the way cannot be found without a true guru.
Kabir saith, and admonisheth all men.[2]

When his guru is blind, what can the disciple do?
The blind urges on the blind, both fall into the well.[3]

What can the helpless guru do? The fault is in the pupil.
The arrow of the word pierces him not; as well blow into a hollow bamboo.[4]

That Yogī is my guru, who will expound this song.[5]

THE FELLOWSHIP OF THE SANTS.—Kabīr not only advocated recourse to a guru for spiritual instruction but speaks much of the spiritual value of association with holy men, or *sants*. Intercourse with evildoers is to be avoided, but with those who are sincere and true of heart and have themselves tasted something of the blessings of fellowship with God, intercourse is elevating and helpful.

You never kept the company and fellowship of *sants* (holy men);
Thus with your own hand you have thrown away your life.
To-morrow you will not gain an abode like this:
You have not known the companionship of sādhus.[6]

If you meet a sant, speak two words with him;
If you meet the profane, then remain dumb.
To speak with a paṇḍit is full of profit:
Speech with a fool is mere babble.[7]

If you would be a sādhu, frequent the company of a sādhu who is perfect.
If you press unripe mustard seed, you get no oil nor cakes.[8]

Saith Kabīr, To whom shall I tell this, That heaven is in the company of the sants?[9]

[1] *Ādi-Granth*, *Āsā* 15.
[2] *Ādi-Granth*, *Basantu* 3.
[3] *Bījak*, *Sākhī* 155.
[4] *Bījak*, *Sākhī* 329.
[5] *Bījak*, *Śabda* 24.
[6] *Bījak*, *Ramaiṇī* 44.
[7] *Bījak*, *Ramaiṇī* 70.
[8] *Bījak*, *Sākhī* 282.
[9] *Ādi-Granth*, *Gauṛī* 10.

He is pure who singeth the praises of the pure God;
He is my brother and dear to my heart.[1]

Without association with the sants and worship of God, truth nowhere abideth.[2]

Saith Kabīr, through the sants I now know in my heart.
That the worshipper in whose heart God dwelleth [performeth] the best worship.[3]

THE ŚABDA.—The doctrine of the power of the Śabda, or Divine Word, is not so much in evidence in the verses of Kabīr himself as in the later writings of the Kabīr Panth; but still it is to be found there. This also is a doctrine found in other phases of Hinduism, and can be traced back to early times. It seems to be connected with the idea of the mystery of language as a means of expressing thought. Only as thought is expressed in teaching, can men find salvation; and hence even the letters have a mystic significance. But behind the letters and the words is thought; and the plurality of words must not obscure the unity of thought from which they proceed. The word 'Rāma' has (in Hindi) but two letters; and, as this approaches as nearly as possible to the ideal conception of unity, it has helped to lend a special sacredness to this name amongst the bhakti sects as a name of God. But behind this is also the conception of God as 'the Letterless One,' which we find in later Kabīrpanthī thought. There is little of all this in Kabīr's verses, but he does speak of the power of the Śabda, or Divine Word, as expressed through the guru, without which salvation cannot be obtained.

In the one Śabda are thirty-six melodies; it makes the music that is infinite.
The mouth is the neck, the ears the shell; the True Guru has set the frets.[4]

This is the property of the thirty-four letters:
That a thousand names are to be seen in them.[5]

Everything connected with the three worlds is contained in the fifty-two letters;

[1] *Ādi-Granth*, *Gauṛī* 26.
[2] *Ādi-Granth*, *Gauṛī* 59.
[3] *Ādi-Granth*, *Gauṛī* 63.
[4] *Bījak*, *Śabda* 69.
[5] *Bījak*, *Ramaiṇī* 25.

These letters shall perish; but He who is beyond letters is not in them.
Where there is speech, there letters are used;
Where there is no speech, there no mind abideth.
God is contained both where there is speech and where there is not;
Nobody appeareth like unto Him.[1]

Make thy body the churn, thy heart the churning-staff;
Into the churn (put) the Word instead of milk;
Make hearty meditation on God thy churning;
Pour the guru's favour into it as thy cold water.[2]

He in whose heart God hath planted His word hath ceased to thirst.[3]

Kabīr, slight is the stroke of a lance; though struck by it man may breathe [for a time];
But he who can endure the stroke of the Word is a guru, and I am his slave.'[4]

THE GOAL OF THE SOUL.—What was the final goal of the salvation which Kabīr was striving after? It was, we may say, re-absorption into God as the Soul of the world. He does not desire heaven, nor does he fear hell, but he longs for this union. Whether after this re-absorption he regards the human soul as retaining its identity and distinct personality, is not at all clear from the verses of Kabīr:

For those who know Him not, are heaven and hell;
They who know Hari have no part in them.
I take no thought for sin or virtue; neither to heaven nor hell go I.[5]

When the body dieth, to what abode shall the [pious man's] soul go?
Kabīr, It shall unite with Him who is beyond expression and indestructible;
He who knoweth God understandeth this.[6]

I shall not die like the rest of the world.
I have now met Him who reanimateth.[7]

The soul is not born, though men think it is; it is free from birth and death.

[1] *Ādi-Granth*, *Gauṛī* 1, 2; known as Kabīr's acrostic.
[2] *Ādi-Granth*, *Āsā* 10.
[3] *Ādi-Granth*, *Sūhī* 4.
[4] *Ādi-Granth*, *Ślok* 183.
[5] *Bījak*, *Śabda* 42.
[6] *Ādi-Granth*, *Gauṛī* 18.
[7] *Ādi-Granth*, *Gauṛī* 12.

When the idea of birth and death departeth from man's mind, he shall for ever be absorbed in God.
As the reflection (of an object) in a vessel of water blendeth with the object when the vessel is broken.
So, saith Kabīr, through virtue doubts flee away, and the soul is absorbed in God.[1]

Since my attention is fixed on God, I no longer suspect that I shall suffer transmigration;
Even in life I am absorbed in the infinite.[2]

KABĪR AND MUHAMMADAN DOCTRINES AND PRACTICES.—It cannot be doubted that the whole of Kabīr's thought is deeply tinged with ideas he has absorbed from Hinduism; but this does not mean that he was unacquainted also with Islam. He refers to the Muhammadan custom of burying their dead instead of cremating them as the Hindus do. He often mentions the Quran, their sacred book, the reading of which profits them little in his opinion. He mentions Adam and Eve thus showing at least some acquaintance with the contents of the Quran. He is acquainted with the Muhammadan custom of fasting for thirty days in the month of Ramazān, and with the slaughter of animals in sacrifice at the Bakr-i-Id. He refers to pilgrimage to the Kāāba (the sacred temple at Mecca in which is the black stone), and to the rite of circumcision. His denunciation of idolatry and rejection of incarnations are on the lines of one who regarded them from the Islamic point of view. But we have no indications that Kabīr had any deep acquaintance with Muhammadan theology and religious philosophy. Some quotations may illustrate his acquaintance with Islam:

Adam, who was first, did not know
Whence came mother Eve.
Then there was not Turk nor Hindu.[3]

O Darwesh, give me knowledge of that house;
In what dress is the king?

O Qāzī, what sort of deeds are thine?
In every house thou orderest the slaughter of buffaloes.

. . . .

Thou knowest not pity, yet thou art called Pīr;
Reading the verses thou teachest the world.

[1] *Ādi-Granth*, *Āsā* 1. [2] *Ādi-Granth*, *Bilāvalu* 11.
[3] *Bījak*, *Ramaiṇī* 40.

Says Kabīr, One was called *Sayed*[1]:
Himself misled, he misleads the world.
They fast all day: at night they slaughter the cow.
Here murder, there devotion; how can this please God?[2]

If birth from a Turk-mother makes you a Turk,
Why were you not circumcised in the womb?[3]

Shaikh and Sayed read their book.[4]

O Qāzī, nothing is done by [mere] talk;
It is not by fasting and repeating prayers and the creed that one goeth to heaven.
The inner veil of the temple of Mecca is in man's heart, if [the truth] be known.
Just decisions should be thy prayers; knowledge of God, the inscrutable One, thy creed,
The subjugation of thine evil passions the spreading of the prayer-carpet; then should'st thou know what religion is.[5]

O Qāzī, thy One God is in thee, but thou beholdest him not by thought and reflection.
Mad on religion, thou heedest not: wherefore thy life is of no account.
Thy books tell thee that God is true, and that he is neither male nor female;
Thou gainest nothing by reading and study, O madman, since thou regardest him not at heart.'[6]

Make thy mind thy Kāāba, the body its enclosing temple.[7]

The Musalmans fast in the month of Ramazān.[8]

If thou pray with deception in thy heart,
What availeth thee thy pilgrimage to Mecca?[9]

KABĪR AND SŪFIISM.—The question arises as to whether the teaching of Kabīr was in any way influenced by Sūfī mysticism. It has already been mentioned that the Sūfīs were in India long before the time of Kabīr; and Shaikh Taqqi, or some of the other pīrs he mentions, may possibly have been Sūfīs. There is undoubtedly a good deal of similarity between his teaching and theirs. The Sūfīs are Muhammadan mystics, whose teaching departs a good deal from the orthodox faith of Islam. They are not a sect, and

[1] *Sayed*, A descendant of the Prophet Muhammad.
[2] *Bījak*, *Ramaiṇī* 49.
[3] *Bījak*, *Śabda* 4.
[4] *Bījak*, *Śabda* 60.
[5] *Ādi-Granth*, *Āsā* 17.
[6] *Ādi-Granth*, *Āsā* 29.
[7] *Ādi-Granth*, *Bhairau* 4.
[8] *Ādi-Granth*, *Prabhātī* 2.
[9] *Ādi-Granth*, *Prabhātī* 4.

have no definite dogmatic system; but in place of the Transcendent God of Islam they have a pantheistic conception of God as one who dwells more in the human heart than in heaven, and it is an ecstatic union with Him that they seek, a union so close that the soul becomes indistinguishable from the Supreme Being. They recognize four stages at least, sometimes more, in the attainment of this. First that of the law (*shariāt*) or keeping of outward rites; then the worship of God in the mind (*tarīqāt*); then knowledge (*mārifat*); and finally the certainty of this union (*fanā*). To reach this stage a religious guide, whose commands must be implicitly obeyed, is considered essential. He must be one who not only possesses knowledge but has himself experienced the union with God after which the novice is seeking. In his upward progress, it is necessary for the novice to cultivate great humility and subjugation of self; and great value is attached to the repetition of the name of God (*dhikr*). The Sūfīs regard all ordinary religious duties as mere forms and attach no importance to them. Divine rewards and punishments (such as paradise and hell) and human standards of right and wrong, are regarded as non-existent for the one who has found union with God.

Many of these ideas of the Sūfīs appear in the teaching of Kabīr. In order to obtain union with God as the Supreme Reality he condemns pride, and declares the uselessness of the ordinary religious rites. God is to be looked for in the heart, for the one who has found God, heaven and hell are nothing. He, too, advocated the value of a guru, or spiritual guide, and the repetition of God's name. Without enquiring how far the Sūfīs have such points of teaching in common with all the bhakti sects of Hinduism, it may be noted that there are several matters in which Kabīr differs in his doctrines from those held by the Sūfīs. For instance, the Sūfīs, like other Muhammadans, hold the doctrine of predestination: namely, that God has destined men beforehand for salvation or damnation; and they also make Him the author of evil; otherwise they say His Divine prerogative would be imperfect. Kabīr, on the other hand, held firmly the doctrine of Karma and Transmigration, which makes man's destiny the result of his own deeds, and taught that all men by following the right path of salvation might obtain release from transmigration. Besides this, we do not find that Kabīr recognised definite stages in spiritual progress, such as those marked out by the Sūfīs; though this idea is now held by Kabīrpanthīs. The Sūfīs learned (probably from Buddhist monks) the use of rosaries, but though rosaries are used by Kabīrpanthīs, the practice was undoubtedly condemned by Kabīr himself.

It does not seem therefore that Kabīr was actually a Sūfī, though he held some ideas in common with them, and may possibly have come to a certain extent under their influence.

CHAPTER VI

THE HISTORY AND ORGANIZATION OF THE KABĪR PANTH

EARLY HISTORY.—The history of the early development of the Kabīr Panth[1] is buried in obscurity. It seems probable that Kabīr himself did not deliberately organize a sect, though he doubtless made disciples amongst the many who were attracted to his teaching.

The Panth is divided into two main sections, one of which has its headquarters at the Kabīr Chauṛā at Benares, and the other in the Chhattisgarh district of the Central Provinces The former is sometimes called the *Bāp* (or father) section, and the latter the *Māī* (or mother) section. But there are other divisions of the sect besides these, as we shall see later.

A. THE BENARES SECTION OF THE PANTH.—The following is a list of the gurus of the section which has its headquarters at the Kabīr Chauṛā at Benares, which is the older section of the two. The list, which is slightly different from that given in Bishop Westcott's book, is taken from a book published at the Kabīr Chauṛā.

NAME OF GURU

1. Kabīr	11. Kokil Dās
2. Surat Gopāl Dās	12. Rām Dās
3. Jñān Dās	13. Mahā Dās
4. Syām Dās	14. Hari Dās
5. Lāl Dās	15. Śaran Dās
6. Hari Dās	16. Pūran Dās
7. Sītal Dās	17. Nirmal Dās
8. Sukh Dās	18. Rangī Dās
9. Hulās Dās	19. Guru Prasād
10. Mādho Dās	20. Prem Dās
21. Rām Bilās	

[1] *Panth*, sect or brotherhood.

Surat Gopāl Dās is sometimes regarded as the real organizer of the Panth. None of the early gurus in the list were buried at Benares, and it seems the Panth had not then taken up its headquarters there. Probably the Nīrū Tila was acquired about the time of Sukh Dās, in the middle of the seventeenth century, and the Kabīr Chauṛā later. The first burial of a guru there was early in the nineteenth century; and about this period Rājā Bulwant Singh, who died in 1770, and his son, Chet Singh, were patrons of the Panth, and may have helped in its acquisition. Of the earlier gurus no history seems to be recorded.

The office of guru is not hereditary, as it is in the Chhattisgarh section. The guru is required to be a man of learning, qualified to teach the doctrines of the Panth. He is responsible for the general arrangements of the *maṭh*, or monastery. When a guru dies, the chief members of the Panth are called together and elect a new guru. A *diwān* looks after business matters, and a *kotwāl* is responsible for the maintenance of discipline. The *pujāri* is responsible for the conduct of worship. Most of the chief office-holders at the Kabīr Chauṛā are Brahmans. Men of all castes are accepted as sādhus, but those of low caste origin eat separately from the others.

THE KABĪR CHAUṚĀ AT BENARES.—The Kabīr Chauṛā, which is the headquarters of the Kabīr Panth at Benares, is situated not far from the hospital, and is approached by a narrow street. It consists of two courtyards, the Nīrū Tila, which is the traditional site of the house of Nīrū and Nīmā, and was probably the first part occupied by the Panth; and the Kabīr Chauṛā proper. Both courtyards are shaded by *nīm* trees and surrounded by buildings, in many of which sādhus of the sect are living. The chief point of interest in the main courtyard is the shrine which is said to be built over the spot where Kabīr taught. It has a pair of wooden sandals upon it to represent the feet of Kabīr. On one side of the courtyard is a room which contains the *gaddī*, or state pillow, of the guru. As the gaddī is supposed to belong to Kabīr, the present occupant of the office of guru does not sit upon it but behind it. In this room there is hanging a large picture of Kabīr, which however was only placed there in 1913. Other smaller pictures, which are found there, are Kabīr sitting with Surat Gopāl and Dharm Dās, Rāmānanda, Nānak, Mīra Bāī sitting before her guru Rai Dās, Śiva and Parvatī, Raṅgī Dās (a former guru of the sect) in his youth, Raṅgī Dās as an old man, Nirmal Dās (a former guru) teaching his disciples, and the present guru. Over the large picture of Kabīr are hung designs to symbolise the five elements of earth, air, fire, water and *ākāsh* (sky or ether), and the nine doors of entrance to the human body. Two vases of flowers are placed in front of the gaddī, and a rosary of a thousand beads is hung upon the wall for the use of the guru. A *topi* (or cap), and a *sehli* (or woollen necklace) of Kabīr are treasured at the monastery, as well as a copy of the *Bījak*. In the courtyard there are five tombs, of which four are those of former gurus, and one that of a disciple of one of these. From the upper storey of one of the buildings of the main courtyard there is a bridge across a narrow street to the Nīrū Tila. This is a smaller enclosure with only a few buildings. In the centre are the tombs of Nīrū and Nīmā, the parents (or foster-parents) of Kabīr.

Two miles away from the Kabīr Chauṛā is the Lahar Talāo, a shallow tank overgrown with weeds, where according to tradition, the infant Kabīr was found by Nīrū and Nīmā.[1] A small courtyard, in which is a shrine, marks the site of the traditional spot. It is in charge of a pujāri belonging to the Panth.

MAGHAR.—Another branch of the Benares section of the Panth is to be found at Maghar, the traditional site of the death of Kabīr.[2] Maghar is a village about sixteen miles from Gorakhpur, but in the Basti district. The Kabīrpanthī sacred place here is situated on the bank of the Ami river. It consists of two portions divided from one another by a high wall. There are no striking buildings.

One portion is in the hands of a family of Muhammadan weavers who claim to have had charge of the tomb from the time of Kabīr's death. It is the custom for each holder of the office to nominate his successor. He has the title of Ghani

[1] See above, p. 9 f. [2] See above, pp. 23 ff, 44.

Karan Kabīr. The present holder of the office is a woman, but the duties are performed by her husband. No record seems to have been kept of the names of previous holders of the office. The Muhammadans in charge of this shrine do not regard Kabīr as God, but simply as a pīr, or Muhammadan saint. They deny the legend about the heap of flowers, and say that the body of Kabīr was buried here in accordance with Muhammadan custom. They say that Rājā Bīr Siṅha was away hunting when Kabīr died and was buried; and that when he returned he demanded that the body of Kabīr should be exhumed and cremated; but his demand was successfully resisted.

The Mussulman shrine stands in the centre of the enclosure built like a temple and surrounded by a platform. At the right-hand corner of the shrine is a small covered building, where the custodian of the tomb has his gaddī during the time when melas are held. At the back of the platform, on the same side, is a much smaller shrine, which is said to be the tomb of Kamāl. By the custodians of this shrine Kamāl is regarded as the real son of Kabīr. Over the tomb of Kabīr a white cloth is placed. Incense is burnt and flowers are strewed at this tomb. But while the rites seem to approximate to those performed at Hindu temples, they are probably only similar to those which take place at the tombs of other Muhammadan saints. In the courtyard is another smaller tomb which is said to be that of Bijli Khān, the Pathān, a Muhammadan ruler, who was a follower of Kabīr. The original shrine of Kabīr is said to have been much smaller, and this seems likely, as the present building is certainly much later than his time.

In early days it is said there was only one shrine, which both Hindus and Muhammadans visited, and a mela was held which lasted over a month. Later on friction arose; and this probably led to the building of the second Hindu shrine. A custodian of the Hindu shrine, named Man Dās, is said to have been killed in an affray between the Hindu and Muhammadan followers of Kabīr.

The Hindu shrine is in the hands of a pujārī, who is a sādhu of the Kabīr Panth, and derives his authority from the Kabīr Chauṛā at Benares. The shrine of Kabīr is situat-

THE TWO SHRINES AT MAGHAR

The Hindu shrine is in front, with the small Sadhu's tomb, and a corner of the Mussulman maṭh can be seen in the distance.

THE TWO SHRINES AT MAGHAR

The Mussulman shrine is in the foreground, and the Hindu shrine, beyond a dividing-wall, is in the background.

ed towards one side of the enclosure, and is similar to, though rather smaller than, the shrine in the Muhammadan enclosure. On the right of the platform, as one approaches the shrine of Kabīr, is the shrine of Kamāl. The shrine of Kabīr is said to be on the spot where he sat waiting for death. It is covered with a red cloth, and worship is carried on here in accordance with Hindu rites. Worship takes place at the shrine every morning and evening. There is also worship at Kamāl's shrine. At the full moon of the month *Aghan* (November—December) the guru of the Kabīr Chauṛā at Benares visits the shrine and administers the *Jyoti Prasād*, a sacramental meal. The Kabīr Chauṛā maṭh possesses some property near Maghar.

Connected with the Kabīr Chauṛā there are monasteries in many parts of India. Amongst these an important one is at Burhānpur, in the west of the Central Provinces. At this monastery lived about a hundred years ago a certain Pūran Sāhib, who is the author of a commentary on the *Bījak*, as well as of other Kabīrpanthī works.

B. THE CHHATTISGARH SECTION OF THE PANTH.—DHARM DĀS.—The reputed founder of the Chhattisgarh (or *Mai*) Section of the Panth is Dharm Dās; and there can be no question that the Kabīr Panth owes a great deal for its development to him; indeed, next to Kabīr, he is almost certainly its most outstanding leader. He is not only the reputed founder of this section of the Panth,—which has its headquarters at Damakhera in the Chhattisgarh District of the Central Provinces—but he also figures very largely in the literature, a great deal of which is in the form of supposed dialogues between himself and Kabīr.

According to tradition, Dharm Dās was an immediate disciple of Kabīr; but the legends are confused and cannot be relied upon. He belonged to the Kasaundhan Baniya caste and lived at Bandhogarh, and his descendants still intermarry with this caste. Bandhogarh was formerly the capital of the Baghel kings, but in 1597 it was taken by the Emperor Akbar. Since then the capital has been transferred to Rewah, and the State is now also called by this name. Bandhogarh lies in the south-west corner of Rewah State, not far from the town of Umaria, where there are now coalfields and a railway station. The stories of the conversion of Dharm Dās relate that he became a disciple of Kabīr when he met him, during a pilgrimage to the north, at Muttra, and afterwards at Benares. We are also told that Kabīr appeared to Dharm Dās in Bandhogarh after passing away at Maghar, and instructed him as to the arrangements for the Panth and as to the teaching he was to give. It is said that his name was originally Judāwan, but that with the permission of Kabīr he changed it to Dharm Dās. The name of his wife was Āmīn, and she also became a disciple. Nārāyaṇ Dās, the son of Dharm Dās, refused to accept Kabīr as his guru; and so it is said that, through the grace of Kabīr, a second son was born in 1516, named Chuṛāmaṇi, who was to succeed Dharm Dās as guru.

The members of the Dharm Dās section of the Panth say that Kabīr foretold that the descendants of Dharm Dās should hold office for forty-two generations. After his marriage, each guru was to live with his wife till a son was born. Then his wife should become a female ascetic. Each guru was to hold office for a period of twenty-five years and twenty days, and after that install his son as successor. Then he should take a betel-leaf according to a solemn rite, and his spirit would depart. The names of the gurus from Dharm Dās onwards have been preserved, and the list is given below. Dhīraj Nām is known to have lived only for three years, and Ugra Nām died in 1914; but the other dates given are reckoned by calculation, twenty-five years for each holder of the office.

Little is known of the history of this section of the Panth, except the names of the gurus. To the name of the fourth guru after Dharm Dās, namely, Pramodh Nām, the title 'Bālā Pīr,' or 'Exalted Saint,' is added, which suggests that he may in some way have been an outstanding man, and there is evidence that some of the literature dates from his period of office. Possibly he may himself have been the author. The Kabīrpanthīs have an impossible legend to explain this title, which connects him with the Emperor Akbar.

NAME OF GURU	APPROXIMATE DATE OF INSTALLATION	BURIED AT
Dharm Dās	1619	Puri (Jagannath)
Chuṛāmaṇi Nām	1644	Kudarmal (near Janjgir)
Sudarśan Nām	1669	Ratanpur (Bilaspur District)
Kulpati Nām	1694	Kudarmal
Pramodh Nām Guru Bālā Pīr	1719	Mandla
Kewal Nām	1744	Dhamda (Drug District)
Amol Nām	1769	Mandla
Surat Sanehi Nām	1794	Singori (14 miles out of Chhindwara on the Seoni Road)
Haqq Nām	1819	Kawardha
Pāk Nām	1844	Kawardha
Praghat Nām	1869	Kawardha
Dhīrāj Nām	1894	Kawardha
Ugra Nām	1897	Damakhera
Dayā Nām	1914	

It does not seem likely that each guru did hold office for exactly twenty-five years and twenty days, but, as in the case of the gurus of the Kabīr Chauṛā section of the Panth at Benares (who are sādhus, and therefore only succeed when adults) the average length of office according to the list given is about twenty years; so we may at least accept twenty-five years as a possible average. It will be noticed that these dates only take us back to 1619. In a country like India, where the average length of life is short, it is difficult to suppose that the average tenure of office in the case of these gurus was longer than twenty-five years; and we are faced with the following alternatives. Either some names have dropped out of the list, or else Dharm Dās was not an immediate disciple of Kabīr (who died in 1517), but lived about the end of the sixteenth and the beginning of the seventeenth century. The latter alternative is the more probable one; and there are other things which may corroborate this. One is the list of the Hatkeshar gurus, given below; and another the confusion of the legends which connect Dharm Dās with Kabīr as an immediate disciple. What probably happened was, that Dharm Dās, a man of considerable force of character, became a convert to the Panth, when on a pilgrimage to the north, and when he returned to his own land gained many other converts and became the leader of the Panth in this region. Then, afterwards, in order to enhance the authority of his successors in office, the legend arose that Kabīr had actually appeared to him and given him instructions; and finally another legend grew that Dharm Dās was an immediate disciple, and had been converted during the lifetime of Kabīr.

With regard to the place where the tombs of the gurus are found, it does not follow that, because a guru was buried in a certain place, this was necessarily the place where he had his gaddī. He may have died when on tour. But it seems that Kudarmal and Mandla were headquarters of the Panth before the gaddī was located at Kawardha.

THE HATKESHAR GURUS.—There is another line of gurus who trace their descent from Dharm Dās, who have their gaddī at Hatkeshar, a village on the northern outskirts of Dhamtari, a small town in the Central Provinces. Their genealogical table, which for the sake of comparison is here set side by side with that of the Damakhera gurus,[1] is as follows:

DHARM DĀS

Churāmaṇi Nām

(*Damakhera Gurus*)	(*Hatkeshar Gurus*)
Sudarśan Nām	Sutidās
Kulpati Nām	Anand Dās
Pramodh Nām Guru Bālā Pīr	Narhar Dās
Kewal Nām	
Amol Nām	
Surat Sanehi Nām	
Haqq Nām	
Pāk Nām	Yudhishthir Dās
Praghat Nām	Fakīr Dās
Dhīrāj Nām	Amrit Dās
Ugra Nām	Jñān Dās
Dayā Nām	Kripāl Dās

Kripāl Dās: Komōd Dās, Dādā Sāhib

Dādā Sāhib: Mahakum Dās, Karnām Dās, Chiṇtāmaṇi Dās, Asthir Dās

[1] For Damakhera, see below, p. 102.

I understand that in this table, some names are omitted between Narhar Dās and Yudhishthir Dās. Unless there are more than two or three, the list would be about the same length as that of the older line of gurus, thus confirming the late date for Dharm Dās suggested above. The present occupants of the gaddī at Hatkeshar are four brothers, and they say their ancestor came to settle down near Dhamtari about one and a half centuries ago; but according to another statement it was Sutidās who first settled there. They say also that up to the time of Surat Sanehi Nām the two branches had communications with one another and intermarried, but that Surat Sanehi Nām had no issue by his lawful wife, Haqq Nām being his son by a servant woman. After the death of Surat Sanehi Nām, when Haqq Nām was installed as guru the Hatkeshar branch broke off its connection with the older line, and after that the two branches managed their affairs separately.

Of this second line of gurus, Yudhishthir Dās, Amrit Dās, Jñān Dās, and Kripal Dās were buried at Rudri, a small village about four miles away from Dhamtari, towards the south-east. Fakīr Dās was buried in a place near Nagpur, as he died on tour when visiting his disciples there. Komōd Dās and Dādā Sāhib were buried in Hatkeshar, as this was their wish expressed during their lifetime and the enclosure at Rudri was practically full. A *bairāgi* (ascetic) looks after the cemetery at Rudri to offer prayers at the tombs of the gurus. It is said that there are no theological or ceremonial differences between the two branches and their followers. About a thousand Kabīrpanthīs, near Nagpur, are attached to the Hatkeshar guru, though they also acknowledge the authority of the guru at Damakhera in all religious matters.

Another schism amongst the followers of the successors of Dharm Dās took place in 1894. In that year Praghat Nām, the guru of the older branch, died at Kawardha, where his gaddī was. Ugra Nām, who was born of a woman of low caste, was acclaimed as the successor of his father, but his claim was challenged by Dhīrāj Nām, whose parentage was legitimate. The dispute led to a case in the High Court at Bombay, which was decided in favour of Dhīrāj Nām, who occupied the gaddī at Kawardha. Ugra Nām retired to Kudarmal, near Janjgir, and afterwards to a newly-founded monastery at Damakhera, in the Raipur District. Dhīrāj Nām was unpopular and little attention was paid to him. Ugra Nām enjoyed the real homage of the followers of the sect, who said that Dhīrāj was the official guru, but Ugra the people's guru. Dhīrāj Nām died shortly after. The representative of the legitimate line now has his gaddī at Bamni, a village only a few miles from Kawardha, but seems to have few followers and little influence. After the death of Dhīrāj his mother wished that a sādhu, named Yugal Ānanda, should officiate as guru during the remainder of the term of office, but the majority of the members of the Panth strongly objected, on the ground that he was not a descendant of Dharm Dās. This lady was called the Dādī Sāhib, and continued to exercise influence at Kudarmal. Yugal Ānanda with other sādhus retired to Bombay, where he edited and published many Kabīrpanthī works.

Besides these lines of succession, there are other Kabīrpanthī mahants (or leaders) who claim descent from Dharm Dās, and are known as *Banshgurus.* One of these lives at Bandhogarh, in Rewah State, the original home of Dharm Dās, and claims to be a descendant of Nārāyaṇ Dās, the elder son of Dharm Dās, but information about this line is not available. Others live at Khetoli and Silondi, villages in the Jubbulpore District. What their relation is to the gurus at Damakhera is not clear.

The Dharm Dās section of the Kabīr Panth seems to have extended in many directions, and to have preserved its own organization, even where it exists alongside of other Kabīrpanthīs who are in communion with the Kabīr Chauṛā at Benares. Thus in Rajputana, where the Panth is not indeed numerous, the Kabīrpanthīs who are connected with the Kabīr Chauṛā, are known as *Mūl* (or 'original'), while those who are in communion with the Chhattisgarh guru are known as the *Bachan Bansh* ('Stem of the World'). Although the Mūl section draws more disciples from the better castes, and the Bachan Bansh from the lower castes, the followers of the latter speak rather contemptuously of the former, saying that they have not found Kabīr.

DAMAKHERA.—Damakhera, the present headquarters of that line of the descendants of Dharm Dās, which has the greatest following, is a village which lies just off the main road from Raipur to Bilaspur, about midway between them, and is about sixteen miles from Bhaṭapara station on the main line of the Bengal-Nagpur Railway. The village is a large open one; and others besides Kabīrpanthīs live there. In one part of it the Hindus have a temple. The guru lives in a fair-sized house of two storeys, and possesses an elephant

GROUP OF MAHANTS, SĀDHUS, ETC. AT DAMAKHERA

and a motor car. Close by the gate leading to the courtyard of his house is a covered platform. On this is the gaddī, where the guru sometimes sits to receive his followers. Adjoining the courtyard of the house is a small building something like a temple. When a mela is held the guru sits inside this. Apparently access to his person is not made easy even for his followers, who are always expected to bring a substantial offering. A large mela is held at Damakhera during the month of *Māgh* (February) on the day called *Basant Pañchamī*, when the guru sits on his gaddī and receives the homage and offerings of his followers. For three days all comers are fed from the bounty of the guru. The tomb of Ugra Nām is in the village, not far from the guru's house, but there is nothing imposing about it. Opposite the house is an enclosure with a well, and between the two an open space, where there is also a large pipal tree surrounded by a *chabutra* (platform). There is a *maṭh* (monastery) in the village where sādhus of the sect stay when they visit this place. It is said that there are about thirty-eight mahants, who receive their commission from the guru at Damakhera.

MANDLA.—At Mandla (also in the Central Provinces) the headquarters of the Panth are situated on the side of the river Narbada. The sacred enclosure here is in the form of a square with a side of about thirty or forty feet, and has a wall all round, that on one side being higher and having an arched gateway. In one corner is a small building covered with a dome like a temple. In the enclosure are two large tombs as well as a smaller one. The tombs are said to be those of former gurus, named Pramodh Nām Guru Bālā Pīr, and Amol Nām. The third tomb is said to be that of the foster-mother of Pramodh Nām. In front of the tombs is a small chabutra in which there is fixed a flagstaff with a white flag. On each of the tombs is placed a pair of wooden sandals, and flowers and lights are offered in worship. Just outside the enclosure are three small tombs which are said to be those of some sādhus of the Panth.

There are traditions at Mandla that the headquarters of the Kabīr Panth were once inside the fort, before being moved to the present site, but the information is very vague.

KAWARDHA.—The Kabīrpanthīs at Kawardha say that Haqq Nām was the first guru who had his gaddī there. This town is the capital of a small feudatory State in the Central Provinces, and being far from the railway is not easy to reach. The name Kawardha is said to be a corruption of *Kabīrdhām* or 'Abode of Kabīr,' but this etymology seems doubtful. There is now no guru at Kawardha, and the mahant there apparently has relationships both with the guru at Bamni and the one at Damakhera, but it is the latter guru who seems to have the real allegiance of Kabīrpanthīs who live at Kawardha. The former residence of the gurus at Kawardha is in a narrow street and is not a very pretentious building. It is at present deserted and in a dilapidated state. The graves of the four gurus who are buried at Kawardha are in the courtyard of the former residence of the gurus. There is also a fifth grave, which is said to be that of the mother of Haqq Nām. All five graves are built of heavy masonry and are in a straight row, occupying the whole length of the courtyard. The grave of Haqq Nām's mother is somewhat smaller than the other four, and is the first in the row.

There is a belief among Kabīrpanthīs of the Chhattisgarh section that forty-two generations of descendants of Dharm Dās are to occupy the gaddī, or seat of the guru, which he established. They also believe that there are to be eventually three other lines of gurus. Dharm Dās, the first guru, was given the chief guruship in the north, and is to be followed by forty-two generations. The second guru is to be Chaturbhuj Dās, who is to have the chief guruship in the south. He is to be followed by twenty-eight generations. The third guru is to be Bānkejī, who will have the chief guruship in the east, and will be followed by sixteen generations. The fourth guru is to be Sahti, who will have seven generations and the chief guruship in the west. Of these four gurus, only Dharm Dās has up to the present been manifested, and the gaddī of his generations established. But when the other three gurus are also manifested, then the religion of Kabīr will spread rapidly. It is to be noticed that this prophecy quite ignores the gurus who hold office at the Kabīr Chauṛā at Benares.

There does not seem to be any essential difference in doctrine between those Kabīrpanthīs who are connected with the Kabīr Chauṛā and those groups which are organized in the Chhattisgarh area. The Kabīr Chauṛā section does not think it right for gurus to be married men and does not recognise the gurus who claim descent from Dharm Dās. Kabīrpanthīs of the Kabīr Chauṛā section do not visit the holy places of the Chhattīsgarh section but the followers of the Chhattisgarh gurus do visit the Kabīr Chauṛā and Maghar.

DHANAUTI.—Another important division of the Panth has its headquarters at Dhanauti, in the Saran District of Bihar. According to information received there, they also do not differ in any essential points from other Kabīrpanthīs though they have their own organization. The founder of this section of Kabīrpanthīs was a certain Bhagwān, and all the gurus of this sect, who are unmarried sādhus, are called 'Bhakta' or 'Gosain'; while his followers are called *Bhaktāhīs*. Bhagwān Gosain lived at a place called Pithaurabad in Bundelkhand. He had four disciples; three of these were named Kokil, Dhanī and Sumaran. A fourth disciple (name unknown) established himself in a village called Larhia in the Champaran District and built a monastery there. A man named Banwārī became his disciple, and when Banwārī succeeded to the guruship he had four disciples named Bhikham, Nain, Dayā and Kamāl. The three latter established monasteries in other places in Bihar. But Bhikham Gosain set up his gaddī at Dhanauti. He was succeeded by Bhupāl Gosain and the next successor was Parameśwar Gosain. Gunpāl Gosain, who was the next in office, left the gaddī and disappeared, and then Sisaman came from the monastery at Kanchanpur and occupied the gaddī at Dhanauti. He was succeeded by three of his disciples in turn, whose names were Harnām, Jaimān and Swārūp. Sādhu Gosain who succeeded Swārūp is said to have been unsuccessful as a leader, and was driven from office. He was followed by the present guru, whose name is Rām Rūp. For the sake of clearness we may set out the succession of gurus at Dhanauti as follows:

Bhagwān Gosain

- Disciple (gaddī at Larhia)
  - Banwārī
    - Nain
    - Bhikham (set up gaddī at Dhanauti)
      - Bhupāl
        - Parameśwar
          - Gunpāl
            - Sisaman (from Kanchanpur)
              - Harnām
              - Jaimān
              - Swārūp
                - Sādhu
                  - Rām Rūp
    - Dayā
    - Kamāl
- Kokil
- Dhanī
- Sumaran

If we take the gurus who have held office at Dhanauti as well as Banwari, the predecessor of Banwārī, and Bhagwān Gosain himself, we have thirteen names. The list is about the same in length as that of the descendants of Dharm Dās in Chhattisgarh. Reckoning an average of 25 years for each occupant of the gaddī (which is probably too long a period) this only takes us back to about 1,600 for Bhagwān Gosain, or over eighty years after the death of Kabīr. At Dhanauti it was even stated that Bhagwān Gosain was 175 years later than Dharm Dās, but no information could be given as to this interval. Sometimes Bhagwān is regarded as the compiler of the *Bijak*. If this tradition is correct, it is evident that the compilation took place very much later than the time of Kabīr.

An old manuscript of the *Bijak* is said to be in the custody of the guru of this division of the Panth, but it is shown only to sādhus belonging to the sect.

The Kabīrpanthī settlement at Dhanauti consists of two monasteries; a large one where the guru and most of the sādhus live, and a smaller one about half a mile away to the north, where there are only a few sādhus. The larger monastery consists of a long building parallel with the village street, with two courtyards, which are separated from each other by a wall behind it. In the centre of the

THE COURTYARD AND TOWER, DHANAUTI MAṬH

The long ' hall ' lies to the left of the tower, outside the illustration.

THE MAHANT AND A GROUP OF SĀDHUS AT DHANAUTI

Mahant Rām Rūp is the fourth figure from the left. His robes and cap are of dark brown cloth. The other sādhus all wear white. In the background is the large hall where the mahant lives.

building is a tower, some thirty feet high; south of this is the long hall where the guru lives, and north of it is the entrance by an archway from the street. The courtyards are used for the storage of farm produce, and the verandahs as cowsheds. The smaller monastery consists only of a plain dwelling house of one storey with verandah. If the leader of the Dhanauti section of the Panth dies, he is succeeded by a sādhu whom he has nominated before his death.

The Bhaktāhīs[1] have monasteries in many different places, mostly in Bihar. In each section of the panth under the head guru there are *bhandārīs* or mahants who visit disciples of the sect all over the country, and there are also sometimes hereditary lieutenants of the chief guru with fixed seats or gaddīs in various places. They have in many cases become quasi-independent.

CHARACTERISTICS OF DIFFERENT SECTIONS OF THE PANTH.—Each of the divisions of the Panth has an order of sādhus or *bairāgīs*, who sometimes itinerate the country making disciples and sometimes live at the maṭhs. In the Chhattisgarh section there are also female *bairāginīs* of the sect, who are usually the wives of men who have become bairāgīs; The Kabīr Chauṛā and Dhanauti sections do not admit women as sādhus. Each of these three divisions has a slight difference in the sect-marks of its ascetics.

The subordinate mahants receive their authority from the chief guru and, in the case of the Chhattisgarh section, they may be either celibate or married. In the Raipur District, a 'dissenting' branch of the Panth has arisen, called the Nadia Panth, the mahants of which are all celibate.

Kabīrpanthī mahants wear a high-peaked cap, something like a bishop's mitre, and a long white robe without sleeves. They have with them also a *chauṛī* or whisk, a *chaubā* or silver stick, and a staff called a *kauṛī* or *aska*. (The latter is said to be carried in memory of one occasion when there was a very high flood at Purī, and the sea threatened to

[1] See above, p. 105.

submerge the temple of Jagannāth; Kabīr then planted a stick in the sand and said: 'Come thus far, and no further!' and the flood was stayed.) When officiating, the mahants wear a small embroidered cap. Each mahant has with him when he travels, a diwān, or assistant. A mahant, like all other Kabīrpanthīs, must abstain from flesh, fish, or liquor, and must not annoy anyone by begging, but should rather remain hungry. If he comes across any living thing which is hungry, he should give to it from his own food.

The mahant is supposed to visit the followers of the Panth in his district once a year, when he gives instruction and receives new converts into the Panth. He is entertained by members of the Panth, who also provide his travelling expenses. The mahants of the Chhattisgarh section, at the time of appointment, receive from the head guru a document bearing his seal, which is known as the *panja parwāna*. On this are entered the names of all the members of the Panth under his charge, and he is required to present it annually to the head guru for inspection and for the entry of new names. At his initiation the mahant makes an offering of cocoanuts. When he makes his annual visit to the headquarters of his guru, he has to present twelve cocoanuts and one rupee, for each new name he wishes to have entered on his parwāna. At the same time he hands over to the diwān all the offerings made at the services at which he has officiated during the year. Most of the mahants are not learned men, but they know by heart at least a number of sayings attributed to Kabīr, and must also possess a detailed knowledge of the ritual required for the performance of religious ceremonies. Some of them however know more, and besides the Kabīrpanthī works, they may be acquainted with the *Rāmāyaṇa* of Tulsi Dās and the *Bhagavad Gītā*. In the case of the Kabīr Chauṛā section, any bairāgi can initiate new members of the Panth.

PRESENT EXTENT OF THE PANTH.—According to tradition, the Panth has twelve divisions with gaddīs in various places; but this seems to be rather fanciful. The list of these divisions given by Kabīrpanthīs never tally with one another, and they differ also from the lists given by Wilson in his *Hindu Sects*. There are, however, various branches of the sect in widely scattered parts of India, and some portions of the sect in some places seem to have broken away and formed new sects.[1] The supposed division into twelve branches may have been suggested by the idea of glorifying the memory of Kabīr, just as Rāmānanda is said to have had twelve chief disciples.

The number of persons belonging to the Kabīr Panth is not far short of a million, of whom about six hundred thousand are in the Central Provinces and belong to the Chhattisgarh section. Converts are still being made, chiefly from the lower castes. Brahmans have been gathered in, and have often been given positions of importance in the Panth; but the majority belong to the lower castes. The weaving castes are usually Kabīrpanthīs, because Kabīr was a weaver. The Brahmans often speak contemptously of it as 'the Weavers' Religion.' In the Central Provinces a large number of members of this sect are found among the weaving castes such as the Pankās, Balāhīs, Korīs, Koshtīs, and Mahārs; and it is also largely professed by other low castes such as Telīs or oilmen, Dhobīs or washermen, and Chamārs or leather-workers. But there are members of the Panth from some castes from which a Brahman will take water, such as Ahīrs, Kūrmīs, Lodhīs, and Kāchhīs, who are farmers and cultivators. Though Kabīr did not directly preach the abolition of caste, he spoke against it, and the logical outcome of his teaching would be that it should cease. But in this direction, as in the case of other reformers in India, his efforts met with little success. A man who becomes a member of the Kabīr Panth does not cease to be a member of his caste, or to conform to its observances, even though these are contrary to Kabīr's teaching, such as idol-worship. Formerly all members of the sect took food together at a *chaukā* (sacramental meal) at the conclusion of each service. But it is now the custom for different chaukās to be arranged for different castes. On the thirteenth day of *Bhādon* (August), however, which is the birthday of Kabīr, as many members of the sect as

[1] See chap. x, 'Other Sects Influenced by Kabīr.'

can meet at the headquarters of the guru do take food together in honour of Kabīr. Sometimes the Kabīrpanthīs belonging to a particular caste form a separate group within the caste; but in the case of the lower castes they take food and intermarry with members of their caste who are not Kabīrpanthīs. Thus the Mahārs and Pankās permit intermarriage between members of the caste who are Kabīrpanthīs and those who are not, the wife in each case conforming to the customs and beliefs of her husband. Kabīrpanthīs conform to ordinary Hindu usages in conducting wedding ceremonies. They wear also the *choti* or scalp-lock, and shave the hair for the death of a relative, notwithstanding Kabīr's contempt of the custom.

THE PANKĀS.—The Kabīr Panth has, even in spite of its failure to live up to the teaching of its founder, given to the members of the lower castes a somewhat higher spiritual ideal than the primitive superstitions and animism which often form their only religion, and from which Hinduism has done little through its Brahman hierarchy to deliver them; and by accepting this faith many persons have been raised in the social scale. As an illustration of this we may cite the Pankās, who are an instance of a body of persons from a low caste embracing a new religion, and thereby forming themselves into a separate caste, and obtaining an advance in social position.

The Pankās are a Dravidian caste of weavers and labourers, found in the Central Provinces, who numbered 215,000 in 1911, and of which eighty-four per cent. are Kabīrpanthīs. They are derived from another caste called the Gandās, with whom however they desire as far as possible to disown their connection. As Kabīr was discovered in the water of a tank, and as a newly initiated convert is purified with water, so the Pankās say their name means *Pānī kā*, which means 'from water.' This has given rise to a doggerel rhyme about them:

Pānī se Pankā bhāe, bundan rache sharīr;
Āge āge Pankā bhāe, pāchhe Dās Kabīr.

This means, 'The Pankā indeed is born of water, and his body is made of drops of water, but there were Pankās before Kabīr'; or as the second line may also be rendered, 'First he was a Pankā, and afterwards he became a disciple of Kabīr.'

But the Pankās have been able to secure a somewhat higher position than the Gandās, in that their touch is not considered to convey impurity. Besides those who are members of the Kabīr Panth, there are other groups of the Pankās. The *Manikpurīa* say that their ancestor came from Manikpur in Darbhunga State, about three centuries ago; the *Saktaha* are those who profess to belong to the Sakta sect, which simply means that they eat flesh and drink liquor, being unwilling to submit to the restrictions imposed on Kabīrpanthīs; the *Bajania* are those who play on musical instruments, an occupation which tends to lower them in Hindu eyes, and the *Dom Pankās* are probably a section of the Dom or sweeper caste who have somehow managed to become Pankās. But the main distinction is between the *Kabīrha* or followers of the Kabīr Panth, who abstain from flesh and liquor, and the *Saktaha*, who do not. The Saktaha group is naturally recruited from Kabīrpanthīs who take to eating flesh and drinking liquor. There is no intermarriage between these groups, but if a girl of either section goes to a man of the other she will be recognised as his wife though the regular ceremony is not performed. The Saktaha worship all the ordinary village deities, but the Kabīrha, at least in theory, do not, and have no religious rites except when a mahant of their sect comes round to visit them. There is an exception however at the time of a marriage, when the betrothed couple worship Mahādeo and Parvati under the direction of a Brahman who also fixes the date of the wedding, this being the only purpose for which a Brahman is employed by Kabīrpanthīs.

CHAPTER VII

THE LITERATURE OF THE KABĪR PANTH

THERE is a great deal of literature belonging to the Kabīr Panth; but, until recent years, most of it existed only in manuscript, and was not therefore easily accessible. Now much of it has been printed, though there are probably still a great many works which have not been made known to the world.

Wilson in his *Hindu Sects* gives a list of Kabīrpanthī works, and Bishop Westcott in his *Kabīr* does the same. Such lists, however, do not give a real idea of the extent of the literature, for three reasons. First of all, many of the works mentioned are quite short works. The writer was shown some time ago some Kabīrpanthī works in manuscript, twenty-five in all. They could all have been printed in quite a moderate-sized volume. Some only occupied a page or so. These works are all included in Bishop Westcott's list. One or two of them have been printed. Then there is often a confusion in the names of the works, so that one may appear twice in a list under different names. Thirdly, we find that, when several works are printed in one volume, sometimes the name of one of the works is given to the volume and sometimes a new title is found for the collection. Under these circumstances it is not easy to identify all the works which are shown in any particular list.

An interesting feature is that most of the literature which has been printed (except the *Bījak*, *Granth*, and *Sākhīs*) seems to have been printed under the authorization of the gurus of the Chhattisgarh section of the Panth, and these volumes generally contain a list of the successors of Dharm Dās and a dedication of the work to them. As will be seen below, many of them are in the form of dialogues between Kabīr and Dharm Dās. This seems to be another indication that it is the Chhattisgarh section which has shown the greatest activity in the production of literature. A collection of verses has been published which are said to be those of Dharm Dās. But it is doubtful how far they are genuine. Conversations of Dharm Dās with Kabīr come into a good deal of the literature; but this was the literary form chosen by the writers, and does not mean that the verses put into the mouth of Dharm Dās were his compositions.

The following are the more important literary products of the Kabīr Panth.

1. THE *SUKH NIDHĀN* (*Treasure of Happiness*) probably belongs to about the middle of the eighteenth century A.D. According to tradition its date is 1729. Mr. Ahmad Shah considers the Hindi of the *Sukh Nidhān* to be about 150 years later than that of the *Bījak*; so that, on linguistic grounds, it would belong to the date suggested. Wilson mentions that it is ascribed to Surat Gopāl, the traditional founder of that section of the Panth which has its headquarters at Benares; but as he must have lived earlier, he is not likely to have been the author. Moreover, as Dharm Dās appears in it as the interlocutor, it seems quite likely that it may have been produced in the Chhattisgarh section. It may be noted here that it is often the custom of Kabīrpanthīs to describe all these later works as being those of Kabīr and they are generally published as *Kabīr Kṛit*, that is, 'written by Kabīr.' The *Sukh Nidhān*, which is a work of some literary merit, begins with teaching about God, who is the Creator, apart from whom nothing exists, and who is to be found in the heart—but men have been led astray by Māyā. It then goes on to tell the story of Dharm Dās. He was an earnest seeker after truth and engaged in many good works. He went on pilgrimage to many places, but all in vain. When he was at Muttra he met Kabīr, who instructed him, but at first Dharm Dās rejected his teaching. Again Kabīr appeared to him, but still in vain was his instruction. Dharm Dās passed on to Benares, and there found Kabīr overcoming in argument learned paṇḍits and Brahmans. He was much impressed

and asked Kabīr what his teaching was and who he was. Kabīr replied that he was *Sat Purush*, *Sat Kabīr*,[1] and the Creator of the World, that he lived within all and all lived within him. Dharm Dās asked further questions especially as to the origin of things, and Kabīr replied that the elements were but forms of himself, that he was all, and all was contained in himself. After somewhat lengthy instruction on this point, Dharm Dās was so far convinced as to throw away into the Ganges the *Śālgrāma*[2] which he used to worship, and continued to ask for further instruction, as to how Kabīr could be described as without form, seeing he is in all things. In answer to this query, Kabīr explains how Māyā has deceived Brahmā, Vishṇu and Śiva; and that it is to save them and their descendants that he has appeared in the world. In reply to further questions, Kabīr says that his body is immortal, and requires no material food, that it is on account of Māyā that men have been deceived and have instituted places of pilgrimage, and different sects and so on. He then appeals to Dharm Dās to save himself and others, and warns him against false teachers. No man can be saved by these false forms of worship nor by merely singing God's praises. Dharm Dās then asks how salvation is to be obtained, and is told to be constant, not to utter false words, to show love to others, to associate with good people, and especially with sādhus. Sādhus are specially to be honoured and served; for Kabīr is The Sādhu, and all sādhus dwell in him. There are some false sādhus who must be avoided; but by meeting a true sādhu, one's thoughts, words and deeds would become perfect. Thereupon Dharm Dās acknowledges Kabīr as the *Sat Guru*[3] and the Creator, but asks what is the fate of those who fail to recognize him or obey his commands. Such men he is told will be rewarded according to their works and have to pass through 8,400,000 forms before they obtain salvation. Kabīr is then entreated by Dharm Dās to accompany him to his house at Bandhogarh. On his return home he tells his wife, Āmīn,

[1] Both these are titles of the Supreme Being.
[2] *Śālgrāma*, a sacred stone typical of Vishṇu.
[3] Literally 'True teacher.'

what has happened, and she, too, becomes a disciple of Kabīr. Food is prepared and a cocoanut and betel-leaf are also brought; and Kabīr prepares for them the *mahāprasād*, or sacramental meal.

2. THE *GURU MAHĀTMYA* (*Greatness of the Guru*).—This is a work in about two hundred and fifty stanzas which consist of those metres known as *chaupāīs*, *soraṭhās* and *chhands*. Dharm Dās asks the way of salvation, and in reply Kabīr says he must recognize the guru as Lord and receive the betel-leaf.[1] The disciple must not listen to abuse of the guru, nor have enmity against the guru; he must also honour the guru's wife. Those who do not honour the guru will fall into rebirths. In the fourth generation of Dharm Dās his descendant Pramodh Dās will be manifested and will lead many souls to the *Satya Loka*.[2] Those who take the cocoanut and receive the betel-leaf will obtain salvation. There must also be love and devotion in the heart and reverence towards the guru. Kabīr then goes on to tell the story of a certain Rājā Rāy Mohan of Srinagar, who went to Badrinath, where he met Kabīr in the guise of a sādhu, and became his disciple.

From the mention of Pramodh Dās in this poem it is likely that it was composed during his period of office, perhaps by himself. He alone of all the gurus of the Chhattisgarh section has the title of Bālā Pīr, or Exalted Saint, which seems to show that he was an outstanding man. May we not suppose that during his time the Panth made great strides, and that much literature also was produced? He probably held office in the first half of the eighteenth century. It is possible that the same author may be responsible for the *Sukh Nidhān* (which also probably belongs to this period) and for the *Gorakh Gushṭi* and perhaps other works. Unless further evidence is forthcoming this can however only be conjecture.

3. THE *GORAKH GUSHṬI* OR *GORAKHNĀTH KI GOSHṬI*.—This is an imaginary conversation between Kabīr and

[1] i.e. in the sacramental meal.

[2] *Satya Loka*, or *Sat Loka*, 'Heaven,' the highest of the fourteen regions of the universe in Hindu cosmology,

Gorakhnāth, who was a celebrated Yogī, or ascetic. As it is mentioned by Wilson in his *Hindu Sects*, it is probably to be dated somewhere in the eighteenth century. It is not a very long work, containing less than 150 couplets. It is written in *chaupāīs* and *samāīs*.

Kabīr first speaks and says that, though many are seeking for God, few find Him. Yogīs, ascetics, and sannyāsīs have been deceived by Māyā. The paṇḍit is proud of his knowledge of the Veda, but does not know God. He appeals to Gorakh to enjoy the blessing of fellowship with God. Though he has performed yoga he has not obtained union (*yukti*)[1], but has sold himself into the hands of Yama, the King of Death. God has manifested Himself in the soul of man; and, through not having known this secret, gods, men, and sages—all have been deceived.

Gorakh replies that, while God indeed pervades the heart He cannot be known without the practice of yoga; for all have been deceived by Māyā. The five elements and the twenty-five *prakṛitis*[2] have to be overcome. As long as Māyā holds the mind, the root of happiness cannot be obtained.

Kabīr answers that Gorakh is in error, and asks how he is going to overcome his senses. Where does God dwell? Whence has He come into Being? Who has created the five elements and the twenty-five *prakṛitis*? Whose is this created world?

Gorakh says that few know God as *nirguṇa*.[3] The Creator is always free from Karma. He has no form nor parts. He has no eyes nor ears. He has no elements nor Māyā. He has no righteousness nor mercy, and so on. All is under him and he pervades all.

Kabīr asks, If God has no attributes, how can He be known? and presses his point at great length.

Gorakh expresses his astonishment at this teaching, and Kabīr makes a great appeal to him to forsake error and accept the truth. Gorakh asks for further instruction, which Kabīr gives to him, showing that the complete Deity (Pūrna

[1] There is a play on words here.

[2] *Prakṛiti*, matter; here, the demerits of the universe.

[3] *Nirguṇa*, without attributes.

Brahma) dwells in every soul. The poem ends by Gorakh laying his cap and wallet and banner at the feet of Kabīr.

This work is a philosophical one and very different from the style of Kabīr, but is not without poetic merit.

The theology of this poem is not so advanced as that of the *Amar Mūl* described below: and as it is mentioned in the list given by Wilson in which the *Amar Mūl* is not mentioned, it is probably earlier and perhaps by the same poet as the *Sukh Nidhān*.

4. THE *AMAR MŪL*.—The *Amar Mūl* (*Root ot Immortality*), is another well-known Kabīrpanthī work. It is generally considered to have been composed about 1800, and this is borne out by internal evidence, for in one section of the poem it is said that the Sat Guru[1] foretold that the descendants of Dharm Dās up to the eighth generation would be tainted with pride, whereas, in the eighth generation, one would be born who would bring men back to the true path. This seems to indicate that the *Amar Mūl* was written when the eighth guru was in office, that is, somewhere about 1800.

This poem consists of about 5,000 stanzas and is in the form of a conversation between Kabīr and Dharm Dās, the disciple of Kabīr, who was the founder of the Chhattisgarh section of the Kabīrpanth. It is written in chaupāīs and sākhīs. The following is a brief analysis of the contents.

Part I. Dharm Dās begins by saying that the shadow of death is upon all souls in the world, and asks the Sat Guru[1] to remove as quickly as possible the pain of their heart. Kabīr replies that those into whose heart the immortal Word has entered receive immortality. In order to obtain salvation, an understanding of the 'Letterless One'[2] is necessary, with the help of the Betel-leaf and the Cocoanut. God is unconditioned (nirguṇa) as containing the essence of the Letterless One, but conditioned (saguṇa) as manifesting Himself in creation. In order to obtain salvation, true belief in God as both conditioned and unconditioned is necessary, and absorption in the Word. Four gurus have been entrusted with the work of conveying souls safely across the ocean of existence; and Dharm Dās is the chief of the four; so he, and his forty-two descendants, must rescue souls from Kāl; for all are deceived by Māyā. In answer to the request of Dharm Dās for further explanation of 'the Betel-leaf' and 'the

[1] Here a title of Kabīr.

[2] i.e. The Indescribable God.

Cocoanut,' Kabīr says that the Betel-leaf proceeded from the Word, and the Cocoanut, when broken by the True Word, is accepted as a substitute for souls which have been made over to the King of Death (Dharm Ray). The Cocoanut, the Betel-leaf and the Word are the three boats by which the ocean of existence can be crossed. Salvation is obtained by receiving the betel *parwāna* (passport), by serving sādhus, and by becoming absorbed in the True Word.

Part II. Dharm Dās then asks for information as to the Priceless Name and the Soul (jīva). He is told about the five elements, and twenty-five prakṛitis, and that the jīva has sprung from Brahma. Atma and Brahma are really one, being united in *Paramātma*.[1] Jīva (which is used as synonymous with Ātma) and Brahma are regarded as two, but are really one, having the same relation as the wave to the ocean, the spark to the fire, and the ornament to the gold out of which it is made. Kabīr goes on to speak of the Sabda and the 'Letterless One.' All who have assumed bodies have been produced by Sabda, which is undivided, whereas all else is divided. The true Sabda reverberates through the universe. He who knows the Letterless One finds an entrance into the Satya Loka. Dharm Dās asks for more information about the Satya Loka and is told of its wonders. The glory of the soul there is equal to that of sixteen suns, while that of the *Purusha*[2] cannot be described. The True Name is the support of the soul. Souls in the Satya Loka eat as it were ambrosia; and thereby all their errors and doubts are removed; and they receive complete satisfaction. They are filled with feelings of love and hope; and desire ceases. All is due to the knowledge of the True Name. In answer to more inquiries of Dharm Dās, Kabīr expatiates further on the value of the True Name, which is like a lamp in the darkness.

PART III. Dharm Dās asks what are to be the rules of devotion, and what rites the Panth which he is to establish shall observe. Kabīr begins by saying that, in order to reach the ocean of happiness, the Sat Guru must be served and the mahāprasād (sacramental food) must be received. The guru must be recognized as identical with God; and he and sādhus must be served, and the water in which they have washed their feet must be drunk. They must never speak ill of their guru and must meditate on the love of the Letterless One. They must always remember the Name, and place no hope in the deceit of Karma. Kabīr goes on to speak of other systems, the Vedas and the Purāṇas (of which the *Bhāgavata* is the best). But men are only puffed up through pride of intellect and are groping in the dark. Only those obtain wisdom who meet the Sat Guru, for the boat is of no use without the boatman. Only those who know the secret can obtain salvation. Doubt has possessed the hearts of men; but, through a knowledge of the Name, doubt can be banished from the heart. Dharm Dās interposes, and says that only a few souls possess know-

[1] *Paramātma*, the universal Soul.
[2] *Purusha*, the Creator.

ledge. How then can people be saved? Kabīr replies that he is imparting to him the knowledge which he himself possesses. He who receives the betel-leaf parwāna will obtain salvation; and he in whose heart there is faith will cross safely the ocean of existence. After receiving the betel-leaf, he will speak the truth, will keep the feet of the Sat Guru in his heart, will sacrifice all for the Sat Guru and serve the sādhus. He will give up love for wife and family; and forsake all for the Sat Guru, and drink nectar in the Satya Loka. In answer to the inquiry of Dharm Dās, as to whether women also can obtain salvation, he is told that they also can cross the ocean of existence by faith in the True Name and giving up all to serve the guru and sādhus. Dharm Dās is then exhorted to be faithful in teaching men devotion; for on him this burden has been placed. Into his hand has been given the touchstone by which jīvas can be turned into *haṁsas*,[1] for this can be done through the vehicles of the Name.

PART IV. Dharm Dās asks for an explanation of 'the touchstone,' and is told it varies in different cases. In the case of the wise it is the Sabda; in the case of children reception of the Betel-leaf; and in the case of the passionate it lies in devoted service. When Dharm Dās asks how it is possible for the guru to live and teach in this world, Kabīr is angry with him for being slow to understand, and says he is still under the influence of Māyā. He then disappears from view. Dharm Dās is greatly distressed, and cries for pardon, and to his great joy Kabīr again appears before him. He clasps his feet and worships him, and having washed the guru's feet drinks the water. He then asks to be given the sacrament of *mahāprasād*. The wife of Dharm Dās, Āmīn, then prepares a meal, and *āratī* (lights) are offered in a golden vessel. All fall at the guru's feet, and receive his instruction, and he then gives the *mahāprasād* to all who were present. Then the Sat Guru sits on a bed, while Dharm Dās fans him and Āmīn shampoos his feet. Āmīn offers herself in devotion to the guru, and he puts his hand on her head and gives her his blessing. Dharm Dās is promised that he shall have forty-two generations of descendants, to whom is committed the task of bringing salvation to the world. Dharm Dās asks that his descendants might be granted this blessing that through them souls might be set free; and Kabīr renews his blessing and urges faithfulness in proclaiming the message he has given to the world.

PART V. In answer to further questions of Dharm Dās, Kabīr shows that all three worlds had been made over to Dharm Ray by Purusha, and that he had tried to stop Kabīr coming into the world. All who performed religious acts were in his power, even Śiva the destroyer. Kabīr, who is here called Jñāni, replied that the authority of Dharm Ray was usurped and that on this account Purusha, with whom Dharm

[1] *Jīva* here means a soul which is under the spell of illusion; and *haṁsa* a soul which has found liberation and union with the Supreme.

Ray vainly tried to identify himself, had sent him into the world to save souls. Dharm Ray implored the kindness of Jñāni, who would only consent to leave him undisturbed on condition that he would leave unharmed all who received the Betel-leaf. Dharm Ray accepted this offer, but was warned that when the Śabda was established in the world his rule would cease. Dharm Dās then thanks the Sat Guru for this teaching, and asks for more information about Kāl. Kabīr says that Kāl, who is really a form assumed by Purusha, is the cause of all actions in the world, has deceived the ten incarnations of Vishṇu, and is the cause of virtue and vice. But he has no power over Śabda and wherever the True Word has been received, duality disappears. A fear of Kāl has led to asceticism, sacrifice, alms-giving and other forms of devotion. Kāl devours all who live the life of the senses. Kāl is the cause of creation, and in Kāl it will fade away. Dharm Dās asks as to which came first, Purusha or Kāl? He is told that first was 'Space' (*Śunya*) and that from space Purusha produced Śabda, and Śabda from Sabda. Space and Time (Kāl) are really one. No one knew the mystery of Kāl, and all feared Kāl. Through fear of Kāl devotion of various kinds arose, but by a knowledge of the Name that fear could be overcome.

PART VI. Dharm Dās goes on to ask for instructions as to the *chaukā*, *ārati*, and other matters connected with religious observances, and is told about these. A cocoanut, he is told, is broken for sins a lakh and a quarter in number,[1] and the sins of many births are got rid of by the splitting of the straw. He is then given various *mantras* which are to accompany various religious acts, in connection with the cocoanut and the straw, at the time of drinking water at the time of bathing, and at the time of receiving *prasād*. With regard to the performance of āratī, he is told that, in the first place, the house should be whitewashed and various articles provided, namely, seven cocoanuts, thirty and a quarter maunds of sweetmeats of eight different kinds, three and a quarter pounds of sugar candy, twelve thousand betel leaves, and besides this, sandal wood, camphor, cloves, betel nuts and cardamoms. A silk *dhoti* must be given to the mahant who officiates. The canopy over the chaukā should be made of gold cloth, and the vessel in which the dew is collected should be made of gold. If any one celebrates an āratī in this way, but not from a selfish motive, he will pass at once to the Satya Loka. Dharm Dās then points out the difficulty in this Kali Yuga of celebrating the āratī in such a lavish way, and is told that a simpler form is permissible. For this, three and a quarter pounds of sweets, one cocoanut and a hundred betel leaves will be sufficient. The mahant must get a new dhoti and all present must make an offering in money to the Sat Guru. The āratī should be celebrated each month; if not, twice a year will be sufficient, in the months of *Phāgun* (February) and *Bhādon* (August). The mahant who conducts the āratī must have a knowledge of the Letter; otherwise he and his followers will go to the world of Yama, the Angel of Death.

[1] A lakh = 1,00,000.

PART VII. Dharm Dās asks how, in this world of death, souls can be preserved from error and heresy. He is told that he in whose mind the True Word dwells will be saved from error, and the Sat Guru proceeds to speak of the four castes. He shows how Brahman, Kshatriya and Vaisya have all neglected the duties for which they were appointed, but the Śūdra, whose duty is to serve the other three castes, has cast out of his heart the desires of the flesh, anger and avarice, and has discovered the way of bhakti to the Sat Guru and so finds his way to the Satya Loka. Dharm Dās is a Śūdra by caste, but all who accept him as their guru will cross the ocean of existence. All souls, whether Śūdras or not, can be saved by meditating on Brahma, for Kāl attacks in vain the soul that knows the mystery of the Śabda. Dharm Dās asks why his family has not obtained the salvation which he himself has found. He is told that the next seven generations of his family will be tainted with pride instead of trusting in the Name. Only those who practise devotion can obtain salvation and impart it to others, who speak to all the truth, who keep the True Name in their hearts and keep from anger, who speak under the influence of the Name, teach knowledge, and preach the doctrine of the Word. But in the eighth generation of his descendants will be one who will be a light to the Panth, and bring men back to the true path. He who does not obtain the True Name is blind, but the Sat Guru dwells in the heart which is illumined by the immortal Sabda.

PART VIII. Dharm Dās expresses the belief that as the Purusha dwells in the guru, there is no distinction between them, and says what an honour it is for him and his descendants to succeed the guru. Kabīr again described the future blessings of the descendants of Dharm Dās, and again urges them to be faithful. Dharm Dās expresses the hope that with the help of the Sat Guru all his children will reach the Satya Loka. Kabīr replies that this can only be if they cherish the True Name. He then goes on to say that some day all creation will enter the Satya Loka, and all beings be absorbed in the Sat Guru. Dharm Dās says that the work of saving souls belongs to the Sat Guru and asks to be relieved of the responsibility of the guruship; but Kabīr does not consent to this. In answer to the question of Dharm Dās why Kabīr, being a dweller in the Satya Loka, had visited this world, Kabīr again explains to him the mystery of creation. When Kāl began to persecute the jīvas (souls), Purusha had pity on them, and sent the Sat Guru to rescue them. Creation is the sport of the Purusha. Dharm Dās then asks for knowledge about the Ātma. Kabīr explains the unity underlying all things. All is equivalent to the Ātma. Master and disciple are one, friend and enemy are one. The Ātma is active, and is also passive. The Ātma shows himself and himself sees, himself is all manifest and himself is hidden in himself, and so on. Dharm Dās asks why the Jīva remains in ignorance of its true condition. Kabīr replies that Brahma is the seed out of which all develops and that Śabda is of subtle form. The relation of Jīva to Brahma is as the wave to the sea, the ray of light to the sun, the oil to the oil-seed, the scent to the flower.

PART IX. Dharm Ḍās asks how this sense of duality can be removed and is told that all is due to Māyā. When man realizes his true condition he becomes Brahma. When Brahma abides in the heart it is illuminated with knowledge. Karma and *Dharma*[1] are obliterated. All Māyā disappears, and all apparent contradictions are reconciled. Brahma is himself the Word that cannot be uttered, and the Word that is spoken to all. He is without form and yet in all forms. He is both conditioned (nirguṇa) and unconditioned (saguṇa). Dharm Dās is told that before he can teach others the way of salvation he must first purify his own heart. False teachings and false ways of worship must be avoided, for these are the work of Māyā. True devotion and a knowledge of essentials is required. All delusion is removed through meditation. Kabīr then gives an account of a vision he had when in the Satya Loka, which was indeed indescribable. The form of Purusha can only be imagined, and the abodes of the Satya Loka are without number, but in all the emancipated souls was discernible the one Letter. In the world of Kabīr he saw the forms of many Kabīrs, but on looking again he saw that it was only one form multiplied. He was Kabīr and he was the Creator. In the light of the true Śabda, all is one, there is no second.

People are taught by means of stories, but for those who understand, all such stories fall short of the truth. All apparent distinctions are creations of the mind, but he who knows the letter thoroughly is saved from duality. Brahma and Jīva have no difference except that the latter is the reflection of the former.

PART X. Dharm Dās is told what to do in the case of one wishing to become a disciple. First he should give to him the betel-leaf, then if the applicant has wisdom he should reveal to him the glory of the Śabda. When his faith in the Śabda is confirmed he should impart to him the full knowledge of Ātmarām. When he understands this he himself is Ātmarām, he knows no second. Kabīr goes on to tell how once in the Satya Loka, Purusha appeared to him and said, 'Kabīr, you and I are one; entertain no thought of duality. All creation is delusion. Beside me there is no second. Gods, men and sages are all involved in this delusion.' Dharm Dās asks if there is no second witness to such an important statement. Kabīr replies that he was told this in the *Tretayuga*[2] and that Madhukar, the Brahman, is the second witness. He then continues to say that Kabīr and Dharm Dās are one. Kabīr is in all bodies, the speaker is Śabda. There is only one form, one Śabda, and one Purusha manifest in all. He who recognises the unity is one with it. The second is this world (of illusion). Dharm Dās asks how it is that the jivas do not recognise their unity with Brahma. He is told that souls come from Brahma Loka devoid of Karma, just as the clouds lift up pure water from the ocean and pour down pure water in rain. But as the water when it comes in contact with the earth

[1] *Dharma*, a comprehensive word meaning duty, law, etc.

[2] The *Tretayuga*, the Second Age of the world (the present age being the Fourth—Kaliyuga.) See below, p. 137.

becomes impure, so the jīvas are embraced by Māyā and are defiled by Karma. But as air purifies water so does knowledge remove Karma and the purity of the jīva is restored. The Ātman mingles with the Paramātman as the rivers flow into the sea. The Atman without Śabda is blind, but when it obtains the eyes of Śabda and meets the Sat Guru it finds the true path. He who is illuminated by knowledge, he is Kabīr, he is Dharm Dās. He who sees the Ātmarām knows that all is contained in himself. All he sees is like himself, and there is nothing else beside Brahma.

The poems ends by Dharm Dās worshipping Kabīr. In this poem the theology is much more advanced than that of the *Sukh Nidhān*; and this in itself seems to show that the *Amar Mūl* is the later of the two. It is not amongst the works mentioned by Wilson, and this also may indicate a later date. It contains some good verse, but nowhere rises to the height of great poetry.

5. THE *KABĪR BĀNĪ*.—The *Kabīr Bānī* contains nearly fifteen hundred stanzas, and is written in chaupāīs and sākhīs. It is a conversation between Kabīr and Dharm Dās. There is a note at the end of the printed edition saying that there is only one manuscript of this, which is dated 1790, and that there are many uncertainties in the text. It begins with a most elaborate account at considerable length of the creation of the world, but says that all is overshadowed by Māyā and in the power of Kāl. Dharm Dās is urged to find salvation by taking refuge in the Sat Guru, whom he must love with all his heart. After that, various topics are dealt with without very much connection or order. Among these are the four kinds of knowledge, the four gurus, the four bānīs, the seven kinds of desire (ichchhā), the four eggs (aṇḍa), the end of the Kāli Yuga, the twelve panths, the forty-two generations of Dharm Dās, the number of souls who are to be saved in each of these generations (which is in gradually increasing magnitude till it reaches huge figures) the arrangement of the chaukā, etc.

6. THE *ĀLIF NĀMĀ*.—This poem of which there is more than one version in existence, is in the form of an acrostic (like the *Chauntīsī* which is found in the *Bījak* and the *Granth*) but is based on the letters of the Persian alphabet. It is however written in Hindi.

7. *REKHTAS*.—*Rekhtas*, of which there are many, are short

didactic poems, or verses in praise of the guru or of God. The *Dās Mukāmī Rekhta* is an account of the ten *mukāms* or places of existence, and the glory of the souls in the Satya Loka. The *Kāyā kā Rekhta* is a mystical poem on the body.

8. THE *BAṚĀ SANTOSH BODH*.—The *Baṛā Santosh Bodh* (*Knowledge of True Satisfaction*) is in the form of a conversation between Dharm Dās and Kabīr. It contains over 200 couplets, and is written in chaupāīs, samāīs, and dohās (sākhīs). Dharm Dās asks for and receives an explanation of the elements. Some of the verse has a good rhythm, but to the uninitiated the contents of the poem are most uninspiring.

9. THE *MUKTI MŪL*.—This is about the same length as the previous poem, and is again a conversation between Kabīr and his disciple, Dharm Dās. Dharm Dās asks for an explanation of the ground of salvation (*mukti mūl*). Kabīr expresses his great readiness to comply with the request of his disciple and says that the ground of salvation is one letter (akshara) which differs from all others.[1] From not knowing this all the world has gone astray. Dharm Dās asks for more knowledge and for an understanding of bhakti, and Kabīr answers first of all by saying that man must look within himself for knowledge. Bhakti is sought after by many, but few understand the right way, and so have taken to idolatry and other vain practices and have not obtained salvation. To understand the right way of bhakti is indeed the root of salvation. Very few even among holy men have attained unto it. It can be obtained by having a lowly mind and by serving sādhus.

Dharm Dās next inquires the proper method of practising yoga and austerities, and then receives a long instruction in the various postures and methods of Yoga and their value.

The next question of Dharm Dās is as to the elements (*tattvas*); and he is told there are eight, of which five are manifest, and three hidden. The three are *omkāra*.[2]

In answer to his question as to the six *darśanas*,[3] Dharm Dās is told that water, air, earth and ether (ākāśa) the

[1] Perhaps the mystic syallable *Om*, which is a single letter in Hindi.

[2] *Omkāra*, the sacred syllable *Om*.

[3] *Darśana*, appearance.

moon, and the sun are the six darśanas, for they illuminate the soul. While people speak about the six darśanas they do not find salvation, and he is rather to look within for this.

Then Dharm Dās asks about the Purusha which is within him, and is told that He is both Soul (*Haṁśa*) and Oversoul (*Paramahaṁsa*). When He was born He became a portion (aṁsa) of the Purusha. This is the ground of salvation, but without the true guru none can obtain it.

The Hindi in this work is easy, and it seems to be quite a modern work.

10. THE *BHAVATĀṚĀN* (*The Crossing of the Ocean of Existence*).—This poem contains over four hundred stanzas, and is again a conversation between Kabīr and Dharm Dās. Dharm Dās asks how the ocean of existence can be crossed, and is told that it is by means of bhakti, and the serving of sādhus. Pride of heart must be given up. The way however is not easy. Yogīs and worshippers of Vishṇu perform many religious ceremonies, but do not cross the ocean of existence. Some are worshippers of Vishṇu and call 'Hari, Hari!' but do not obtain salvation. Many are proud of their learning, but they, too, are not saved. Kabīr then proceeds to expound the doctrine of nirguṇa. Nirañjan has made the universe, and has made the three qualities. He is the *ego* in the heart. All incarnations are parts of him. Seers, sages, gods, all serve Nirañjan, but devotion is hidden from them. Dharm Dās then asks what is the way of devotion. Kabīr first warns him against false ways which are current in the world. The Purusha is contained in all and yet separate from all; the world has not known Him. Dharm Dās then asks again what the true way is, and is told he must let love come into his heart and serve and honour sādhus. This will establish devotion towards the Purusha. Dharm Dās asks what the difference is between nirguṇa and saguṇa devotion. Kabīr cites the examples of Dhruva and Prahlād. Both had saguṇa devotion, but failed to find the Purusha. The same is the case with all whose devotion is of the saguṇa type. Dharm Dās asks what nirguṇa devotion is. Kabīr in answer tells him the story of the creation of the world according to the usual Kabīrpanthī cosmogony, and how Kāl had deceived the

world. Dharm Dās, must give up love of family and devote himself wholly to the guru. Then Kabīr goes on to describe how the chaukā is to be prepared and ārati performed.[1] In this way the ocean of existence can be crossed. Dharm Dās expresses his thanks, and the poem ends with a dissertation by Kabīr on the Letterless One, and an exhortation to Dharm Dās to follow the true path.

11. THE *BHED SĀR* (*Essence of the Secret*).—This is written in chaupāīs and samāīs, and contains about 250 couplets. It is not, as many of the other works are, in the form of a dialogue between Kabīr and Dharm Dās, but is nevertheless addressed to the latter, the phrase, 'Kabīr said to Dharm Dās' frequently occurring. It is a somewhat lengthy discourse with much repetition on the value of the name of God[2] which is said to be the essence of the secret (*Bhed Sār*) of religious knowledge.

12. THE *PRITHVI KHAṆḌ*.—This is another dialogue between Kabīr and Dharm Dās. It is written in chaupāīs and sākhīs and contains over 300 stanzas. In answer to a question of Dharm Dās as to the origin of the world, Kabīr explains it to him. The cosmogony is very elaborate.

13. THE *ĀDI BHED*.—This is a fairly short work. In answer to a request of Dharm Dās, Kabīr gives him instruction with regard to cosmogony, etc. Some of it is in verse, but for the most part it consists of a catalogue of names in connection with the matters which Kabīr reveals. Amongst other things there is a list of the forty-two generations of gurus who are to succeed Dharm Dās.

14. THE *JNĀNA SARODĀ*.—A mystical discourse on the five elements, written in chaupāīs, sorathās and sākhīs.

15. THE *SWĀS GUNJĀRĪ KĪ SAIL*.—A poem in the form of a mystical discussion of the vital airs.

16. THE *KARMA BODH*.—This is a dissertation, partly in verse and partly in prose, on the evils of Karma. All are in the toils of Karma, including Adam, Noah, Abraham, Moses, Christ and Muhammad. Kabīr alone is free from it. Men have tried different ways of securing release from

[1] See p. 109.

[2] Either the *Mūl Nām* (Original Name), or the *Gupt Nām* (Secret Name).

Karma, the way of ritual, the way of worship and the way of knowledge. Some have taught the Jain religion, others have followed the *Mimāṁsa*, and so on; but all have failed to obtain salvation. There are eight different kinds of Karma. Only through the mystery of the Sat Guru can release be found.

17. THE *NIRANJAN BODH.*—A poem of about two hundred stanzas, in chaupāīs and sākhīs. It begins by showing how Kāl Nirañjan, the unconditioned (nirguṇa) king had afflicted the three worlds, including Brahma, Vishṇu, and Śiva. The Purusha sends Jñānī to remedy this state of affairs, and the latter goes forth and meets Nirañjan, who is terrible in appearance, and accuses him of having troubled the universe. Nirañjan says that the three worlds were given to him by Purusha, but Jñānī says he has been sent by Purusha to save the souls therein. On being asked by Nirañjan how he can get them out of his power, Jñānī says that it is through the power of the Śabda. Nirañjan replies that many sādhus and holy men have devised means to find salvation, but none have succeeded, but Jñānī again replies that the power of Nirañjan is usurped, but that the power of the Śabda can effect deliverance. Nirañjan asks how the Śabda of the Purusha can reach these souls. They are in the grip of lust, anger, etc. Others have established sects, but all have come into his noose and souls again and again come under the power of Yama. But Jñānī again asserts the power of the Śabda. Nirañjan says all the world recognizes the Vedas and other religious books, and performs many religious practices, but these have not saved the world. Jñānī however declares that when souls put trust in the Śabda they will give up their faith in the Vedas and other books, and will observe the Immortal Name, and through devotion will obtain deliverance. Nirañjan says that even if they receive the Śabda souls will not give heed but will fall into pride and the toils of Karma again. Jñānī answers that those souls who have devotion will keep the Śabda always, and will not come under the power of lust, anger, etc. Nirañjan says that all the incarnations fell into the toils of Karma, and so with all holy men and wise men who have

lived. Jñānī asserts his power to deliver souls through the Śabda of Purusha. A generation will be born in the world, and by taking refuge in them souls will be saved. Nirañjan acknowledges this, but asks how souls are to be awakened. Jñānī says that the weapon of 'the generation' (i.e. the descendants of Dharm Dās) will be the Śabda. Then Nirañjan assumed a terrible form and tried to frighten Jñānī, and claimed to be the Purusha himself. Jñānī overcomes through the power of Śabda, and Nirañjan acknowledges himself defeated, and is dismissed by Jñānī. Jñānī then addresses Dharm Dās, who expresses his thanks for the revelation given him.

18. The *Jnāna Bodha* in the first part is addressed to Dharm Dās as by Kabīr, and in the latter half is in the form of a conversation between them. It is written in chaupāīs, sākhīs, and sorathās, and contains about six hundred stanzas. The ocean of existence cannot be crossed without the help of the Sat Guru; but Kabīr has come to conduct men across. People despise his religion as 'the weavers' religion'; but the whole world is lost in error, and through the doctrine of Kabīr alone can salvation be found. Kabīr then begins to unfold his way of salvation, and commissions Dharm Dās to teach others this doctrine.

19. The *Mukti Bodh.*—This is a conversation between Kabīr and Dharm Dās, in about four hundred stanzas, and is written in chaupāis and sākhīs. Kabīr begins by discoursing on the value of the Name. Dharm Dās asks for an account of the origin of the 'Letterless Name.' Kabīr replies that it can be known through Śabda by him who has real love in his heart. When Purusha is known the power of Kāl is weakened. There are many kinds of worship in the world but salvation is only to be obtained through the Name, and by the help of the Sat Guru.

20. The *Chaukā Swarodaya.*—A mystical poem about the sun and moon, followed by an account of how the chaukā is to be prepared for worship. It contains about two hundred stanzas and is written in chaupāīs and sākhīs.

21, 22, 23. The *Dāyā Sāgar, Jnāna Stotra* and *Jnāna Godrī.*—Short poems in praise of the guru, who is identified with Kabīr. One Indian editor ascribes the *Jñāna*

Godrī to Dharm Dās, but the Hindi seems to be quite modern.

24. THE *CHITĀWANĪ* is a short didactic poem.

25. THE *ANURĀGSĀGAR* is in the form of a conversation of Kabīr with Dharm Dās on the Vedānta. It is edited by Nand Kumār Lāl of Gorakhpur, and is said to be for the benefit of students of the Vedānta. It is a short work written in chaupāīs, sorathās and chhands. It was published in 1903.

26. *SAMĀDHI KĀ ṬĪKĀ* by Mahant Paramottam Dās of Chhapra was published in 1908 and is written in chaupāīs, sākhīs, and chhands. It is a conversation between Dharm Dās and Kabīr before the *samādhi* (death) of the former. The wife of Dharm Dās named Āmīn, and his son, Chūrāmaṇi, also take part, as well as a certain Rājā Rām, the Purusha, and others.

27. THE *JNĀNA-PRAKĀŚA*, by Bairāgī Mahā Dās, was published at Narsinghpur in 1908 and is written in chaupāīs, sorathās and chhands. It is an account of the Kabīrpanthī doctrine, cosmogony, etc., and amongst other things gives an account of the story of Kabīr's interview with the paṇḍit Sarvānanda at Benares.

28. THE *JĪVA DHARMA BODH* is a long poem of over three thousand stanzas written in chaupāīs and various other metres. It is evidently quite a modern work, and contains a great deal of matter very loosely arranged. A good deal of it has probably been worked up from the *Kabīr-i-Manśur*.[1] Amongst the subjects are a dissertation on lust, anger, avarice, infatuation, and fear, an account of the five elements (each of which is said to have five prākṛitis) an account of Karma, of the *Swasam Veda*, of *Satsaṅg* and *Kusaṅg* (good and bad company). Instructions are given on keeping control over speech, the eyes and ears, the hands and feet. A warning is given against the eating of flesh and the drinking of intoxicants, and there is an account of temperance societies. The need of doing good to others is urged. The doctrine of *Tat tvam asi* is discussed and the way of salvation described.

[1] See below, p. 131.

10

The four castes are referred to, and the ideas of several religious systems refuted, including the religion of the Vedas, the Jain religion, the doctrine of the *Smārta* sect, the *Mīmāṁsa*, Islam and the teaching of the Aghoris. An account of creation is given and a conversation between Kabīr and Nānak. The unity of all religions is taught, and the unity of all languages, all the latter having come from Sanskrit. In the section on unity there are some strange comparisons, or rather equations, put forward. Brahmā is identified with Adam, Manu with Noah, Mahādeva with Muhammad, Hanumān with Ali, Paraśu Rāma with Moses, Kṛishṇa with Christ, and the king with the paṇḍit. At the end there is an account of the ocean of existence and the way to cross it.

Many of the publications of Kabīrpanthī works are said to have been edited by a certain sādhu of the sect, named Yugal Ānanda. Many of these works though evidently quite modern are said to be written by Kabīr, but the names of the real authors are not made known.

OTHER KABĪRPANTHĪ WRITINGS.—Besides those already described, there are many other writings of the Kabīr Panth which are now accessible either in print or in manuscript. These include the *Muhammad Bodh*, which is an imaginary conversation with Muhammad; the *Jain Dharma Bodh*, which shows the superiority of the Kabīrpanthī faith to the religion of the Jains; and other similar works. Probably, however, enough has been described to give an indication of the style of literature which is produced by the Panth.

As mentioned at the outset, almost all these works make reference to Dharm Dās and seem to be connected with the Chhattisgarh section of the Panth. Most of them are probably quite modern, but some may belong to the eighteenth century A.D. They contain much verse that is well written, but nowhere rise to the height of being great poetry. In some of them there is a certain interest and movement, but others are most uninviting, and to the outsider have little meaning. There is a great sameness about them all. The glory of the Sat Purusha, an elaborate cosmogony of the world, the ravages of Kāl, the worthlessness of other ways of obtaining salvation, the need of the Sat Guru, the power of the Sabda, the need of true devotion, and of giving honour to the guru and to sādhus, the commission to Dharm Dās and his forty-two generations, the value of receiving the betel-leaf—these and a few other topics occur again and again in nearly all the poems.

A few other modern Kabīrpanthī works also deserve mention, some of which are in prose. Among these is the *Kabīr-i-Manśur* or *Kabīr Manśur*.[1] This work was written originally in Urdu by Paramānanda Dās of Firozpore in the Punjab in 1887, but was translated into Hindi in 1903. It is a large tome of over fifteen hundred quarto pages and is a veritable miscellany of information. The contents do not seem to be arranged on any very definite plan, and the same or similar matters are often referred to more than once. It is written in prose, but verses are occasionally quoted. It is in the main a manual of theology of the Kabīr Panth. It begins with an account of the Sat Purusha and an elaborate cosmogony. It gives stories about the life of Kabīr and an account of the forty-two generations of Dharm Dās. It tells of the four gurus and twelve divisions of the sect. It speaks of things which may and may not be eaten, and at the end there is a long catechism on the matters connected with the religion of the Panth. But it not only contains an account of the Kabīrpanthī faith, but tells of other religions, often showing what things in them are considered to be false. There is thus an account of the Vedas, of the Quran, of the Tauret, Zabur, and Injīl, stories of various heroes of Hindu mythology, as well as of Buddha, stories of prophets under which are included Adam, Noah, Abraham, David, Moses, Christ, and Muhammad, and accounts of devotees. There is a dissertation on Karma, various forms of worship, yoga, etc., and an account of various sects and *sampradāyas*.[2] The commandments of various religions are given, as well as those recognized by the Panth. Amongst other things there are accounts of animals, birds, and fishes, with stories

[1] See below, pp. 132, 144 ff.

[2] *Sampradāya*, traditional doctrine or custom; a term often used for a group of sects which hold certain views in common.

about them something like the bestiaries of the Middle Ages in Europe. This work, though written in the Punjab, seems to emanate, like so many others also, from the section of the Panth which has its headquarters in Chhattisgarh.

LIVES OF KABĪR.—There are several lives of Kabīr in existence, all of which relate legendary stories about him. The *Kabīr-Charitra*, or *Life of Kabīr*, seems to gather most of its material from the *Kabīr-i-Manśur*, of which it is to a large extent a rearranged and abbreviated edition. It is written in prose, except for occasional quotations. The *Kabīr Kasauti*, or *Touchstone of Kabīr*, is a much shorter work, but is written in poetry. Both of these works are quite modern. In both there are verses quoted about the life of Kabīr from Garīb Dās,[1] and it would seem as though the latter must have written a life of Kabīr in verse. But if so, it has not yet been published except in these extracts.

COMMENTARIES ON THE *BĪJAK*.—With regard to commentaries on the *Bījak* there are several. Two standard ones are those of Pūran Dās and Viśvanath Siṅha. Bābā Pūran Dās of Nagjhari in the district of Burhanpur wrote his commentary about 1837. Viśvanath Siṅha was Maharaja of Rewah State, and reigned from 1833 to 1854. He wrote many poetical works. His commentary is said to expound the *Saguṇa Upāsana of Rāma* (*Religious contemplation of Rāma as the embodiment of all good qualities*); whereas the exposition of Pūran Dās is called the *Nirguṇa Upāsana*. These commentaries are both in prose. A third commentary which is recognised at the Kabīr Chauṛa is that of Mehīn Dās. It was published in 1915. Another expositor of Kabīrpanthī teaching was Rām Rāhās of Burhanpur, who wrote a work in five volumes called the *Pāñch Granthī*, which contains the following: *Nirnaysār*, *Bairāgya Śatak*, *Kabīr Parichay*, *Śākhīs*, *Gyārah Śabda*, and *Pārakh Vichār*. All except the last are in verse and are expositions of portions of the *Bījak*.

DEVOTIONAL MANUALS.—Many small manuals of Kabīrpanthī devotion are in existence. One called the *Gutka* is summarized in the *Alwar Gazetteer*, and seems to be in

[1] For Garīb Dās, see below, p. 165.

use in that district. The word *gutka* means a small book used as an amulet. This work, which is in thirteen *aṅgs*, or parts, follows the usual line of Kabīrpanthī doctrine, the need of a guru, the right attitude of mind, the deceits of Māyā, and so on. The first aṅg is introductory, and touches on all the chief points of Kabīrpanthī doctrine. The second is about the guru and shows how he should be reverenced as God. The third is about the *jatti* (one who has conquered his passions) and shows the need of a man conquering his desires. The fourth is about the *satī* (pure and truthful one) and emphasises this virtue. The fifth deals with *pramodha* (instruction). The sixth is on the *man* (mind) the seventh on *krodh* (anger); the eighth on *karuṇa* (long suffering); and the ninth on *chit kapaṭī* (hypocrisy). All these show the need of having right thoughts and actions in order to obtain salvation. The tenth aṅg is about *mānsāhārī* (flesh-eating) and warns the reader very earnestly against this vice. The eleventh aṅg deals with *binti* (prayer) and contains some specimen prayers. The twelfth aṅg is about the *sādhu* (wandering monk) and shows the blessings of this state of life and what the sādhu should be like. The thirteenth and concluding aṅg is on *parcha* (union with God) and dwells on this at considerable length and with much ecstatic fervour.

THE *KABĪROPĀSANA PADDHATĪ*.—Another manual much used by Kabīrpanthīs is the *Kabīropāsana Paddhatī*. This work, which was compiled by a Kabīrpanthī named Makanji Kuber Penṭar, was published at Bombay under the patronage of the guru of the Chhattisgarh section. It is quite a recent work and professes to be a compilation from other works. It mentions other manuals previously published but now out of print. It is arranged in eleven sections (or *Viśrams*) of unequal length.

In Section I some idea of the object of the book is first given, and the necessity is urged for good conduct and the performance of duty as a preliminary of worship. Various kinds of duty are referred to, such as duty to the body, to the soul, to society, to the guru, to one's village, to one's country, to the government.

In Section II there are rules for early morning duties, prẹcise and minute directions being given with regard to such duties as getting up, cleaning teeth, bathing, dressing, putting on a sect-mark, etc. The value of rising at half-fast four in the morning, so as to have time for worship and religious duties, is inculcated.

Section III gives detailed instructions as to morning worship, its place, correct posture, need of ceremonially rinsing out the mouth, as well as the correct method to be used for prayer and reading and meditation. A householder, it is said, should finish his worship by six o'clock.

In Section IV the compiler gives information as to the benefit and necessity of exercise, and speaks of fourteen instincts or impulses which must be properly regulated if health is to be preserved.

Section V gives precise rules for food and drink, the kinds of food which may be eaten, regulations as to cooking it, and proper manners to be observed while eating. Meat, intoxicants, honey, and butter are forbidden.

In Section VI the duties of householders and sādhus are described. The householders must do their daily work remembering to serve the sādhus. Sādhus must be engaged in worship. Rules are laid down for their asking of alms and also for the mid-day worship.

Section VII describes the evening worship, which is similar to that of the morning. This should be followed, if possible, by a *satsaṅg*, or assembly of good men for singing hymns and good conversation, etc. The advantage of this, and the right method of conducting it, are dwelt on at great length.

Section VIII gives various *sumirans* (short verses like mantras) to be recited on various occasions; for example at worship, before sleep, before rising, before cleaning the teeth, washing the face, looking in the looking-glass, dressing, drinking, eating, etc.

Section IX is a Sanskrit work giving the thousand names of the guru which are to be used in devotion.

Section X is the longest, called the *Stuti Ratnākar* and contains a selection of hymns of praise and poems to be used in worship. Some are in Sanskrit but most are in Hindi.

Section XI is also a collection of verses called the *Vinaya Ratnākar*, which are in the forms of prayers rather than praises. It contains verses of Dharm Dās, of Garīb Dās, and of others, as well as of Pūran Dās, the commentator on the *Bījak*. The *Vinaya Śabdāvalī*, a collection of forty-seven short poems of Pūran Dās, which comes at the end, contains verses of some merit.

The manual ends with some short prayers in prose.

OTHER COLLECTIONS.—Various other collections of hymns used by Kabīrpanthīs are also published.

Many Kabīrpanthī works are to be found in Gujarati, Bengali, Telugu and other languages, and this shows how widespread is the influence of the teaching of Kabīr.

Several works also exist in Sanskrit, such as the *Daśmātra* and the *Kabīrukottara Śataka*.

CHAPTER VIII

THE DOCTRINES OF THE KABĪR PANTH

JUST as the ritual of the Kabīr Panth at the present time is very little in keeping with the simplicity of Kabīr's teaching as found in the *Bījak* and the *Granth*, so in doctrine also there has been a very great change.

COSMOLOGY.—The Kabīrpanthīs have now a very elaborate system. According to this there exists one essential Being who is called 'Sat Purusha.'[1] It is to be noticed that though Kabīr used 'Rāma' and 'Allāh' and other names for the Supreme God, modern Kabīrpanthīs seldom, if ever, do so, at least in their writings; but almost invariably use the title 'Sat Purusha.' The Sat Purusha of his own will created a universe, and in this he placed six Brahmans, who are also called his sons, whose names are given as Sahaj, Omkāra, Ichchhā, Sohang, Achintya, and Akshar. We may regard these almost like the emanations of the Gnostic systems. These, however, did not preserve discipline in the universe, so he proceeded to create a seventh. The Sat Purusha brought deep sleep upon Akshar when he was sitting where all was water, and when Akshar awoke he saw an egg floating on the water, upon which he began to meditate. The egg burst with a loud noise and from it there came forth a being of a fearful appearance who was named Nirañjan.

He is also called Kāl or Kāl Purusha. It may be noticed that the word Kāl means Time, and this being seems to be a kind of hypostasis of Time. Nirañjan, although fierce in temper, engaged in asceticism, which was so effective that he was able to obtain from the Sat Purusha a boon in the

[1] Literally, 'The True Being.'

form of the sovereignty of the three Lokas, or worlds, which were to be created, namely, heaven, earth, and hell. As the materials for making these were in the keeping of the Tortoise, Nirañjan was told to make polite request to him for them. But instead of being conciliatory, he acted otherwise, and this led to a fight between him and the Tortoise. Nirañjan cut off sixteen of his heads, and from them there poured forth the necessary materials, the sun, moon, earth, etc. When the Tortoise reported the matter to the Sat Purusha, he was angry and decreed that Nirañjan should never enter his abode or look upon him. The abode of the Sat Purusha is called the Sat Loka.

But though Nirañjan had now possession of the material elements, he was unable to make man. So he swallowed three heads of the Tortoise and went into a trance, after which he asked the Sat Purusha for a field to sow in. The Sat Purusha then created for him a woman whose name was Māyā. At first she kept her eyes fixed on the Sat Purusha, and would not become the wife of Nirañjan, but gradually she was overcome by the fascination of Nirañjan, and became separated from the Sat Purusha. From her, Brahmā, Vishṇu, and Śiva were born, and after their birth Nirañjan became invisible. Māyā created three daughters to be wives for her sons, and Nirañjan at the same time created the four Vedas. All however were drowned in the ocean, and Brahmā, Vishṇu and Śiva then churned the ocean and recovered the women and the Vedas. The Vedas were absorbed in Saraśvati, who became the wife of Brahmā. The other two women were given to the other two brothers.

Then Brahmā created the present world and men began to worship the trio. But when Māyā realised that her three sons were shutting her out from the attention of mankind, she created three more women, who originated music and singing, and so fascinated the world that they all began to worship the mother (Devī). Nirañjan also claimed to be the Sat Purusha himself. The souls of men were thus distracted and they could find no means of salvation. But they cried to the Sat Purusha in their distress, and in answer to their prayers he sent Kabīr into the world to teach men to look beyond Māyā, Brahmā, Vishṇu, Śiva, and Nirañjan, to the Sat Purusha himself. Kabīr has been revealed in each of the four ages. In the Sat Yuga he was called Sat Sukṛit; in the Treta Yuga, Muṅīndra; in the Dwāpara Yuga, Karuṇāmai Ṛishi; and in the Kali Yuga, Kabīr Sāhib. Kabīr is also called Jñānī (The Wise One).

One day a great flood (*mahāpralaya*) will come and destroy all the universe, and only the Sat Purusha and the Sat Loka will remain. But the souls who are in the Sat Loka will all be under the protection of the Sat Purusha. The flood will be preceded by many fearful signs, and sin will be great upon the earth. A hundred and twenty five years before the great flood, the sun and moon will be constantly troubled with eclipses, which will increase in number till the sun and moon cease to be, and after that the great flood will come. There will be so much water that the waves will mount up ten thousand *yojans* (one yojan = eight miles) above the earth and all living beings on the earth will die. Everything will become void, and nothing will be seen in earth or heaven. Kāl Purusha will absorb all the creation into himself again, including Adya[1] and the three qualities (*guṇas*). In his forehead there is a place in the shape of a hemisphere like a lotus in which the whole creation will be absorbed and will remain in a subtle form. Having reabsorbed the creation, Nirañjan wanders about in the void continuously for seventy ages. After this his mind becomes troubled on account of his solitude. At first he imagines himself to be the Sat Purusha. But finding he has not in himself the power to recreate the world, he approaches the Sat Purusha. Then the Sat Purusha will say to Jñānī: 'O Jñānī, go into the void and tell Nirañjan to spread out the creation on the back of the Tortoise.' Jñānī will obey, and Nirañjan having received this permission will at once go and recreate the world. He will spue out Adya from his mouth and Adya and Nirañjan together give birth to Brahmā, Vishṇu and Śiva, and all five together will bring back the whole creation as it was before.

[1] There seems to be a play on words here. In Sanskrit, *adya* signifies 'food,' and also 'to-day,' 'now.'

The Stages of the Soul's Enlightenment and the Way of Salvation.—Corresponding to the Sat Purusha and his seven sons, are different stages to which a soul can rise and there are also two stages corresponding respectively (1) with Brahmā, Vishṇu, and Siva, and (2) with all the Jīvas. Thus there are ten in all. There are also ten different stages of knowledge or enlightenment,[1] and a soul reaches that stage for which his knowledge fits him. A guru can only take his disciple as far as he has reached himself.

The keeping of ceremonial rules does not bring a soul beyond the lowest stage. Upāsana, or worship, brings him to the next stage. Yoga, or asceticism, brings one safely to the third stage from the bottom (*Jīvarut*). In this place there is a lotus with a thousand petals and Nirañjan remains invisible in his own light. Yogīs who go into a trance (*nirvikalpa samādhi*) reach as far as this stage. Here Nirañjan dwells and he is worshipped by all the world. Through him four kinds of salvation and the happiness of heaven can be obtained. But this happiness is only bodily happiness, aud the satisfaction of the desires of the flesh. He who has attained the illumination of Mārifat goes as far as the *Lahut* Stage. This can be done by the wise by

[1] These stages and the corresponding enlightenment required are as follows (beginning at the top):

	Stage of	Name	Knowledge
1.	Sat Purusha ...	Sat Loka	Śabda Sār
2.	Sahaj...	Sahaj Dwīpa ...	Dae Nākā
3.	Omkāra	Omkāra Dwīpa ...	Hukm Murtid
4.	Ichchhā	Ichchhā Dwīpa ...	Julkār Chandṛagī
5.	Sohang	Sohang Dwīpa ...	Dhyān Dorahiyat
6.	Achintya	Achintya Dwīpa ...	Taraawahat
7.	Akshar	Lahut	Mārifat
8.	Nirañjānand Māyā	Jīvarut	Haqīqat
9.	Brahmā, Vishṇu and Śiva	Malakut	Tarīqat
10.	All the Jīvas ...	Nasut	Shariat

reading and meditating on the Vedas. Some amongst sādhus get sometimes as far as the *Achintya Dwīpa*; and men of all religions make promises that salvation is to be found only in their religion, but no one knows how to get beyond this. Brahmā, Vishṇu and Śiva can reach as far as the *Sahaj Dwīpa*, but they do not shew their mystery to men, but keep it to themselves. Only through the teaching and help of the Sat Guru can souls be brought to the Sat Loka. Many of these terms, as well as the whole idea of stages, seem to be taken from the teaching of Sūfīs.

With regard to the Sat Loka it is said to be such that its glories cannot be told. Only in the *Swasam Veda*[1] is there some little account of it. The glory of the dwellers there is such that each hair is so full of light and splendour that before it millions of suns and moons hide themselves. Nirañjan, Adya, Brahmā, Vishṇu, Śiva, seers and sages, Rāma, Kṛishṇa, and holy men all have desires still in their mind, and so take birth again and again, but from the souls in the Sat Loka all desire has been taken, and they are not therefore subject to rebirth, but dwell for ever there. When a man dies it is said that his soul goes upwards towards the north, first to Vishṇu to Baikunth (the heaven of Vishṇu) to give an acccunt of his sins and merits. But the soul under Kabīr's protection, through the power of the Śabda of the Sat Guru, mounts upward with great force. When it wishes to go beyond the universe it meets the three hundred and sixty daughters of Dharm Ray, whose garments and ornaments and beauty are indescribable. There is no one in the world except Kabīr who does not become powerless when he sees them. They are placed there to try and prevent the soul mounting up to the Sat Loka by entangling it in their net. But when the soul is under Kabīr's protection their blandishments have no power to fascinate. Kabīr bids them be off, and they go away hopeless. Then Dharm Ray comes to oppose the progress of the soul. But Kabīr conducts it past him also. When the soul reaches the Sat Loka the other souls go out to meet it and conduct it along, and every soul is drawn

[1] See below, p. 142.

towards it and is very pleased, and they say, 'To-day a soul which has been separated from us for many days has come back to us,' and then they all conduct it to the Sat Purusha. The soul obtains a view of the Sat Purusha and makes obeisance, and having accomplished its purpose dwells in the Sat Loka. In its passage upward the soul sees the whole creation, and all the heavens and paradises, but passes beyond all things and beyond space till it arrives at the Sat Loka.

Like other sects which have arisen from the midst of Hinduism, the Kabīr Panth, following Kabīr himself, makes much of the doctrine of transmigration and Karma. A modern Kabīrpanthī work says: 'The chief point of Kabīr's teaching is that transmigration of souls may be brought to an end. Transmigration causes great sorrow. That teaching of religion which shows how pain of continuous births and deaths may be removed is the religion for man, and it is the duty of human wisdom to hold fast to that guru or sacred teaching which explains this. If a man obtains a body and does not seek for salvation he is most unfortunate, for he will not obtain such an opportunity again, and will be dipped continually in the ocean of existence.'

Kabīr then is regarded as the deliverer from the evils of transmigration, and the Kabīrpanthīs hold it firmly, as an 'article of faith,' that there is no other deliverer. He is equated by them with the Sat Purusha himself. He manifested himself to men as Kabīr, but the Kabīrpanthīs do not call him an *avatar*, and still less would they say he was an incarnation; for they hold that he is without a body and only *appeared* in a bodily form to men. Many of the legends about him illustrate this. It was not necessary, for example, for him to eat or drink, and when his enemies tried to kill him the sword passed through his body as through air.

Meanwhile man is entangled in the noose of Nirañjan or Kāl. The relation between this being and Māyā is shown in the account of the cosmology of the Panth; but in ordinary practice it is difficult to distinguish between the two. The point is that the souls of men, or jīvas, are really portions of the Sat Purusha himself, but are deceived into thinking themselves different from him, and so entangled in desires of the flesh. Dharm Ray, who is a kind of Angel of Death who judges men's actions after death, and Yama, the god of death, are also mentioned. As long as men are under the power of Kāl, they fall again and again into their clutches. It is especially over the three worlds of heaven, earth, and hell that Nirañjan rules, and these are the sphere of the operation of the law of transmigration. As long as he possesses this, no one can find salvation apart from the guru, but one day the power of Nirañjan will end, and the Kingdom of Akshar Purusha will come, and in that kingdom there is hope that all living beings will find deliverance. Brahmā, Vishṇu, and Śiva and the other gods of the Hindu pantheon are also under the power of Nirañjan; and even if a man by good deeds and asceticism reaches one of their heavens, his pleasure will not last for ever, but he must again fall into the ocean of existence and be reborn.

Kabīrpanthīs regard all the religions of the world, except that of Kabīr, as 'religions of Nirañjan' whom they have mistaken for the Sat Purusha; and even if a man follows them zealously he cannot by their means escape from transmigration, though he may attain for a time the pleasure of heaven. The four Vedas and other religious books are simply 'nets of Kāl,' and by entangling men in those nets he has so deceived them that he has manifested as his own all the names which belong to the Sat Purusha. Under the guise of the Sat Purusha all men are really engaged in the worship of Kāl Purusha, who has hidden the name of the Sat Purusha and has not told its mystery even to Brahmā, Vishṇu, and Śiva.

In order to escape from Kāl, men must have recourse to a true guru. 'Sat Guru' is a title often used of Kabīr himself, but the gurus of the Panth since he disappeared from this world are his representatives on earth. They are in fact to be identified with Kabīr, as Kabīr himself is identified with God. The guru, therefore, must be regarded with great reverence. His commands must be implicitly obeyed and the disciple must look to him alone as a refuge and help from all the sorrows of this life, and as the means of bringing him safely across the ocean of existence to the Sat Loka. He must be served and honoured to the greatest degree of one's power.

Devotion (bhakti) towards the Sat Purusha, and to Kabīr as his manifestation, is also required in all those who would obtain salvation. In practice this really means devotion to the guru as Kabīr's representative.

A man must also be in a right moral condition if he would obtain salvation, and the Kabīrpanthīs have a very high code of morality which they set before the members of their sect. In addition to universally recognised moral duties, the disciple must rigidly abstain from the eating of flesh and the taking of intoxicants.

Not only must the guru be reverenced, but great honour must also be paid to sādhus, who must be served in every way. This apparently applies to the sādhus of any sect, but especially to those of the Kabīrpanthī sect, who must be honoured in a way only short of the way in which honour is paid to a guru.

In addition to these requirements, it is essential that a disciple should be initiated, and especially that he should receive the betel leaf, *parwāna*, or 'passport.' The rites connected with this are detailed in another chapter, but here it may be said that the efficacy of this sacrament as a means of salvation to all worthy recipients is very strongly insisted on, and urged again and again in modern Kabīrpanthī works.

The performance of other prescribed rites of the sect is also considered important, and in addition a man should study what is called the *Swasam Veda*, which means 'our own Veda.' This seems to include far more than the *Bījak*, or the recognised scriptures of the sect, and apparently embraces all the utterances of Kabīr, including those quite erroneously supposed to be his in the many modern works which are so often published as *Kabīrkṛit*, or written by Kabīr. We have seen the estimate of the four Vedas of the Hindus which is held by the Panth. These are called the *Purushama Veda* (Human Veda) to distinguish them from the *Sukshma Veda* (Immaterial Veda) which is the term applied to what is otherwise known as the *Swasam Veda*.

THE SUCCESSION OF GURUS.—There is a belief amongst the Kabīrpanthīs of the Chhattisgarh section that forty-two generations of descendants of Dharm Dās are to occupy the gaddī, or seat of the guru, which he established, and they have also a belief that there are to be four gurus in all. It is said that the first guru was Dharm Dās who was to have the chief guruship in the north and to be followed by forty-two generations. The second guru is to be Chaturbhuj Dās, who is to have the chief guruship in the south. He is to be followed by twenty-eight generations. The third guru is to be Bānkejī, who has the chief guruship in the east, and will be followed by sixteen generations. The fourth guru is to be Sahti, who will have seven generations and the chief guruship in the west. Of these four gurus, only Dharm Dās has up to the present been manifested, and the gaddī of his generations established. But when the other three gurus also are manifested then the religion of Kabīr will spread rapidly.

Kabīrpanthīs and Hinduism.—The cosmology and many of the ideas of the Panth are distinctly due to Hinduism, though they differ from it in many respects. There are many inconsistencies in their teaching, but it may be said that modern Kabīrpanthīs certainly tend towards Vedantic ideas. Some of them reject the terms 'nirguṇa' and 'saguṇa' as applied to God; yet it is impossible not to see that in their system the Sat Purusha really corresponds to the Nirguṇa Brahma of the Vedantic system, and Nirañjan to the Saguṇa Brahma. The Hindu pantheon receives some kind of recognition, though it is said that worship of these deities cannot lead to deliverance from transmigration. Idolatry is however condemned, and Kabīr is put forward as the only one who can bring salvation.

The doctrines of the Kabīr Panth to-day display a great 'advance' on the teaching of Kabīr. No doubt, modern leaders of this sect could prove by means of a 'doctrine of development' the agreement of their teaching with his system. There may be passages even in his genuine works here and there which might countenance some of the present teachings of the sect; but taken as a whole, it certainly differs greatly from what Kabīr taught. The cosmology has become greatly developed and systematised, even if all passages in the *Bījak* and the *Granth* which deal with this are the work of Kabīr. The philosophic standpoint tends towards the pure 'Monism' or advaita, of the Vedānta, whereas that of Kabīr seems to be more Visishṭādvaita (or modified monism). Kabīr seems to have regarded God under the name of Rāma, Allāh, etc., as having personality, and approached Him as a humble sinner seeking salvation. But the Kabīrpanthīs have transferred whatever personality there is in God to Kabīr, who is equated with God; while the Supreme Spirit himself, under the name of Sat Purusha (the titles Rāma, etc., not being used) has retreated into a background of impersonality.

Not only has the sect now elaborate rites which are binding on its members, but the use of the rosary, and other practices which Kabīr condemned, are now recognised as not only lawful but important. Moreover a sacramental system has been developed which is far removed from the ideas of Kabīr.

Kabīr recognised the value of the guru, and often spoke also of God as the Sat Guru, but he never regarded the human guru as equivalent to God, as is now done in the sect.

The literature of the Kabīr Panth, which has been outlined in another chapter, gives many corroborations of the summary of teaching here given, and we can, too, see traces of growth. In the *Sukh Nidhān*, for instance, there is the equation of Kabīr with God, and a reference also to the sacramental meal of the cocoanut and betel-leaf, but in the *Amar Mūl* these ideas are greatly extended. Here the cocoanut, the betel-leaf and the Word (*Śabda*) are said to be the three boats in which souls can safely cross the ocean of existence; elaborate directions are given for the preparation of the chaukā, and mantras are prescribed. Vedantic ideas, too, are taught, and in other ways development of doctrine can be traced.

THE FIFTY ARTICLES OF KABĪRPANTHĪ DOCTRINE.—Kabīrpanthīs have a kind of summary of doctrine and precepts which contain fifty articles. This is printed both in the *Kabīr-i-Manśur* and in the *Kabīr Charitra*. In order to show some of the teaching which they regard as important, it is given here in full:

1. One ought to have devotion to the One all-Pervading, Unconditioned Brahma, or Sat Purusha, and not to meditate on any other beside him. This Brahma or Sat Purusha is only known by means of the true guru and by reading the *Swasam Veda.* He cannot be found by any other path.

2. The Sat Purusha and Kabīr are one; there is only the difference of a name. The one is called by two names, and there is not the smallest difference between them. If anyone thinks there to be a difference it will be difficult for him to obtain salvation.

3. One ought to serve his guru with body, mind and wealth, place reliance on his word, and obey him. He must not think there is any difference between Kabīr and the guru, nor consider the glory and perfection of the guru, as belonging to the guru. He who regards his guru as God and gives devotion to him as to God, his work will be perfected. He who thinks there is any difference between the guru and God—all his efforts will be in vain.

One ought to give a tenth of his earnings to the guru, and must always humbly return thanks to him.

4. One ought always with love and devotion to serve sādhus without making any distinction. He who has the favour of a holy man or guru is alone fortunate and successful in both worlds.

One ought heartily to serve all kinds of sādhus without deceit, but especially to remain always at the service of that holy man who is wise, thoughtful, tested in judgment, and who by giving instruction stirs up the devotion of men to the Sat Purusha. Especially ought one to listen to, and attentively consider, the teaching of those holy men of our own faith who are of true judgment; for by the word of holy men, who are well versed and firm in our own faith, there comes a firm support for religion, and acquaintance with our own faith. On the other hand from the word of those sādhus who are advocates of other religions, unbelief, and error with regard to our own religion arises.

The sādhu in whom the qualities of his guru are found one ought not to consider different from his guru, but to have unfeigned devotion towards him with faith, and without making any distinction.

5. One ought to have the same feelings of kindness to all living creatures, movable or immovable, in whatever form they may be found, and to reckon them as one's own body and soul. One ought not to give pain to living creatures at any place or at any time. One ought to carry on his occupation in the world in such a way that no harm comes from him to any living thing. One ought to show equal kindness to all creatures of the water, the land, or the forest, whether beasts or birds, or belonging to the vegetable kingdom, and to consider all as one's own body and life.

6. One ought to consider the eating of flesh the greatest of all great sins. He who eats flesh, whatever good qualities and merits he possesses, can never obtain the true path. One who eats flesh can never be a possessor of knowledge of the ātman, nor can he ever receive salvation.

7. Intoxicating drink, and other intoxicating things, ought to be renounced, as well as the eating of flesh. He who is a slave of intoxicants can never meditate; and without meditation spiritual knowledge cannot be obtained, and without knowledge salvation cannot be obtained.

8. The adulterer will go to hell.

9. There are many forms and shapes in the universe of different names, but no one by worshipping any of them will become an inheritor of salvation. As idolatry is a mockery of the way of knowledge, so meditation on the guru and devotion to him is the key of the door of knowledge.

10. Food, clothes and whatever is necessary for maintenance should only be received after it has first been offered to the Sat Purusha. He who receives what has been first offered to the Sat Purusha gets nectar-like fruit. Therefore it is fitting that he should have food which is quite clean and pure. Whatever thing has been offered to any god or goddess must not be received by a devotee of the Sat Purusha, nor used in any way, for it is a great sin to receive what has not first been offered to Sat Purusha and whatever has been offered to any god or goddess cannot be offered to the Sat Purusha. To make such an offering to him would be as great an offence and indignity as to offer to an emperor the shoes of one of his menial servants.

11. Do not speak falsehood or give a false word, nor have anything to do with falsehood of any kind.

12. Do not steal, nor go with thieves, nor take counsel with them, nor receive their goods, nor go near them.

13. Do not gamble. Gambling is a cause of great sorrow, and gamblers come to a very evil condition. See how gambling destroyed and brought to an evil condition even such meritorious and virtuous persons as King Nala, and King Yudhishtira. Gambling, lying, theft, adultery, murder, etc., are sins which have a great connection between them, a fault in one of them leads gradually to faults in all of them. The man who indulges in even one of these sins will have great misery and trouble in this world, and in the next will be a partaker of hell.

14. Twelve sect marks should be placed upon the body. There should be a line like a straight stick on the forehead, on the eyes, on the navel, heart, both arms, from both breasts toward the shoulders, on the back, and on the ears.

15. Clean and fair clothes should be used.

16. A rosary of *tulasi* beads and a necklace of tulasi beads should be worn round the neck.

17. The True Name should be repeated, and used in singing and worship.

18. There should be devotion to the Sat Purusha, and preaching of the true path. The reward of a man who does this is greater than the merit of him who saves millions of cows from the hands of the butcher.

19. No regard should be given to charms and amulets, and such superstitions (*jantra, mantra, tantra*). These are the enemies of salvation and he who uses them becomes entangled in deceit and hypocrisy and, becoming an evil-doer, inherits hell. The use of these things is a path to hell.

20. There is no hope of finding out the path of salvation from any other books except the *Swasam Veda*, but other books may be read for the sake of increasing knowledge and wisdom.

21. Apart from Sat Kabīr and his *Hañsa* (Soul) as Boatman, no one can understand the way of salvation.

22. Salvation cannot be obtained without the teaching of the Sat Guru.

23. All other devotion except devotion to the Sat Purusha will only cause men to be drowned in the Ocean of Existence.

24. Sacred places for pilgrimage, vows, etc., are all 'bands of Yama' (Death).

25. The nine kinds of devotion, and the four kinds of salvation are only bands.

26. Those who worship God as Nirguṇa and Saguṇa are always in bondage.

27. Hindus, Muhammadans, Christians, Jews and people of any other religion can join the Kabīr Panth. Devotion and salvation are alike for all.

28. Heaven and hell, and all other worlds, only exist for those who have no knowledge. To him who has obtained the knowledge of the true Ātman, they are only falsehood and error.

29. There is no way to attain salvation apart from the Essence of the Word (Sār Śabda).

30. Abuse, envy, hypocrisy, pride, etc., are enemies of salvation.

31. By means of humility all virtues and merits are obtained.

32. The way of salvation is very narrow, but the way of hell is very wide.

33. Kabīr is without a body. His body never suffers.

34. Whatever troubles you have to face, do not look to any other for help except to the Sat Guru. Do not place hope of any kind on any other except the Sat Guru.

35. He who takes refuge in the Sat Guru ought to obey all the rules which he imposes. He should have full faith that the Sat Guru will extract him from the net of Kāl and bring him across the ocean of sorrows.

36. One should never forget to thank the Sat Guru for his kindness but should thank him every moment. Let it not be that first he prays and then forgets to return thanks. The ungrateful person never obtains salvation.

37. The fear of God is the sign of salvation. One should always remember death.

38. Without true love devotion is fruitless.

39. Blessed are those who renounce the lusts of the flesh and remain in devotion.

40. Without liberality no one can attain unto devotion. The liberal man is happy in both worlds, and even a little merit of his is very fruitful. The worship and asceticism of a miser is useless, and no matter how much pretended devotion and worship he performs yet he gains nothing, all is fruitless. The miser partakes of misery in both worlds.

41. Silence is a very great virtue. One should only speak when there is necessity, as opportunity comes, and not uselessly. From false speaking there is harm both to soul and to body.

42. One should read the words of the Sat Guru (Kabīr Sāhib), meditate on them, consider their meaning, think about their mystery and try to understand it, and always keep them in mind. One should not resort to any wrong device to understand their meaning. As opportunity arises one should sing and take part with others in singing the Śabdas of the Sat Guru and always praise and pray to the guru.

43. Kabīr is the teacher of all the religions which are current in the world. But Kabīr himself has been appointed as giver of salvation and also the four gurus and their descendants; there is no other saviour.

44. Do not curse anyone, nor speak evil to anyone, nor think unkindly of anyone.

45. Recognise the Supreme Spirit as present everywhere, and regard pain given to any living thing as equal to pain given to God.

46. The proud person can never recognise the Supreme Spirit as all-pervading.

47. Obedience to the guru is equal to great religious austerity.

48. So long as one thinks much of his body, and nourishes it, obedience is impossible.

49. The fool, the deceitful man, and he who is ignorant, cannot attain unto salvation.

50. So long as one fears and gives regard to his body, (that is, so long as he is proud of his body) he will never be able to attain the state of being bodiless.

CHAPTER IX

THE RITES AND CEREMONIES OF THE KABĪR PANTH

THE WORSHIP AT BENARES.—At the monastery (maṭh) of the Kabīr Chauṛā at Benares, daily service is conducted by the pūjāri. The sādhus, who are present, after taking their morning bath, assemble in front of the *mandir* or preaching platform, where the first part of the service takes place. This includes the ceremony of *Āratī* (waving of lights), which is described below, and the washing of the feet of the guru. Then the various *samādhīs* or (tombs) are visited, and also the gaddī; and then they all return to the mandir for the concluding portion of the service.

As already mentioned, a pair of wooden sandals are kept to represent the feet of Kabīr. These are washed daily and the water in which they have been washed (known as *charaṇāmṛita*)[1] is kept in a brass vessel. All visitors to the monastery during the day receive three teaspoonfuls of charaṇāmṛita together with three leaves of the *tulasi* plant, or basil, which is sacred to Vishṇu, and it is on this account that its leaves are given. But as Kabīr, when speaking of Rāma, meant, not the incarnation of Vishṇu, but the Supreme Deity, some Kabīrpanthīs do not approve of this practice. The monastery remains open all day long to visitors and is closed at eight o'clock in the evening. Any charañāmṛita which remains over at that time is given to any sādhus who have not received it before during the day. The guru then drinks the remainder, and rinses out the vessel with fresh water and consumes that also. The occupants of the monastery also hold an evening service, which lasts longer than the morning service.

[1] *Charaṇāmṛita*, 'Nectar of the feet.'

THE SHRINE OF KABĪR AT THE PLACE WHERE HE TAUGHT AT KABĪR CHAUṚĀ, BENARES

TOMBS OF FORMER MAHANTS AT KABĪR CHAUṚĀ, BENARES

In the month of January a *mela*, or religious fair, is held at the Kabīr Chauṛā monastery, which lasts for several days. On this occasion many Kabīrpanthīs attend, and the large court is crowded with devotees. Various other melas are held in connection with the Panth. In connection with the shrine at Maghar a mela is held at the full moon of the month of *Aghan* (November).

When the guru from the Kabīr Chauṛā visits Maghar, on the day of the mela he goes to the shrine, followed by the *dīwān* (minister) who carries a large dish which contains *khichari* (rice mixed with lentils). Another man, called the *bandālī*, carries an earthenware vessel of water which is covered over with a white cloth. These vessels are placed before the shrine and on the tomb a fire of cowdung is made in which incense is burnt. The ashes of this are passed through a piece of fine muslin and kept in a brass vessel. A service is held by the guru in which all present take part. After the prayers are over, the guru sits down and the dīwān gives to each of the worshippers a small portion of the khichari, and the bandālī pours into the palm of the hand of each a few drops of water, which each drinks. After all have been served in this way, the dīwān and the bandālī consume the remainder, and after more prayers by the guru the proceedings end. Persons who visit this shrine are expected to present a rupee, and also an offering of rice and lentils. In return, they receive a small portion of khichari and a pinch of the ashes that have been left after burning the incense with the cowdung. A mela is also held here on the fourteenth day of *Bhādon* (August).

A mela is also held at Kudarmal, the reputed burial place of Chūrāmaṇi, which lasts for about seven or eight days, and another at Rudri, near Dhamtari, on the Mahanadī, in the Central Provinces, where another of the gurus is said to be buried.

The 'Kabīr Chabutra,' in the Dindori tahsil of the Mandla District, is another place sacred to Kabīrpanthīs. Here, it is said, Kabīr lived and meditated for many years. An arch and platform in the temple of Rāma at Ramtek (also in the Central Provinces) is considered to belong to the Kabīrpanthīs, though the Brahmans of the temple say that the arch was really made by a daughter of a local king of the Solar Dynasty, in order that her swing might be hung up in it. How it came to be associated with Kabīr is unknown. The temple of Jagannāth at Puri is regarded as sacred by Kabīrpanthīs of both sections and Dharm Dās is said to be buried at this place. Many Kabīrpanthīs make a pilgrimage there. Melas are also held at the headquarters of the chief guru on the occasion of the celebration of the chaukā service as described below.

Distinctive Marks and Dress.—The members of the Kabīr Panth wear necklaces of beads made of tulasī wood. This necklace is called a *kanthī*, and like the rosary is associated with thoughts of prayer. This kanthī is given at the time of initiation; and, if lost, a member of the Panth is not allowed to eat or worship till it has been replaced. Many, however, in lieu of the kanthī, wear one large bead on a strong thread, and this is regarded as permissible. Kabīrpanthī householders are called *bhagats.* They wear the kanthī but not the marks of a sādhu. Sādhus wear only a laṅgoti, or loin-cloth, and have sect-marks. The sect-marks vary slightly in the different groups of the Kabīr Panth. In the case of the Chhattisgarh section, the mark is usually a single broad streak of white from the top of the forehead to the nose. It is made with a kind of paste in which sandal wood is mixed. A sādhu is initiated by the mantra being spoken in his ear. He often has to have some months of instruction first. In the case of the Kabīr Chauṛā and Dhanauti sections, women are not admitted as sādhus; but in the Chhattisgarh section they can be admitted. If women are admitted as members of the Panth, they are not allowed before marriage to wear the kanthī, nor may a woman become the disciple of her husband's guru. Sādhus of the higher caste will eat together, but not with those of lower castes.

The Initiation Ceremony.—The initiation ceremony is considered to be of great importance. In the presence of the guru and other members of the Panth the candidate must first promise to observe the rules of the Panth, and is warned of the serious consequences for those who do not keep them. Violation of these is held by many Kabīrpanthīs to be often visited with sickness or death. The requirements are that he should renounce idol-worship, and acknowledge his belief in one God, that he should eat no flesh and drink no intoxicating liquor, that he should bathe daily, and perform morning and evening devotions, that he should forgive up to three times those who trespass against him; that he should avoid the company of all women of bad character, and all obscene jesting, and never turn away his lawful wife from his home, that he should always speak the truth, never conceal the property of another, and never bear false witness against a neighbour, nor speak evil of another on mere report. After the candidate has made these solemn promises, the guru whispers half the sacred *mantra* into his left ear. In the Kabīr Chauṛā section, there is only one mantra, but in the Chhattisgarh section two mantras are given at the time of initiation, the *Guru Mantra* and the *Tinka Mantra*. Subsequently three more are given, called the *Pañch Nām*, the *Sat Nām*, and the *Har Nām*. The mantras used in the two sections are said to be different. The guru then places in the outstretched hands of the candidate some grass, betel-leaves, and white flowers. A bairāgī then takes a brass vessel of water and leads the candidate to a place where he allows the articles previously given to him to fall on the ground. The bairāgī then pours water from the vessel into the hands of the candidate, who first rinses out his mouth, and then washes his face, after which he is brought back to the guru. Next a kanthī is given by the guru to the bairāgī, who takes it round to all members of the Panth present, each of whom touches it. This ceremony, known as *gawāhī*, or witness, is evidently meant to call those present as witnesses of the initiation. After this the guru takes the kanthī again, and after doing obeisance to the gaddī, puts it on the candidate's neck with the thumb and first finger of both hands, and then whispers the whole of the mantra into the right ear of the candidate. The candidate is now further warned that he must not eat the fruit of the fig-tree. The reason for this prohibition is said to be that the fruit often contains so many insects that it cannot be eaten without much destruction of life. A cocoanut is next handed to the candidate and, after touching with it his right shoulder, breast, and forehead, he hands it back to the guru with an offering of one rupee. The guru then washes the cocoanut with betel-leaves dipped in water and breaks it on a stone; he then cuts up the flesh of the cocoanut into small portions with a knife and puts them in a dish. The candidate is then given charaṇāmṛita,[1] which he drinks. The guru takes a betel-leaf and placing upon it a *parwāna* (specially consecrated betel-leaf), a portion of the cocoanut, some *batāsa* (small sugary wafer), *gur* (raw sugar), and raisins and currants, gives it into the outstretched hands of the candidate who at once eats it. No portion of the cocoanut may be destroyed or eaten by those who are not Kabīrpanthīs. Whatever is over is kept by the guru and given to members of the Panth in other places he visits, when he tells them the name and residence of the new disciple at whose initiation it was offered. A feast follows this ceremony, in which it is said that members of other religious sects are also allowed to take part. The guru is honoured and hymns are sung in praise of God and Kabīr. This ceremony is called *Tinka Arpan*. The customs with regard to it vary in the two sections of the Panth. Whereas in the Chhattisgarh section only one cocoanut is presented by the candidate, and his offering must not be less than one rupee, in the Kabīr Chauṛā section a candidate has to present sixteen cocoanuts, and with each cocoanut an offering which is not less than four annas. In the Chhattisgarh section this ceremony is performed only once for each candidate by the chief guru, whereas in the Kabīr Chauṛā section it is first performed by a local mahant, or by a bairāgī, and then again by the chief guru at the Kabīr Chauṛā monastery.

Daily Worship and Ceremonies.—The members of the Panth are expected to worship God morning and evening. The hymns which they generally use at morning and evening worship are given by Crooke, in his work on the *Tribes and Castes of the N.W. Provinces and Oudh.*[2] Those, however, given in the *Kabīropāsana Paddhati* differ from

[1] See above, p. 150. [2] Vol. III, pp. 75, 76.

the former, and in this manual appropriate hymns are given also for use at mid-day and on many other occasions. It is likely that the practice of the Kabīrpanthīs is not the same everywhere in these matters.

In the various ceremonies of the Kabīrpanthīs the cocoanut has a special significance attached to it. This idea they share in common with other Hindus. It is believed to be a substitute for the human head, and to have been created by Viśvamitra, and the *buch* (the tuft of fibre at the end) represents the hair. The Kabīrpanthīs will not eat any part of a cocoanut from which this tuft has been removed, as they fear it may have been broken off by others in the name of some god or spirit. Once the tuft is removed the cocoanut becomes useless as an offering, for its likeness to the human head is considered to be destroyed. The members of the Kabīr Panth further say that the cocoanut has a face resembling that of a man, that its surface is divided into three parts representing Brahmā, Vishṇu, and Śiva, that its flesh is formed gradually as human flesh is formed, and that it differs from other fruits in containing no seed. The breaking of a cocoanut is regarded as a bloodless sacrifice, a peace offering to Nirañjan, in order that members of the Panth may enter the Satya Loka. The shell of the cocoanut is said to represent Kāl, who wishes to keep men from the blessing contained in the mild and milk-formed flesh of the fruit.

At the Kabīr Chauṛā, charaṇāmṛita is obtained by washing in water the wooden sandals preserved there. But it can also be obtained by using the water in which the feet of the chief guru have been washed; for he is Kabīr's representative upon earth. This water is mixed with fine earth and then made up into pills, which may be either swallowed whole, or drunk after they have been pounded up and mixed with water.

Parwāna (Passport) is the name given to the betel-leaf which is specially prepared by the chief guru at his headquarters for the use of members of the Panth. A pile of betel-leaves, sixteen handbreadths in height, is arranged upon the ground. At night a pewter saucer is placed in a specially prepared spot, and the dew, called *āmar*, is collected in it, and is regarded as water from heaven direct. Then in the morning the guru meditates in front of this pile of betel-leaves, and with the amar writes upon the topmost betel-leaves the secret Name of God. The leaves are then made up into small portions, about a quarter of an inch square, and distributed to the mahants as required for use at a *Jot Prasād*, or at a ceremony of initiation. The parwāna is said to represent the body of Kabīr, and the modern Kabīrpanthī works, such as the *Amar Mūl*, and others, make frequent references to the idea that the receiving of this, accompanied by other right conditions, ensures salvation.

The Chaukā Service.—Kabīrpanthīs are supposed to observe every Sunday, as well as the last day of the lunar month (*pūran māsī*), as a day of fasting; and after bathing to assemble in the evening for a solemn religious service, known as chaukā. During the fast, water, or water mixed with sugar, may be drunk. In practice, Kabīrpanthīs often fast only up to mid-day, and then the chaukā is not held. But the full chaukā service, preceded by the fast, is held at least twice a year, in the months of *Phagun* and *Bhādon* (March and August). The thirteenth day of Bhādon is kept as the birthday of Kabīr.

The chaukā is really the space marked out for the service. It is five or seven and a half yards square, and is specially prepared and cleansed. In the centre of this, a smaller space, two and a half yards square, is measured out which is covered with wheat flour, and in its centre a pattern is made of nine lotus-flowers to represent the sun, moon and seven planets. Over this, real flowers are laid. An awning covers the prepared space, white (as are also the flowers) on festal occasions, but red when the service is held in memory of the dead. A bunch of flowers is suspended from the centre of the awning. The mahant sits in the enclosure facing the people, and on his right, within the smaller square, are placed a small metal box containing charaṇāmrita and parwāna, a dish containing 125 betel-leaves arranged round its edge with a single leaf in the centre on which rests a piece of camphor, and a pillar made of dough with a hollow top, in the centre of which is placed a stick covered with cotton wool, on which *ghī* is poured. On the left hand of the mahant within the smaller square are placed a dish containing batāsa and gur, a cocoanut and a vessel (called *khalsa*) containing water. At each corner of the larger enclosure is placed a small jar of earthenware containing water, on which rests a plate of grain, and on the grain is placed a linseed oil lamp. There is a similar arrangement in the case of the khalsa, and the water in the earthenware vessels is placed there, in case that in the khalsa is not enough. The grain in the plate is to absorb the oil that may fall from the lamp, and so preserve the purity of the water.

The men sit on one side and the women on the other; and the mahant then reads certain portions from his service book. After this he performs the ceremony of *Āratī* (waving of lights). He lights the candle made of cotton wool standing in the dough on which ghī has been poured. Then he lights a piece of camphor on a stone which is by his side, and takes the cocoanut and after pouring water over it breaks it on the stone. Then he lights the piece of camphor in the centre of the dish containing the betel-leaves; and, while the camphor is burning, waves it backwards and forwards. After this he passes the dish round; and those present place in it small offerings, which are taken by the mahant for the use of his monastery. He then takes half of the flesh of the cocoanut, and divides it with a knife into small pieces. All present then come up to the mahant, and receive from him in the palm of their right hand, a betel-leaf and a portion of cocoanut, batasa and gur. This they eat on bended knee before him, taking great care that no portion falls on the ground. As each retires, he has water poured upon his hands to cleanse them. After all have partaken, the mahant says some private prayers, and then some aloud, and after this gives an exhortation to his congregation. Then he does reverence to the chaukā; and those present do reverence to him; and the service ends. It is interspersed with the singing of many hymns.

A less elaborate form of the chaukā service is sometimes held; and there can even be a chaukā service without the mahant. When there is no mahant, the inner square is not overlaid with flour; and the charaṇāmṛita and parwāna are absent. Instead of the candlestick made of dough is placed a dish on which camphor is burnt; instead of the khalsa an ordinary brass vessel (*loṭā*); and instead of the whole cocoanut fragments of cocoanut bought in the bazaar. The Kabīrpanthī who officiates cannot do all that the mahant is authorized to do, and is only provided with a service-book which contains a portion of the service. Even when a mahant is present, the service is only said on Sundays in part; but the full service is read on the last day of the lunar month. When a mahant lives at a distance, supplies of charaṇāmṛita and parwāna are occasionally kept by a trustworthy Kabīrpanthī, who can be relied on to keep them from pollution. These are for use in cases of serious illness, or when a mahant is not present at the time of the full moon. But only a mahant can prepare and administer the *Prasād* (see below). Kabīrpanthīs, when dying, receive from the mahant, prasād, charaṇāmṛita and parwāna; but in his absence, the two latter can be given by an ordinary Kabīrpanthī, if he has been entrusted with them. It is considered essential that the dying person should receive charaṇāmṛita and parwāna. Receiving the former is supposed to symbolize the complete devotion of the recipient to Kabīr; and receiving the latter is held to secure a safe passage to the Sat Loka.

THE JOT PRASĀD SERVICE.—A still more solemn service, known as the Jot Prasād, takes place after an interval of an hour or so, in which, however, all do not partake, but only those who feel themselves worthy to do so. Jot, or light, means the flame of the candle; and Prasād, consecrated food. The dough of which the candlestick had been formed is taken by the servant of the mahant, and kneaded up with additional flour, ghī, and fragments of cocoanut. From this dough the mahant makes a number of small wafers, each of which measures about two inches in diameter and then summons those present to take part. He reads a short address; and then an interval is allowed for meditation or prayers, during which all who do not feel worthy to take part in the service retire to a distance. Then those who remain approach the mahant in turn, and receive from him into the palm of the right hand, which is placed upon the left, a pill of the charaṇāmṛita, and a portion of the parwāna; and, after eating of this, one of the wafers made from the dough. The dīwān then pours from the khalsa into the palm of their right hand a few drops of water, which they drink, after which they retire to a distance where an attendant pours water over their hands to cleanse them. This food is regarded with great reverence as the special gift of Kabīr: and it is said that all who receive it in a right spiritual condition will obtain an entrance to the Sat Loka. After this service all take part in a substantial meal, which, unless some wealthy member of the Panth supplies it, is paid for by subscription,

Burial Customs.—Kabīrpanthīs sometimes bury their dead, and sometimes cremate them. The bodies of bairāgīs are buried, but householders may be either cremated or buried. In some places formerly the bodies of married people, both male or female, were buried inside the compound of the house where they lived, but this is now prohibited on sanitary grounds. A cloth is placed in the grave, and the corpse laid on it, and another cloth placed over it covering the face. A little platform is afterwards made over the grave, on which the mahant and two or three other persons can sit. Upon the death of a member of the Panth, the relatives purchase two cocoanuts. Of these one is carried by the barber in the funeral procession, and placed by the side of the dead body immediately before cremation or burial, and the other is kept in the house as an offering to be presented at the funeral chaukā which is held later. On the twenty-first day after death the mahant should, if possible, hold a service for the dead. The service is as before described but differs in some details. When burial has taken place, the mahant sits on the platform over the grave, and the chaukā is made in front of it. The awning over the chaukā is red instead of white, and a piece of white cloth is placed on the chaukā to represent the dead man's body. The number of betel-leaves is reduced to 124, the one removed representing the portion of the dead man. At the beginning of the sevice the mahant prays in silence that the deceased may be preserved from all the dangers of his journey to the

Sat Loka. Then those present sing five funeral hymns, and all do reverence to the mahant, and to the piece of white cloth which represents the dead man's body. The cocoanut which has been kept for this service is washed ceremonially by the mahant, and then handed to a relative to the deceased, or, if there be no relative present, to one who is a disciple of the same guru. This man applies the cocoanut to his shoulder, breast, and forehead and returns it to the guru with an offering. The candle is meanwhile lighted and the camphor. The mahant breaks the cocoanut on the stone on which the camphor is burning. Where burial has taken place, this is always on the grave. Kabīrpanthīs believe that the soul of the dead person, which up to this time has remained in the grave, now mingles with the flame, which represents the soul of Kabīr and is absorbed into the deity. When breaking the cocoanut, the mahant says, 'I am breaking the skull of Yama,' because it is thought that the soul of the deceased has been absorbed into the deity and not taken down into the hell of Yama. The remainder of the service then goes on as before. The number of cocoanuts varies from one to nine according to the means of the relatives. With each cocoanut a separate offering has to be made to the mahant. After the ceremony the flesh of the cocoanut is kneaded up with flour into small cakes; and bairāgīs distribute them at the houses of Kabīrpanthīs.

SALUTATIONS.—The ordinary salutation of Kabīrpanthīs amongst themselves is 'Sat Sāhib!' but to other Hindus they say 'Rām, Rām!'

IDOL-WORSHIP AND SACRIFICES.—In theory, Kabīrpanthīs are required to abstain from idolatry, and the majority of them do so. But the force of old customs, and the prevailing tendencies around them, cause many of them to fall from this ideal. Thus it is said that once in three years the Mahār Kabīrpanthīs at Mandla make a sacrificial offering of a goat to Dulha Deo, the bridegroom god, and afterwards eat the flesh, burying the remains beneath the floor. On this occasion they also drink liquor. Other members of the Panth will light a lamp and burn camphor in the names of Brahmā, Vishṇu, and Śiva, but do not make idols of them. They will accept the cooked food offered to Vishṇu as Sat

Nārāyaṇ, and a piece of the cocoanut kernel offered to Devī, but not the offerings of any other deities. In their own services the wooden sandals are treated with a respect approaching idolatry, and some of the features of the chaukā service are closely akin to the idolatrous rites of Hindus. It is said that many illiterate Kabīrpanthīs worship the *Bījak*.

CHAPTER X

OTHER SECTS WHICH OWE THEIR INSPIRATION TO KABĪR

The great influence which the teaching of Kabīr exercised in India is shown by the large number of sects which owe their origin to the ideas which he promulgated. All these have their literature in the vernacular.

The Sikhs.—The foremost of these is the sect of the Sikhs. This was founded by Nānak (1469–1538) who was a younger contemporary of Kabīr. He, like Kabīr, was no doubt influenced by the religious movements of his time; and it cannot be stated definitely that he ever met Kabīr, though there are some stories which tell of their meeting. Kabīrpanthīs say he was a disciple of Kabīr and was appointed by him as leader of the sect in the Punjab; but that he and his followers corrupted the true doctrine of Kabīr and broke away from the Kabīr Panth. But, while this is not historically correct, it seems quite evident that Nānak was influenced by Kabīr, and an acknowledgment of the influence which his sect owed to Kabīr is seen in the large number of verses of Kabīr which were, after Nānak's time, included in the *Ādi-Granth.* The religious ideas of Nānak are in the main the same as those of Kabīr. God is one, and must be worshipped with the heart, not with images. Men of all castes and races can know God, and Hinduism and Islam are only two paths to the same God. Karma and Transmigration are recognised and the delusions of Māyā. The guru is needed in order to find salvation and through him man can be brought into a union with God which means re-absorption into him. But Nānak stands nearer to Hinduism than Kabīr did, and the whole Hindu pantheon was recognised in his poems. Many Hindu ideas and practices which he rejected have since crept back into the sect.

THE DĀDŪPANTHĪS.—The founder of the sect of the Dādūpanthīs was Dādū of Ahmedabad (1544–1603). He is sometimes called Dādū Dāyāl, which is said to be on account of the great spirit of kindness (dāyā) which he always manifested. Common report makes him a cotton-carder by caste, but his followers say he was a Brahman, and there are evidences to show that this may be correct. Though born at Ahmedabad, most of his life was spent in Rajputana, where his sect is still strong. One tradition makes him a disciple of one Kamāl, who is said to have been a disciple and not the son of Kabīr. The date of Dādū's birth makes this quite a possibility; but, without more evidence, it cannot be accepted as true. His teaching is certainly similar to that of Kabīr, though not so much influenced by Muhammadan ideas. Dādū rejected the teaching of the Vedānta, caste and idolatry; but much of the Hinduism against which he protested has crept back into his sect. Some of his modern followers are Vedāntists, and his sect has nothing at all to do with outcastes, while his *Bāṇī* or collection of verses is worshipped with idolatrous rites. The *Bāṇī* is a long work of about five thousand verses in Hindi, and contains the teaching of Dādū.

THE LĀL DĀSĪS constitute a sect which was founded by a certain Lāl Dās who belonged to a predatory tribe called the Meos. He lived in Alwar, and died in 1648. His teaching is also collected in a volume called the *Bāṇī*, the hymns of which are often sung to music by his followers. It is written in Hindi. His doctrines also can be traced to the influence of Kabīr, and he emphasised the value of the repetition of the name of Rāma.

THE BĀBĀ LĀLĪS form a very small sect which was founded by a certain Bābā Lāl, who lived at the time of the Emperor Shāh Jahān and who had interviews in 1649 with the emperor's son, Dārā Shukoh, who was very favourably inclined towards Hindus. Bābā Lāl's sect still survives near Baroda and his teaching was preserved by two Hindus of his time who wrote it down in Persian.

THE SĀDHS.—The sect of the Sādhs in chiefly found in the upper part of the Doab of the Jumna and the Ganges, south of Delhi. There are also many Sādhs in Mirzapur. The sect was founded in the year 1543 by Bīrbhān. Bīrbhān was a disciple of a certain Uday Dās. Uday Dās was a disciple of Rai Dās, who was one of the disciples of the great Rāmānanda. Bīrbhān taught his followers very much the same ideas as those taught by Kabīr, and he was possibly influenced by him. The sect received a great impetus under the leadership of Jogī Dās. He had been a soldier, under the Rājā of Dholpur, and fought for Dārā Shukoh in 1658. After the defeat of Dārā Shukoh, Jogi Dās seems to have fled in disguise and he was accepted by the Sādhs as their teacher. He brought to the Sādhs the law of monogamy, and other Christian elements, which they still teach. He probably got these Christian ideas from some Roman Catholic priest who was friendly with Dārā Shukoh. The Sādhs had thus two founder-teachers. Each of them left a literary deposit. Bīrbhān left a set of hymns in the form of śabdas and sākhīs, while Jogī Dās left a work in prose called *Ādi-Upadeśa*.

DHARNI DĀS who was born in 1656, was a Kayastha who lived at Manjhi in the district of Chhapra. He wrote religious verses in Hindi, and is the founder of a small sect which still survives.

THE CHARAN DĀSĪS.—Charan Dās was a Baniya by caste, who lived from 1703 to 1782, and about the year 1730 founded at Delhi a sect which is still in existence. His teaching shows distinctly the influence of Kabīr. He emphasises the value of the repetition of the name of God, the importance of the word (śabda), the need of devotion (bhakti), and the necessity of having a guru. Charan Dās, like Kabīr, also denounced idolatry, but it has crept back into the sect. The guru is regarded as divine as in the modern Kabīr Panth. Many Hindi verses were composed by Charan Dās and amongst his disciples were two women, who were sisters, named Sahajo Bāī and Dayā Bāī, who also were writers of Hindi religious verse.

THE ŚIVA NĀRĀYAṆĪS form a sect which was founded in 1734 by a Rajput named Śiva Nārāyaṇ, who lived near

Ghazipur. This sect worships God as Brahman without attributes (nirguṇa), but Śiva Nārāyaṇ is himself regarded as an incarnation of God by his followers. As in the Kabīr Panth, people of all castes are admitted as members, as well as Muhammadans; but outward conformity to ordinary Hindu and Muhammadan practices is permitted. Śiva Nārāyaṇ wrote many books of Hindi verse.

THE GARĪB DĀSĪS.—Garīb Dās lived from 1717 to 1782. His guru is said to have been Kabīr, which is of course an anachronism. But the sect which he founded is probably little more than an off-shoot from the Kabīrpanthīs. The sādhus of his sect must belong to the twice-born castes, which shows a departure from Kabīr's teaching. Garīb Dās lived at Chhurani in the Rohtak district of the Panjab. His writings have been preserved in a book called the *Guru Granth Sāhib*, which is said to contain twenty-four thousand Hindi verses, of which seven thousand are couplets taken from Kabīr. It does not seem to have been published in its entirety. He seems to have written an account of Kabīr in verse; for many of his verses are quoted in books which relate the life of Kabīr.

THE RĀMA SANCHIS (Lovers of Rāma), regard as the founder of their sect a certain Rāma Charan who lived in Rajputana and was born in 1718. He rejected idolatry. His sect is now represented only by an order of sādhus. Rāma Charan wrote Hindi verses which have been collected in a *Bāṇī*. The third leader of the sect, Dulha Rāma, who joined it in 1776 and died in 1824, was the author of ten thousand śabdas and four thousand sākhīs.

THE PALṬŪ-PANTHĪS.—Palṭū Sāhib lived some time in the eighteenth century and was born at Nagpurjalalpur, a village west of Azamgarh in the Fyzabad District. His guru, named Govind, had been instructed by a certain Bhīkhā Sāhib. Palṭū Sāhib remained a householder, but was the founder of a small sect which still exists in the neighbourhood where he lived. His headquarters were at Fyzabad. He has left some well-written verses in the *kuṇḍaliya* metre. Like many others, his teaching seems to be due ultimately to the teaching of Kabīr.

THE SATNĀMĪS.—The sect of the Satnāmīs, which

seems to have been founded before the middle of the seventeenth century, was reorganised by Jagjīvan Dās about 1750, and he is often regarded as its founder. He lived at Kotwa between Lucknow and Ayodhya. As their name implies, the adherents of this sect adore only the True Name, the One God who is without attributes; but the Hindu gods are recognised, and also the Hindu incarnations. Though Jagjīvan himself is said to have been a Kshatriya, his sect has spread mostly amongst the outcastes. He wrote many Hindi verses. Between 1820 and 1830 a certain Ghāzī Dās developed the Satnāmī sect in the Chhattisgarh district of the Central Provinces. He did not however acknowledge his indebtedness to Jagjīvan. The sect has spread fairly widely in that region, especially amongst the Chamārs.

The Prāṇ Nāthīs.—Prāṇ Nāth who lived at Panna in Bundelkhand at the beginning of the eighteenth century was a Kshatriya who was well versed in Muhammadan as well as in Hindu literature. He founded a small sect in which not only Hindu and Muhammadan, but even Christian influence is seen. He tried to reconcile Hinduism and Islam, and the members of his sect have occasionally a common meal, though otherwise they conform to the Hindu or Muhammadan practices of their own families. He calls God by the name of *Dhām* (a dwelling place) and on this account his followers are sometimes called Dhāmis. He wrote many verses in Hindi, though using a large mixture of Arabic or Persian words.

The Rādha Swāmī Satsang is a modern sect which was founded about 1861 by Tulsi Rāma (1818–78), an Agra banker, known as Śiva Dayāl Sāhib, and has its headquarters at Agra. It seems to owe a great deal of its inspiration to Kabīr. In the daily meetings of the sect portions of their own sacred books or of the writings of Kabīr and other Hindu devotees, are read. A Hindi couplet of Kabīr (though evidently a forgery) is quoted by them to show that Kabīr called God by the name of Rādhāswāmī. Moreover, their teaching is closely allied to that of Kabīr and while they profess to find all truth in the writings of their own gurus, they use the writings of certain other Hindu and Muhammadan devotees, and amongst these they give Kabīr the highest place.

MUHAMMADAN WRITERS INFLUENCED BY KABĪR.—There are many Muhammadan writers of Hindi religious poetry who may have been Sūfīs. But the fact of their writing in Hindi shows a connection with Hindu thought. Probably many of them were directly or indirectly influenced by Kabīr. These include Yārī Sāhib (1668–1723) who lived at Delhi, who had as disciples Keśav Dās and Bulla Sāhib who were also writers of Hindi religious verse, and flourished about 1730. Bulla Sāhib had as his disciple Gutāl Sāhib, who in turn was the religious preceptor of Bhīkhā Sāhib. Both of these, who lived in the latter half of the eighteenth century, have left Hindi religious verse. Dariyā Sāhib of Bihar, Dariyā Sāhib of Marwar, and Bulle Shāh, were all Muhammadans who wrote similar poetry, and lived in the first half of the eighteenth century.

All the sects and writers mentioned in this chapter probably owe something to Kabīr, in some cases the influence being direct, and in others indirect. Though they differ in many important details, they all have something in common. The value of the repetition of the name of God, the need of a guru and the respect due to him, the supreme importance of devotion (bhakti), the delusions of Māyā, the value of truth, the duty of living a righteous and sober life—all these and other doctrines appear in most, if not all, of them. They stand, in theory at least, for a non-idolatrous theism; but in a great many of these sects idolatrous practices have crept in. Even where they have not resorted again to the use of images, they have introduced worship of the guru, or a reverence little short of idolatry, to some sacred book. In this respect they have departed from the ideals of Kabīr.

Kabīr has sometimes been compared with Martin Luther; and though the comparison is not altogether a close one, it does help in some way to indicate the position Kabīr holds. Martin Luther was not actually the author of the religious Reformation of the sixteenth century in Europe; for the movement had long been preparing, and would have gone on and developed even if he had never lived. But he was undoubtedly the one who, more than any other, brought the movement to a head, and gave it an impulse forward in a definite direction. So also Kabīr was himself the product of a religious movement which had long been preparing; and yet he, too, gave it an impulse, and marked out for it the line of advance which it was to take. He stands chiefly for the development of the non-idolatrous ideal of the bhakti movement, to which he certainly gave a great impetus. It is a tragedy that so few who have come under his influence have been able to live up to the ideals he set before them.

CHAPTER XI

KABĪR AND CHRISTIANITY

WAS KABĪR INFLUENCED BY CHRISTIAN TEACHING?—The possibility that Kabīr may have been subject to Christian influences has often been discussed; and one Indian Christian, Pandit Walji Bhai, of Borsad in Gujarat, went so far as to express the belief that the Kabīr Panth was really instituted by Jesuits. This is an extreme view of the case; but others have found coincidences in the teaching and practices of his sect, which may point to his having come in some way under Christian influence.

There have been Christians in South India from early centuries of the Christian era, and the Syrian Church there claims to have been founded by St. Thomas himself. Even if this claim cannot be substantiated, its origin is certainly very ancient, and in very early times of the Christian era there were Nestorian Christians in Bactria, with whom India may have been in contact. But this contact must have been destroyed by the progress of Muhammadanism long before the time of Kabīr. Jesuit Missions were not founded in India till after the death of Kabīr, in the latter part of the sixteenth century. In those days of slow travel and communication it does not seem very probable, therefore, that Kabīr had any direct contact with Christian teaching; though we cannot say that it was altogether impossible.

PARALLELS BETWEEN KABĪR AND THE BIBLE.—There are many passages in the verses of Kabīr which suggest to our mind passages in the Bible. The following are a few examples:

> 'God is light, the essence (of all things) incomparable; pure without a stain. Where He dwelleth is neither shade nor sunshine.' —*Ādi-Granth, Gaurī* 10.

> cf. 'God is light, and in Him is no darkness at all.'—I John 1 : 5.

'He who made the whole world, that guru was manifested: the guru who saw him with his eyes, that guru revealed him to men.'—Westcott's *Kabīr*, p. 78.

cf. I John 1: 1–3.

'Small is the door of devotion (bhakti) as the tenth part of a mustard seed. The heart of man is swollen with pride to the size of an elephant, how can he pass within?'—Westcott's *Kabīr*, p. 82.

cf. 'It is easier for a camel to go through the eye of a needle than for a rich man to enter into the Kingdom of God.'—St. Matt. 19: 24.

'Learn to distinguish the honest man and the thief from their manner of speech; all the works that are within proceed forth by way of the mouth.'—Westcott's *Kabīr*, p. 94.

cf. 'Out of the abundance of the heart the mouth speaketh.'—St. Matt. 12: 34.

'Whoso drinketh God's water shall not be thirsty again.'—*Ādi-Granth, Mārū* 3.

cf. 'Whosoever drinketh of the water that I shall give him shall never thirst.'—St. John 4: 14.

'Thy stewardship being ended, thou must give thine account,
When the cruel messengers of death come to take thee.
[They will ask thee] what thou hast earned, and where thou hast squandered it.'
'The warrant of God's court hath come for thee.'—*Ādi-Granth, Sūhī* 3.

cf. The Parable of the Rich Fool.—St. Luke 12: 20.

'No one hath brought wealth with him, and no one shall take it away.'—*Ādi-Granth, Sāraṅg* 1.

cf. 'We brought nothing into this world; and it is certain we can carry nothing out.'—I Timothy 6: 7; Job. 1: 21.

'What availeth it to read the *smṛitis* to a dog?'—*Ādi-Granth, Āsā* 20.

cf. 'Give not that which is holy unto the dogs.'—St. Matt. 7: 6.

'The desire to gratify my evil passions forsaketh me not; though I make many efforts to guard myself against them, I am entangled in them again and again.'—*Ādi-Granth, Bilāvalu* 4.

cf. 'The good that I would I do not: but the evil which I would not, that I do; . . . when I would do good, evil is present with me.'—Rom. 7: 18–21.

With regard to such passages as these, it may be remarked that in translating them into English, a translator who is acquainted with the Bible tends to assimilate his language to the words of the Bible, and this often makes the connection seem closer than it really is. We cannot, moreover, say that any one of them is such a parallel that it *must* have been borrowed. It is rather the cumulative effect of a large number of such passages which seems to have weight. But there are certain metaphors and ideas in connection with religion which are common to mankind, and many expressions of a proverbial nature which are current in one form or another all over the world. Many illustrations and ideas which our Lord Jesus Christ used in His teaching were used also by other teachers before Him. In saying this, we say nothing derogatory to His unique position, but only that He spoke in the language which was intelligible not only to His hearers but to all men. References in Kabīr to Adam and Eve come from Muhammadan sources, and need indicate no direct connection with the Old Testament. Christ and His apostles are nowhere mentioned by Kabīr.

KABĪR AND THE DIVINE WORD.—Kabīr teaches the doctrine of the Śabda, or Divine word; and this has many striking analogies with the doctrine of the *Logos* as given in the Johannine writings, as well as with the Hebrew conception of the *Memra*, or Divine Word. This doctrine is not confined to Kabīr, but is taught in many Hindu sects. It can be traced right back to the Vedas, where *Vach* (Speech) is personified. The mystery of speech as the vehicle of thought has often impressed itself on men, and the religious ideas arising out of this are found in many parts of the world even in ancient times. That this doctrine may have developed amongst the bhakti sects through the impetus of Christian influence is not at all unlikely; but it is difficult to prove from a few passages which seem to have close parallels with Christian teaching, that Kabīr in this doctrine was directly influenced by Christianity.

KABĪRPANTHĪ AND CHRISTIAN SACRAMENTS.—The sacramental system of the Kabīrpanthīs certainly bears some very close resemblances to that of the Christian Church. The sacred meal is taken only by those who feel themselves worthy, is taken fasting, and is followed by a love-feast in which all partake. The consecrated elements are even reserved for administration to the sick and dying. This certainly suggests that here there has been some borrowing of ideas from Christian practices. But the institution of these sacraments amongst the Kabīrpanthīs seems to have begun after the death of Kabīr, and only to have been gradually developed. Moreover, the sacramental meal, or *mahāprasād*, is found in other Hindu sects which are connected with the bhakti movement.

In the legendary life of Kabīr, there are many incidents which recall the Gospel story—his miraculous birth of a virgin, his temptation, his working of miracles, his accusation before a ruler by his enemies, his punishment by that ruler, and his escape from the punishment amounting to a resurrection of the dead, and so on. It is quite possible that a desire to assimilate the life of Kabīr to that of Christ has helped the growth of such legends; but while these would show that Kabīrpanthīs have come under Christian influence, they have no bearing on the connection between Kabīr himself and Christianity.

The Bhakti Movement, of which Kabīr was an outstanding leader, was almost certainly influenced by Christian ideas. The idea of bhakti was indigenous to India, and had already developed there long before the Christian era. But many of those who have investigated the question have no doubt that it was through Christian influence that this and other kindred doctrines received a great impetus, even if the borrowing was not a conscious one. It is not uncommon for a religion to take elements from other religions and to adapt them to its own system. The influence of Christianity on Hindu thought was much greater after Kabīr's time, and was never so great as it is to-day.

While therefore it is almost certain that Kabīr did not directly come into contact with any Christian influence, and probably knew little or nothing of Christian teaching, yet the bhakti movement to which he belonged was undoubtedly under obligation to Christian ideas, and any influence Kabīr received from the direction of Christianity came to him through the mediation of this general movement.

Later Contacts between the Kabīr Panth and Christianity.—It is certain, however, that subsequent to Kabīr, when the Christian faith was more widely preached in India, the members of his sect did come directly in contact with a good deal of Christian influence, and this may

KABĪRPANTHĪ SĀDHU READING A COPY OF ST. JOHN'S GOSPEL

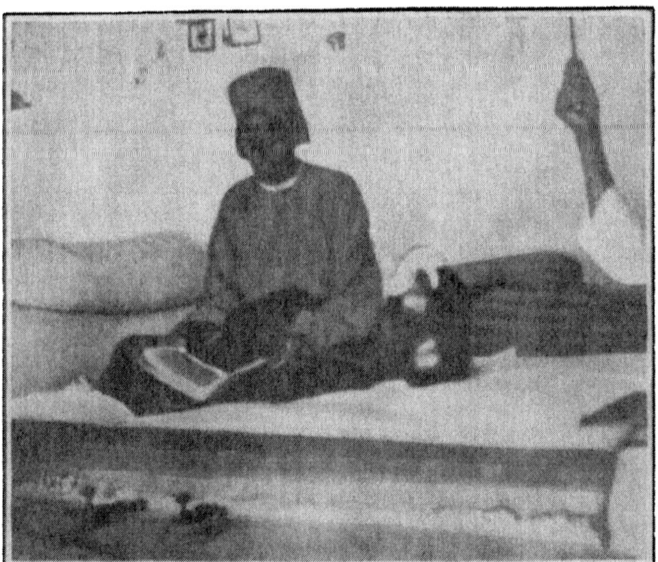

THE MAHANT OF THE DHANAUTI MAṬH ON HIS GADDĪ

have helped in the development of their sacramental system and in other ways. By the latter half of the seventeenth century, there were already many Roman Catholic priests in North India, and pious men such as the leaders of the bhakti sects would naturally talk with them. The sacrament of the Holy Communion clearly impressed many Non-Christians.

Modern Kabīrpanthīs make a good deal of reference to Christianity in their works, taking care however to show the superiority of their own religion. Like other Hindus, they draw the parallel between Christ and Kṛishṇa; but never between Christ and Kabīr. They say, indeed, that like others Christ was subject to the law of Karma, and that though His life was beautiful, the death on the cross which He had to undergo, and from which even His prayer to His Heavenly Father could not deliver Him, showed that He was still entangled in the law of Karma. Kabīr alone, according to their teaching, was entirely free from Karma. The accompanying translation of a poem from a modern Kabīrpanthī work, the *Jīva Dharma Bodha*,[1] is interesting, as showing the attitude of Kabīrpanthīs towards Christianity:

The Customs of the Religions of Moses and Jesus

The qualities of *Raj*[2] and *Tam*[2] are found mingled in the religions of Moses and Jesus.
They make mention of offerings, and sacrifices, and the law, and quote authorities as from the Vedas.
The people of these religions drink wine and eat meat, as they do herbs and vegetables;
They acknowledge the killing of men to be sin; but other living beings they regard as all being like herbs.
The religion of Moses is held by the Jews; this religion is not very much spread.
No disciples of Moses remain; therefore there has been no increase of this religion.
Those who are descendants of Abraham accept the religion of Moses as authoritative.
The Christian religion has the appearance of the quality of *Sat*[2];
there is much in it of forgiveness and good conduct.

[1] Published in 1907 by the Śrī Venkateshwar Press, Bombay.

[2] According to some Hindu philosophers all things in creation possess in various degrees the three constituents of *sattva* (goodness), *rajas* (energy), and *tamas* (darkness)—or in Hindi, *sat*, *raj*, and *tam*.

It teaches that one should be without deceit and violence, and practise humility, beautiful deeds and pure conduct.
But Christians drink wine, and meat, therefore there is the quality of Tam in this religion.
They make little of worship, gifts, and merit, and there is much in their minds of the quality of Raj.
Forgiveness and peace cover all demerits, forsaking error they look towards the Lord.
The disciples of Jesus have many divisions; they have gone to all parts of the world.
In many countries this religion is preached; they speak in all ways of the merits of Jesus.
Where they have opportunity, they extend this religion, amongst simple people who have little cleverness.
They have little knowledge, many are uneducated, then what can be the condition of this religion?
They give little instruction, they make all Christians.
Europe has become entirely Christian; the land of Asia has an abundance of merit.
Only a few men have accepted the Christian religion; India is superior in religion.
Here padris have come; they have converted a few people to their religion;
Since the English ruled, more have become Christians.
In the religions of Moses and Jesus there is no certainty of heaven or hell.
There is no mention in them of the Ātma, of the Jīvas, or of subtle knowledge.
These religions teach material knowledge; they settle the reward of sin and merit.

Many Kabīrpanthīs have become Christians. In some places, missionaries have found them most friendly in their attitude towards the Christian message; though this is not always the case. Those who have become Christians, while giving full allegiance to Christ as Lord and Saviour, generally retain great respect for Kabīr. Nor is such a point of view unreasonable. Though Kabīr himself probably knew nothing about the Christian faith, he was an earnest seeker after truth, and one who anticipated some of the truths which are more fully taught in the Gospel of Christ.

Kabīr and the Teaching of Christ.—Kabīr is certainly one of whom it may be said that he possesses to a large extent 'a mind naturally Christian.' Yet there are, of course, many essential differences in his religious outlook. His hatred of shams and stern denunciation of mere formality in religion is something which certainly appeals to Christians. In his conception of the unity of God, as opposed to Hindu polytheism, and especially in the idea of God as Father, which he seems to have held, he is approaching very near to Christian truth. There are times when he seems to be drawing near to God in personal fellowship. Yet, steeped as his thought was in pantheistic views of God, his conception of Divine personality is often very shadowy. His denial of the doctrine of incarnations did not help him to form a true conception of God as a personal being. We cannot be surprised that his followers, in seeking to supply this defect, have come to deify Kabīr himself. We can see the value here of the Christian doctrine of the Incarnation, with its message of a Divine yet human Saviour.

In his views of salvation Kabīr does not escape from the Hindu doctrine of transmigration. Hence salvation for him means deliverance from this, and from the deceits of Māyā, rather than deliverance from the penalty and bondage of sin, which is so important a part of the Christian message.

Kabīr placed much value upon the Śabda or Divine Word. Yet though he makes it clear that he does not mean the Vedas or the Quran, we do not find anywhere that he indicates what the Śabda was. It seems to have meant with him a subjective impression received by individuals, rather than any objective Divine revelation, and contrasts with the Christian view of the Scriptures as being the living oracles of God.

The central truth of Christian teaching is its message of the Cross; and there is nothing which in any way compares with this in the teaching of Kabīr or his followers. Nor do we find him anywhere emphasising the duty and privilege of self-sacrificing service for others.

Yet although from the Christian standpoint there are many defects in the teaching of Kabīr, we cannot but honour him as an earnest seeker after truth, and one who did much to give a moral uplift to his fellow countrymen, to direct their aspirations to a higher view of life, and to give to them a loftier conception of God.

BIBLIOGRAPHY

A. Editions and Translations of the 'Bījak.'

1. Edition by the Rājā of Rewah. Benares: Viśvanath Sinha. 1867.
2. Edition, with translation, by Rev. Prem Chand of Monghyr. Calcutta. 1890. (2nd edition, 1911.)
3. Edition, with commentary, by Puran Dās. Allahabad. 1905.
4. Edition, with translation, by Rev. Ahmad Shah. Cawnpore. 1911.

B. Translations of Kabīr's Poems in the 'Ādi-Granth.'

1. By Dr. E. Trumpp (certain *Rāgs* only). 1877.
2. By Macauliffe, in Vol. VI, of his *Sikh Religion*. 1909. (Macauliffe's translation is very free; e.g. he renders various names of God, such as 'Hari, Rāma,' etc., indiscriminately as 'God.')
3. An edition in Hindi characters, by the Newal Kishore Press, Lucknow.

C. Books on Kabīr.

1. *Religious Sects of the Hindus*. H. H. Wilson. 1846.
2. *Kabīr and the Kabīr Panth*. Bishop G. H. Westcott. 1907.
3. *Castes and Tribes of the Central Provinces*. R. N. Russell. 4 vols. 1916.
4. *Tribes and Castes of the N.-W. Provinces and Oudh*. W. Crooke. 4 vols., 1896.
5. *Outline of the Religious Literature of India*. J. N. Farquhar. 1911.
6. Articles in:

   Encyclopædia of Religion and Ethics: 'Kabīr,' 'Bhakti Marga,' 'Sūfis,' etc.

   Journal of the Royal Asiatic Society:

   'The Ādi Granth' by F. Pincott. pp. 437 ff. 1886.

   'Modern Hinduism and Its Debt to the Nestorians' by Sir G. Grierson. pp. 311 ff. 1907.

   The Alwar Gazetteer: Translation of the *Gutka*.
7. Hindi Lives of Kabīr; e.g.,

   The Kabīr Kasauti.

   Śrī Kabīr Sāhib ka Jiwān Charitra. Narsinghpur: Sarasvati Vilas Press, 1905.

(For other *Lives of Kabīr*, see above, Chap. vii, pp. 112 ff.)

GLOSSARY

Ādi-Granth—(the 'original volume'.) The sacred book of the Sikhs. Called the *Ādi-Granth* to distinguish it from a later volume known as '*The Granth of the Tenth Guru.*'

Advaita—absolute Monism.

Allāh—the Muhammadan name for God.

Aṁsa—a portion, a part. Used of the human individual soul as a portion of the universal soul.

Āratī—a sacrificial offering of light.

Aśram—a period in the religious life of a Hindu; of which there are four; also used of a place for religious meditation.

Auliyas—auliya is plural of *Wali*, a Muhammadan saint.

Bairāgī—an ascetic, one who has renounced the world.

Baniyā—a Hindu of the trading caste.

Bhagat—a devotee.

Bhajan—a hymn sung as an act of worship.

Bhakti—loving faith and devotion.

Bow-holder—a title of Vishṇu.

Brahma—the name of the supreme God of Hindu theology, generally regarded as impersonal and all-pervading.

Brahmā—one of the Hindu triad of deities, the others being Vishṇu and Śiva.

Brahmachārī—a Hindu student, i.e. one in the first of the four Aśrams (see above).

Chabutrā—a raised platform of stone, or cement, or brick.

Chamār—a member of the low caste of leather-workers.

Chaukā—the space prepared for the sacramental meal of the Kabīr-panthīs; also used of the sacramental meal itself.

Chaupāī—a verse of four lines in Hindi, of a special metre.

Dharma—law, custom, duty, justice, righteousness.

Darśana—a vision; also used of the six schools of Hindu philosophy.

Dhotī—a cloth tied round the waist and falling round the legs.

Dohā—a Hindi couplet of a special metre.

Ekadāśī—the eleventh day of a half-month observed as a fast by Hindus.

Faqīr—a Muhammadan ascetic.

Gaddī—literally, a pillow; the place where a religious leader has his seat of honour.

Ganeśa—the son of Śiva and Parvatī. The god of wisdom and good luck. Generally represented with an elephant's head.

Garuḍa—a mythical bird represented as the vehicle of Vishṇu.

Gāyatrī—a sacred verse of mystical meaning recited daily by Brahmans.

Govinda—a name of Kṛishṇa.

Guṇa—quality, or attribute.

Guru—a religious teacher.

Halāl—the orthodox Muhammadan formula when an animal is killed.

Hanumān—a monkey-chief of prodigious strength who figures in the *Rāmāyaṇa*. He is worshipped as a god by Hindus.

Harnākhas—father of Prahlād. He subjected his son to a variety of cruelties to compel him to renounce the worship of Vishṇu. To save Prahlād, Vishṇu assumed the form of Narāsiṅha, half-lion and half-man.

Indra—the king of heaven and lord of the gods.

Jaṅgama—a devotee who practices a certain form of asceticism.

Jhatka—the Hindu orthodox method of killing an animal.

Jīva—an individual soul.

Kāāba—literally 'a cube'; the square stone building at the mosque at Mecca which contains the sacred black stone.

Kāl—a mystic being personifying time and death, which figures very prominently in the Kabīrpanthī mythology.

Karma—action as involving punishment or reward.

Kaśī—an old name for Benares.

Kaurī—a shell used in India as a coin of very small value.

Khudā—a Muhammadan name for God.

Koṭī—ten millions.

Kṛishṇa—one of the ten incarnations of Vishṇu.

Lahar Talāo—the pond (*talāo*) near Benares where the infant Kabīr was said to have been found by Nīrū and Nīmā.

Lakh—a hundred thousand.

Lakshmī—the consort of Vishṇu and goddess of good fortune.

Loka—one of the divisions of the universe.

Mahant—a leader of a religious sect; the head of a monastery.

Maheśa—a name of Śiva, who is one of the Hindu triad of deities.

Mantra—a secret phrase or password.

Maṭh—a monastery.

Maulvī—a Muhammadan religious teacher.

Māyā—illusion. The idea of Māyā plays a great part in Hindu philosophy and theology.

Mulla—a Muhammadan religious teacher.

Muni—a sage.

Nāla—a small stream or ditch.

Nārad—a divine sage of Hindu mythology.

Nārāyaṇa—a name of Vishṇu.

Narāsiṅha—the man-lion incarnation of Vishṇu.

Nirguṇa—'without attributes.' According to Hindu ideas it is a higher conception of God when he is considered as *nirguṇa* than when he is considered as *saguṇa*, that is 'with attributes.'

Omkāra—the Hindu sacred syllable 'Om.'

Pāṇḍe—a Brahman, a paṇḍit.

Panth—literally 'a path'; a sect.

Paramātma—the Universal Soul.

Pārvatī—the consort of Śiva.

Parwāna—an authoritative document, a passport.

Pīr—a Muhammadan saint, or religious teacher.

Prahlād—son of Harnākhas. He was persecuted by his father, but rescued by Vishṇu, who assumed for the purpose the form of Narāsiṅha, the man-lion.

Prakṛitis—primary and productive elements of the Universe.

Pūjārī—one responsible for performing worship to a divine being.

Purāṇas—the name of a certain class of Hindu sacred books containing mythological stories.

Purusha—a being, person, male. Used as a title of the Supreme Being.

Qāzī—a Muhammadan religious functionary.

Rādhā—the cowherd mistress of Kṛishṇa who figures in the legends about him.

Rāma—one of the incarnations of Vishṇu, who is the hero of the famous epic, the *Rāmāyaṇa*.

Ramazān—the Muhammadan month of fasting.

Śabda—a word or saying, especially a Divine Word.

Sādhu—a Hindu religious mendicant.

Saguṇa—'with attributes.' See *Nirguṇa*.

Sākhī—a Hindi couplet, usually containing a short apophthegm.

Saktī—the female representation of Divine energy.

Śalgrāma—a sacred stone, typical of Vishṇu.

Sampradaya—traditional doctrine or custom, often used for a group of sects which hold certain views in common.

Saṇgati—society, association (especially with holy men).

Sant—a saint, a holy man.

Sat Guru—*sat*, true, *guru*, teacher. By Kabīrpanthīs, 'Sat Guru' is often used of Kabīr, or even of God.

Sayed—a descendant of the Prophet Muhammad.

Śeshnāga—a mythical serpent.

Siddhā—one who has attained spiritual perfection.

Singhāra—the water-chestnut.

Śiva—one of the Hindu triad of deities, the others being Brahmā and Vishṇu.

Smṛiti—religious teaching based on memory or tradition.

'*Soham*'—'I am He.' A Hindu philosophical conception expressing the identity of the individual soul with God.

Sūfīs—a school of Muhammadan mystics.

Śūdra—a Hindu of the fourth group of castes, which includes various kinds of artisans.

Śyāma—an epithet of Kṛishṇa.

Taka—an Indian coin of the period in which Kabīr lived, said to be a double paisa, that is about one halfpenny.

'*Tat tvam āsi*'—'Thou art That.' A Hindu philosophical conception expressing the identity of the individual soul with the universal soul.

Tilak—a sect mark, usually worn on the forehead.

Tinkā Arpan—the offering (*arpan*) of a straw (*tinka*) in sacrifice.

Tulasī—the basil plant, sacred to Vishṇu.

Upanishads—philosophical books which form the concluding part of the *Vedas*.

Vedānta—'the end of the *Vedas*'—the orthodox standard of the teaching of the *Vedas*.

Vedas—the four *Vedas* are the ancient sacred books of the Hindus written in Sanskrit.

Vishṇu—one of the Hindu triad of deities, the others being Brahmā and Śiva.

Viśishṭādvaita—modified monism, which allows some place for the personality of God.

Yādavas—the descendants of a certain Yadu who figures in Hindu mythology.

Yama—the Hindu god of death.

Yogī—a Hindu ascetic who seeks to attain spiritual enlightenment by the performance of certain ascetic exercises and postures.

INDEX

A GLANCE

AT THE PAST AND THE FUTURE

IN CONNECTION WITH

THE INDIAN REVOLT.

BY

MAJOR-GENERAL H. T. TUCKER, C.B.,

LATE ADJUTANT-GENERAL OF THE ARMY IN BENGAL.

LONDON:

EFFINGHAM WILSON, ROYAL EXCHANGE.

1857.

"If you see man or boy striving earnestly on the weak side, however wrong-headed or blundering he may be, you are not to go and join the cry against him. . . . At any rate, remember that he has found something in the world which he will fight and suffer for."—Tom Brown's School-days.

THE INDIAN REVOLT.

CHAPTER I.

At a time when the eyes of all men are open to the glaring errors and imperfections in our Indian system of government, which has resulted in such a revolt and mutiny as cannot be paralleled in history, and when the columns of every newspaper have teemed with suggestions and plans from many who, before the realization of this fearful catastrophe, were content to repose in placid indifference and apathy, I feel impelled, in offering a few remarks for the consideration of those interested in the welfare of our fellow-countrymen in India, to reproduce a few extracts from the cautions and warnings which, in 1852, when all was peaceful and quiet, I ventured, at the cost of grave imputations of being an alarmist, to publish in an Address to the Proprietors of East India Stock. The subsequent alteration in the terms of the Company's charter induced me to forego my design of canvassing that body generally, but I printed and distributed no less than 400 copies, of which many were circulated to persons in the highest positions, and filling the most important situations both in India and in England. The elaborate Address I had prepared commenced as follows. · Paragraph 1:—

"I beg to solicit your support in view to my election as one of your Directors for the management of the affairs of the East India Company.

"It is proper that I should state to you the grounds of my appeal, and I have thought it also incumbent on me to explain generally the views and opinions I entertain in regard to the system and policy it is desirable to pursue in conducting so difficult, so peculiar, and so vast a Government as that of the British Empire in the East."

At Paragraph 7, I observed that—

"The stability and internal tranquillity of our vast Indian possessions require, in the chiefest degree, the constant vigilant attention of the Governing Authorities, both in Europe and in Hindostan. Our extensive conquests since the commencement of the present century have perhaps enlarged our dominions to the utmost extent necessary or desirable, but we may nevertheless find it impossible, consistently with safety and good policy, to arrest the tide of conquest. On the East, on the West, and to the northward of us, still remain powerful, turbulent, and in some cases warlike and ambitious neighbours. As with Bhurtpore formerly, so probably will it be with the kingdom of Nepal. A second war will some day be entered on to decide the final mastery, and our peaceful and fertile plains will witness the descent of an army of warlike and well-appointed Goorkahs, with possibly Thibet and China at their back."

After entering into various details, in which, among other matters, I enforced the necessity for "*confirming* and *consolidating our supremacy*," and observed that "to strengthen and secure our centre, and the long line of the Himalayan frontier, should be now, and during the years of peace, the subject of grave consideration and deliberate and scientific arrangement," I entered, at Paragraph 12, on the subject of the Native Troops. It runs as follows:—

"No considerations can be more important than those connected with the discipline and welfare of the native forces in India. Within the last twenty years much has been done in each of the armies of the three Presidencies in view to improvement, and it is to be hoped with effect. But fanciful and mere theoretical changes, however well intended, prove often fallacious when practically applied; and that some erroneous steps have been taken of late years, in regard to the increase of pay and allowances to the Sepoys, can scarcely, I fear, admit of a doubt. To retrace our steps on such occasions is sometimes impracticable, or, at the least, dangerous and unsafe, and we can do nothing at the price of disaffection. Those who hold the reins of Government, whether at home or in India, should never be forgetful of the fact that our armies are composed of mercenaries, not of national troops; and that when, in the course of events, they shall become nationalized, it must necessarily be in opposition to foreign rule and domination. Our conquests, which have brought so many kingdoms and provinces under one form of Government, together with our system of education and freedom of the press, are gradually *nationalizing India.* For the sake alike of the governed and those who control them, it is desirable that the just and philanthropic views which have actuated our Statesmen in introducing these and other measures of amelioration, should be slowly, even tardily, progressive; and if this, as I conscientiously believe, is applicable to the great mass of the people, it assuredly, and in tenfold force, applies to the native troops of India in European employ."

And again, in the following paragraph :—

"We have carried to the very verge of prudence a system which was and is admirable while kept within due bounds. We have been so successful that there is danger of our becoming too secure; but the tens of thousands which compose our armies in the East, are simple mercenaries, opposed to us as much in faith, nation, and feeling, as in colour. We should be sedulously careful, therefore, *to maintain a just equipoise*, for our real strength does not consist in overwhelming bodies of mercenaries,—these may indeed one day constitute our chief weakness,—but in the numbers, the valour, and the discipline of our fellow-countrymen. These, and our European officers serving with the native troops, we should increase and foster as far as the means and finances of the State will admit, for on them we must depend when troubled and stormy times shall hereafter arise; while we should be ever on the watch to avoid that false and specious system that in its result would convert useful and obedient auxiliaries into greedy, pampered, and overbearing Pretorians."

In the foregoing, I endeavoured earnestly to attract attention to the necessity for maintaining "a just equipoise" between "the overwhelming bodies of mercenaries in our employ, and the European national troops;" and to enforce attention, I added: "It is not without a motive that I advert to these grave matters, for although no alarmist, I hold *that it is fatal to slumber on in a fancied security*." It may be asked by some intelligent reflective reader, But did this paper ever reach the eye of any one in authority, having power to inquire and move in such a business? My reply is, Yes, many; but I give one proof. I printed this paper at Simla, in the beginning of August, 1852. I sent a copy to Lord Dalhousie, then in Calcutta, and had some correspondence with him on the subject; he uttered no word of dissent in reference to my estimate of the dependence to be placed upon the Sepoy troops; but his own words will be a convincing proof that he thought them just, and that my becoming a Director of the Company would be productive of good. I am not aware that in making this use of them I infringe on any received etiquette; I am not using them in order to attack his Lordship, but to show that I did make known my opinions in the very highest quarter, and that if no inquiry or reform followed, I at least may claim to be exonerated from any charge of blindness or supineness. *Speaking before the event*, I think it will be allowed that I could scarcely have said more, for I was filling at that period a very important situation, that of Adjutant-General of the Army in Bengal, and I was liable to be called upon both to explain and justify my opinions. From Lord Dalhousie's communication, to which I have alluded, I extract as follows:—

"Government House,
"16th August, 1852.

"My dear Tucker,

"The intimation you give me of your views towards the Direction, does not take me quite by surprise; and I shall be heartily glad to see them accomplished.

"I doubt I can aid you with little beyond good wishes. When I was appointed to this Government, I did not know one of the Court, except —— and Mr. ——. Besides these I can't say I know any now, but those who have been in the Chair.

"It does not seem to me that they will let you start while you are employed. But if they do, as whenever they do, I will most readily write to those whom I do know among them. —— asked me (with the same object in view as you now propose to yourself) to write to him if I thought well of him, and say I wished him success. I was not vain enough to suppose this would be of much use. He thought so, however, and if it was useful then, it will probably be equally or more so now. If you should think so, I shall be truly glad to do it whenever you express the wish. Always yours sincerely,

"(Signed) DALHOUSIE."

At Paragraphs 15 and 16 of my Address, I entered upon the state of the Civil Government; that was a matter requiring delicate handling, for no persons are more easily aroused than the Bengal Civil Service of the present day, when any hint is given that they do not appear to be altogether infallible. Nevertheless I wrote as follows:—

"As regards the civil administration, there is still avowedly a wide field open for amelioration; much has been done, much remains to do. The state of trade and manufactures, the revenue, the encouragement and improvement of the agricultural system, the condition of the native press and its tendencies, as at present exhibited, the construction of railroads and other scientific works and discoveries which can be made applicable to the East, each and all demand the most careful attention; and the fostering aid, guidance, and support of Government are essential to the well-being of these interests in India, and in many cases to the perfect development of the great resources of the country.

"The state and efficiency of the civil courts, their adequacy to the ends in view on their introduction, also, require to be looked into with a jealous and precise scrutiny; for on the purity and simplicity with which we administer law and justice to the natives of the country, the prolongation, stability, and popularity of our rule will, in a great measure, ultimately depend. I feel constrained to avow candidly that, in my opinion, great defects at present exist, and that the venality which is stated to pervade our courts of law is a theme of condemnation throughout the country, chiefly attributable, however, even among themselves, to native venality and falsehood, and in a great degree also to the insufficiency of European superintendence, a supervision which, I may observe, cannot judiciously be dispensed with until a higher moral sense and far greater integrity of thought and conduct shall characterize the natives, who are quick to observe, keenly apprehensive, and quite capable of distinguishing between those *ad captandum* acts which have merely a popular tendency, and those which emanate from a pure and true spirit of philanthropy. Those rare acts and judgments which stand the test of time, and which, often at first unpopular, confer nevertheless a just fame hereafter, are never lost upon them; and European domination will therefore sustain no shock and lose no ground in the native mind, by the pursuance of a firm, cautious, and circumspect system of government; on the contrary, our rule will be raised greatly in their estimation by observing that we are not hastily carried away by new systems and plausible theories, nor easily led into the adoption of unexpected, fanciful, and ill-digested measures."

Now I will avow that I look upon the Indian Civil Service as composed generally of a most zealous and admirable body of men; but I think, notwithstanding, that great defects exist in its constitution, and that it has of late years much deteriorated: that it has become too exclusive, too much of a "vested interest," and so puffed up with self-complacency, in consequence, that it is almost impossible for the sentiments and opinions of an outsider to penetrate within the circle of its clique-like reserve. Like the unhappy native army, it has been pampered, petted, and indulged, until it cannot stand the least control or opposition, and I am greatly in error if the correspondence of the Court of Directors will not show that of late years, even in the Council Chamber, unseemly, disrespectful, and insubordinate letters were addressed by the civilians of that body to the Honourable Court. Hence, when the present mutiny broke out, the opinions of independent military men were disregarded, and when officers of conduct, courage, and experience were writing from the seat of Government, that "we had *only* now to fight for it," the civilians in the council of Lord Canning were hugging themselves in the belief that the crisis was past, that the mutiny was stifled, and that an undue and unnecessary outcry had been raised! Where, it will be asked, was the Military Secretary to the Supreme Government of India at this time? What were the counsels and opinions of that officer at such a crisis? More of that hereafter. His acts shall be given in the words of an eye-witness on the spot—one who has manfully dared to speak out. The very simple reply to be given to the question here, is, that the Military Secretary was "nowhere." Except for evil, he does not appear to have even found a place. Another proof of the impolicy of advancing men to high and important positions, who have no sterling merit, and whose rise is due to mere favouritism and that pliability of disposition which bespeaks a ready partisan, while it betokens the reverse of that honest independence so necessary to the just and upright discharge of important public duties.

To recur—at Paragraph 17 of the Address to the Proprietors, I observed that the number of civilians should be greatly increased, but "not by a temporary and makeshift system, such as that of borrowing by wholesale from officers of the army, by which practice the military service is so much injured in its efficiency."

And at Paragraphs 18 and 19, I thus wrote:—

"It has been, with great justice, thought a duty to foster and promote education in India; but education generally diffused will necessarily produce new desires and suggest new objects of ambition; the process will, it is to be hoped, prove gradual, but we should prepare for it, not only with reference to our own, but with advertence also to the future interests of the people of India. The apparent apathy and indifference of the Hindu will assuredly give place by degrees under this system to feelings of patriotism, and a natural craving to exercise as well as to emulate that exalted and ennobling virtue, the desire to promote the welfare of their country, which so generally characterizes the natives of the West.

"The effect of that extension of our Empire which the course of events has forced upon us, has been to produce an internal though almost an unconscious pressure, but which must necessarily greatly increase; and the difficulties attendant on the Government of so vast a country will be increased with it, for we cannot expect the natives of India to remain stationary. Our conquests are consolidating and becoming by degrees nationalized; but it should be remembered that dominion, equally with "glory," may be likened to those circles in the water which never cease to enlarge themselves, "till by broad spreading they disperse to nought!" In brief, our difficulties and dangers augment with our greatness, and with every prostrate and conquered kingdom, we are raising up a united internal force and pressure, which it will require all the wisdom and all the prescience our statesmen can bring to bear upon it, to regulate and control; and it is therefore essential to the well-being and interests of our own country, no less than of India, that she should be ruled and governed by those whose practical knowledge, observation, and experience will guide them to correct views and sound policy."

From this document it will, I think, appear, that I was fully alive to the imperfections of both our civil and military system, and that I desired to draw attention to it, and to aid in reforming it. I have had little opportunity for either. The door is now practically closed to the East India Direction, except to such as have interest with the Minister, or are connected with influential and aristocratic families; and, although in the situation I filled in India I did my utmost to lessen the danger of our position, yet, as it was then impossible, *in the face of all received opinion*, to dilate and insist upon the danger to be apprehended from mutiny and revolt among the Sepoys, I was able to effect but little; what I did attempt I shall briefly advert to in another chapter.

Meanwhile, in reference to what is stated at Page 4, of the "erroneous steps" taken to increase the pay and allowances of the Sepoys, it appears desirable to give an idea to the home reader of what these steps sometimes were, to enable him to understand the peculiarly unwise nature of the system often adopted in dealing with these mercenaries: one instance will suffice. It may be broadly stated, in round numbers, that the pay of the Sepoy amounts to seven rupees per mensem: with that sum he is required to feed and support himself. Certain articles of military clothing are besides supplied to him from the State; but for his food and clothing generally, and the support of his family, when he has any, this is the sum which he ordinarily receives. It is very ample; as a general rule, he saves one-half of it, and often more, for so covetous and penurious are these high-caste men, that they will often literally half starve themselves to add to their savings; and I have positively known the medical officers of corps (than whom no class of public servants in India are more intelligent and meritorious) report men for thus denying themselves a sufficiency of food, and who, in consequence, had become so weak and emaciated as to be obliged to go into hospital!

A few years since, notwithstanding, it was thought desirable, for the sake apparently of mere change, for nothing really called for such a measure, to "better the condition" of the Sepoy, and it was resolved on the part of Government to increase their pay, and to add to it one rupee monthly, after sixteen years of service, and a second additional rupee after twenty years of service in the grade of private: these additions were to be called good-conduct pay, and could only be drawn for when the man's conduct had been unexceptionable for a previous period of two years. The theory of this very impolitic and foolish increase, which took annually a very large sum from the public exchequer, without being productive of the least corresponding good, was this:—it was contended by the advocates for the change, that by giving such increases of pay after sixteen and twenty years' service, the Sepoy would be deprived of any just ground for feeling discontent if he were passed over for promotion to the non-commissioned ranks; these additions for "good conduct" would sufficiently compensate him, it was said, for the loss of promotion, and his position would still remain an enviable one, while the addition was a proper reward for previous faithful service and good conduct. To these *ad captandum* arguments the more practical reply was, Let well alone. Do not teach your mercenaries to think that pay can be so easily raised and increased at the pleasure of any Governor or Commander-in-Chief. To imbue with such an idea mercenary troops, is to court demands of a pecuniary description which no State could support, and is to introduce amongst us the instability and fluctuations so common among the troops of the native states; when, moreover, there is no real occasion for it, and when, except in mere theory, its action will be found alike embarrassing and injurious. And so in my judgment it proved to be; for to refuse a Sepoy promotion who was enjoying extra pay for being well conducted, involved, as was soon found, a practical contradiction. Sepoys so passed over were in the habit of inquiring, "Why then did they receive extra pay, if they were not fit to be made corporals?" and the specious arguments employed were of no avail to convince them that they did not suffer an injustice.

Now, that this tampering with pay was a dangerous principle to introduce, no one who reflects dispassionately on the peculiar position we occupy in the East, can, I think, doubt. The reasons for it were simply, to the best of my recollection, those I have stated; they were certainly those of a late Governor-General, Lord Hardinge, to whose firm consistent kindness and support I have been deeply indebted, and for whose memory I shall always entertain a lasting feeling of respectful gratitude. That nobleman, in conversing with me on such subjects at Simla, so expressed himself: and the intention was doubtless good; the policy and wisdom of the act most questionable. It received, however, as was understood, the approval of the home authorities at the East India House; and with advertence to these last, I may here very properly note the contrast between the unwise and profuse liberality shown to the Sepoy, and the obstinate, perverse illiberality, in the matter of half-batta, which affects only his European officer. Just thirty years ago, the Court of Directors, during Lord William Bentinck's tenure of government, issued orders for placing all stations within 200 miles of the Presidency, on what was called "half-batta," by which measure the allowances of every European officer at such stations were considerably reduced. Now the captains and subalterns in India are very ill-paid; and this order was peculiarly hard upon the latter, who were brought from remote, quiet, up-country stations, to the Presidency (Barrackpore), and on arrival there, found themselves on reduced allowances when exposed to all the numerous expenses and temptations of the capital. No idle attempts at argument, no sophistical reasoning could get over the facts of the case. The Government urged, that wine and beer, and European articles of consumption (jams and pickles!), were cheaper than up the country, because the expense of carriage was avoided; forgetful that everything else was more expensive, and the incitements and temptations to expense incredibly increased. To add to the inconsistency, the military staff in Calcutta, the well-paid officers of the military Secretariate, Audit, Adjutant, and Quartermaster-General's offices, were all exempted and excepted from the operation of the order. These influential persons were unaffected by a general measure of so-called financial reform, while needy subalterns were to be unsparingly retrenched! The whole procedure was well fitted for the sarcasm and satire of Horace or Juvenal; and the complacency of Leadenhall-street would have been sadly ruffled, if the remarks made throughout the army had ever penetrated to those musty and antiquated recesses. Lord Metcalfe, then one of the Supreme

Council, strongly and urgently denounced the injustice and harshness of the measure, but the military class of the servants of the Company have rarely any influence at the India House, and the injustice continues to be perpetrated to this day, and is to this day also the cause of just discontent; for no quibbling logic can upset the broad fact, that in support of a foolish theory, the Directors have continued a system of payment whereby the European officer receives least pay when he most requires it, while the Sepoy, who did not require any increase at all, and to whom it was most unwise to give it, continues to receive the same, although the reasoning under which it was bestowed has been found to be utterly fallacious.

CHAPTER II.

It is not only our military system that has failed in India, but our whole civil, fiscal, and judicial policy requires to be remodelled. We have been weak and philanthropical. We have shown ourselves as rulers entirely wanting in that stern vigour, foresight, and insight into the native mind and character, so essential to the maintenance of our supremacy. We have been unwilling and reluctant to believe in that deep duplicity and consistent guile with which the *Mahomedan* native of Hindostan, more especially, so well conceals his deep-rooted malignity and hatred. Now for a time the eyes of the British public are opened, and we should seize the golden opportunity, and amend our system. It is to that end I desire to contribute my humble quota to the general information, for the question is now a national one. The will and voice of the people must now be consulted, and it is not by the Court of Directors, or even by the *Sic volo, sic jubeo* of Lord Palmerston, that the future form of Indian Government will be decided. Indeed, if, as had nearly been the case, the indecision and delay of the Cabinet, and the seeming indifference displayed to the fate of our struggling countrymen, in apparently so wilfully neglecting the means of ready transit through Egypt, had led, as was only too much to be feared, to the total overthrow of our power in Bengal, it is to be doubted if even the patient endurance of the public would have held the Ministry excused.

To proceed with the record of my own official experience. In the beginning of the year 1850 I became Adjutant-general of the army; and Sir Charles Napier, in nominating me to that responsible post, wrote as follows:—

"From General Sir C. Napier, G.C.B., Commander-in-Chief in India, to Lieutenant-Colonel Tucker, C.B., Adjutant-General of the Army; dated Simla, 27th April, 1850.

"My dear Tucker,

"Your situation as Deputy Adjutant-General, your abilities, and your good service in war, have made you Adjutant-General, and you owe me no gratitude. I have only done justice to merit.

"I am, etc.,

"(Signed) C. J. NAPIER."

The note is characteristic. I insert it to show that it was not through Directorial influence, or subserviency of any sort, that I obtained the appointment. I was naturally earnest to discharge my duties efficiently, after such an opinion expressed by such a man, and I worked hard and sedulously with him so long as he remained in India, and I continued to receive letters from him even from that sick couch whereon he not long after breathed away his noble but unquiet spirit. But I had no desire to be a partisan; and when, therefore, I was invited by Lord Dalhousie to discuss military matters, I readily availed myself of the opportunity to prepare for his consideration various elaborate memoranda, in the hope that some practical result would follow. I submitted to his Lordship, among other papers, a memorandum regarding the unsatisfactory state of the Cavalry, regular and irregular, and suggested various changes and amendments in the system. I submitted a similar paper, of great length, relating to the state of the Artillery, and pointed out the great evils resulting from the paucity of officers and insufficiency of men. At a subsequent period I forwarded to his Lordship a document which I very carefully drew up, in which I insisted on the denuded state of the Infantry in regard to officers, and offered for consideration a plan for the formation of a staff corps; and in treating of the state of the native army generally, I advocated the abolition of the grade of native commissioned officer, that rank which, in the convulsion and revolt we have to deplore, has only produced a nest of traitors, whose duplicity, baseness, and ingratitude will for ever stand unrivalled in the annals of military revolt. What use his Lordship may have made of my suggestions, I have no means of judging; but for the Cavalry, nothing was done until, after an interval of two or three years, Government sent home to the Court of Directors a proposal to disband four, I think, of the regular Cavalry regiments, and to substitute for them two regiments of European Dragoons. That proposal came to head-quarters for the opinion of the Commander-in-Chief. I was called upon to give mine, and did so in a paper which gave so much satisfaction to his Excellency, that he drew the particular attention of the Government to it, and it was sent home for the information of the Honourable Court. The breaking out, however, of the Crimean war, put a stop to this plan, a circumstance greatly to be lamented.

To the Artillery, after a long interval, a slight addition was made, and an additional officer or two was given to each regiment of the line; but the arrangements were quite inadequate to meet the evil complained of,—the wholesale drain, that is, of officers from corps to fill civil and staff appointments, and under which system the most experienced officers were withdrawn from regiments, leaving for the discharge of regimental duties an altogether insufficient number.

But it is not to be supposed, that in advocating privately with the Governor-General changes and alterations, I thought I sufficiently performed my part. On the contrary, I pressed on the Commander-in-Chief, and by his authority on the Government, *usque ad nauseam*, the necessity for an increase to the Artillery, etc. etc.; and as opportunity offered, I endeavoured to bring about important changes. I will give two instances, both of them bearing nearly on the present state of affairs. Many people in this country have been surprised to hear of the admirable manner in which the mutineers have worked their artillery; the explanation, though scarcely credible, is as follows:—Application had been made by the military authorities, and Government had sanctioned the instruction in the artillery gun exercise of 100 men in each regiment of Native Infantry, and accordingly ten per cent. of our Sepoys were so instructed! I shall not enter into any discussion on this strange fact—it speaks for itself; but I was so sensible of its fatuity, and of the danger likely to result from it, that I took occasion to represent to the Commander-in-Chief the suicidal nature of the measure, and obtained from Sir William Gomm authority for submitting to Government a proposal quietly to stop the practice. In the letter I drafted to Government, I gave my reason for the recommendation in the plainest terms, and said, that in the event of any revolt or mutiny of the Sepoys, the knowledge thus being acquired would only be an incitement to them to attempt to capture our ordnance. To this despatch a reply, briefly assenting, was received; not one word of remark or inquiry was made. I had been prepared to give *in extenso* my reasons for thinking that the Bengal army was ready, on any sufficiently exciting cause or occasion, to turn upon us in revolt; and the proof that I did entertain this opinion will be found in the letters I wrote in the *Times* at the first opening of this sad tragedy, in which I stood, I believe, almost alone in warning the public of what was to be expected.

The second instance of a warning bearing on what has now come to pass, was in a recommendation I made to Sir William Gomm for permission to apply to Government to disarm all travellers on the great high-roads. I represented, in a letter addressed to the Military Secretary to Government, that the Sepoys all had private arms in their possession, and that it was most desirable to deprive them of these weapons; that the Commander-in-Chief was prepared to do so; but as it was urged, that to deprive them of these means of defence, while proceeding on furlough to their homes, was to expose them both going and returning, and while there, to be murdered and robbed by the armed community and by travellers, for the sake of the savings they were known to carry with them from their regiments, he was anxious that the system of going about the country armed should be first put a stop to. To this proposal an almost scornful and derisive reply was received, and it was asked by the Military Secretary whether the Commander-in-Chief really meant to recommend to Government such an impracticable plan as that of disarming the whole population of the Upper Provinces. Now, there was nothing at all impracticable in the matter. Sir John Lawrence had done the same thing in the Punjaub, and we now know of what signal benefit such a procedure would have been; but the Governor-General was sick, and, it was said, splenetic, and there was a most pernicious and adverse influence at work in the Military Secretariate. I do not pretend to quote the actual words of the despatches in those two cases, but they were precisely to the effect I have described, and will be found on record in the Military Departments in Bengal.

It may be remarked, To what end write of past errors of Government, which can now in their narration be inoperative for good? To this I would reply, that not only may good be educed in the future, by showing the errors we have fallen into, but the wilfulness too often displayed by governors, secretaries, and others, in combating judicious measures merely because they were personally opposed to those who suggested them, ought to be held up to just condemnation; and I will conclude this part of my subject by an instance, showing exactly how such feelings may operate to the detriment of the public service. I was much struck, when I first succeeded to the post of Adjutant-General, at the way in which numbers of the older officers in command of divisions, districts, and stations, applied to me, both privately and publicly, for advice as to how they had best act in such and such emergencies. I found that to rely on themselves was the exception—that almost all seemed to wish to lean on authority before committing themselves to action—in a word, a great bugbear prevented their acting on their own judgment: *that bugbear was the dread of responsibility,* produced chiefly by the "wigging" system of the Government. I set myself to work to combat this system. I wrote in the most friendly spirit numerous letters, showing how badly such a system must necessarily work; pointed out the purpose for which men were placed in these important and lucrative posts; and deprecated the reference of every petty detail for the opinion of the Adjutant-General, and more broadly the system of centralization which had sprung up. I had reason to suppose that my efforts, during the six years I was Adjutant-General, were productive of much good; but there was a higher influence than that of the Army Head-Quarters at work, an authority under which the native Articles of War, with all its faults and errors, had been prepared; I allude to the Military Secretary to the Government, who had previously served all his life in the department of the Judge-Advocate; a department admirably calculated for generating a quibbler where that turn of mind existed, but extremely ill calculated for the training of a Secretary to the Supreme Government, who should be one able and willing to take a broad, general view, free from the petty bias which, as Sir Charles Napier used justly to observe, far too frequently characterizes the class of military lawyers; but we have the opinion of this great soldier, in his life, by Sir W. Napier, of the amount of merit to be discovered in the *ci-devant* Chief of the Judge-Advocate's Department. To proceed: one striking reason for the laxity in point of discipline which too often called for censure, appeared to me to rest with the Government,—the appointing, namely, to important commands, of worn-out and incapable officers, merely on account of their seniority. Soon after I became Adjutant-General, I wrote, with the approval of the Commander-in-Chief, a very strong and earnest despatch, pointing out the evils, and suggesting the remedy. The then Secretary to Government, Colonel J. Stuart, was a man of vigorous understanding and sound sense; he warmly seconded the proposal, and Lord Dalhousie at once assented in terms of praise and approbation. Vacancies existed on the Divisional and Brigade staff, and at once some half-a-dozen incapables were set aside; and the Commander-in-Chief, thus secure, as he imagined, of the support of the Indian Government, nominated junior officers, considered more equal to the performance of such responsible duties. But the affair did not thus terminate; Colonel Stuart fell sick, and was succeeded, though he was known earnestly to deprecate such an appointment, by the present Military Secretary; and at an interval of some two years, the Commander-in-Chief was called upon by this officer, in the name of the Government, to state more specifically the reasons for passing over one of these worn-out, used-up old Generals, a man who, in his best days, had been notoriously inefficient. The Commander-in-Chief observed, in commenting on this unexpected communication, that he did not know personally any of the officers who had been superseded; that he was obliged to depend in such matters on the confidential report and explanations of the Adjutant-General, who was responsible for the fidelity of his representations; but that it was altogether too much to expect of that functionary to give, in detail, each and every item constituting inaptitude and incapacity on the part of those superseded, for public report to Government, *and communication, when solicited, to the aggrieved parties concerned;* and that, finally, the letter from the Military Secretary under comment appeared to be strangely at variance with that from his predecessor on the same subject. Ultimately the supreme Government gave way, and no such explanation as had been required was furnished!

I have little to say in this place of the details of the measures of reform and change which the state of the native troops and the general disorganization prevalent everywhere in Bengal, so loudly demands. "Indophilus" and others have written nearly all that can be said of practical use in way of suggestion; and to re-echo and repeat what is now so generally seen and felt, would be merely pedantic and useless; I will therefore offer only a brief outline of the principal changes I would advocate. Those changes, to be of use, must be most carefully and dispassionately considered; and it is to be hoped that, in the alterations and revision which will take place, the brave and devoted Indian officers who are now so heroically upholding the empire, without one word of despondency, far less of despair, will not be made to bear the onus or to suffer for the faults of a vicious system over which they had no control, or for the blindness, fatuity, and utter want of prescience which has characterized too many of the acts, both of omission and commission, of those in authority. The officers of the Bengal army, unwisely shipped for the East at the immature age of sixteen, are a wonderful body, considering the difficulties with which they have to contend. It is true they cannot perhaps dress, on their return to their native country, like the more finished loungers of Regent Street and the Clubs, they are not so graceful and refined in a drawing-room,—they were exiled ere they could attain to that style of seeming superiority; but for all real, manly feeling and acquirements they have, as a body, few superiors. Those acquirements have been diverted by the Government into improper and unprofessional channels, to the great loss and detriment of the military service; but for that *they* are not the responsible parties.

Of the army before Delhi, Henry Tombs, for daring gallantry, manly and professional readiness, could not be surpassed in all Europe. Nor in all the ranks of the British army here, at home, will a more accomplished, talented, or more thoroughly instructed staff-officer be found than is to be met with in the person of Captain Henry Norman. Of Brigadier-General Nicholson, who shall speak in terms of adequate praise? To the firmness, courage, and judgment of this officer, and to that equally brave and unhesitating man, Sir John Lawrence, we owe our very existence in the North-west. Major Edwin Johnson, Adjutant-General of the Artillery, in the field is an officer who, for calm excellent judgment and great official aptitude, cannot be surpassed. And from among those sacrificed to the inefficiency of our system, how many names of gallant and able men appear. Let me pay a brief tribute, in adverting to the fate of some few—men who were honoured and respected by all.

Colonel J. Finnis fell devotedly at the Meerut outbreak. He had written to me while his regiment was marching to that station; and, with his usual sagacity, observed, that "some very strange feeling had come over the Sepoys," that "something was brooding." That mystery was soon to be solved; and so fell one of my earliest Indian friends.

Lieutenant-Colonel Tudor Tucker, of the Cavalry, fell, after having for eight days worked day and night as a common gunner, with all that zeal and earnestness for which he was through life distinguished. He was as gentle and amiable as he was brave and devoted, and not a man in India fell more generally beloved. To the end he was favoured, in that he died while yet the heroic defence of the few officers at Futtehghur was maintained—ere yet the captivity of his wife and family, ending in revolting massacre, had occurred.

Of that gallant, able, and most talented officer, Major Fletcher Hayes, Military Secretary in Oude; of Edward Fraser, Commandant of the Sappers; of Arthur Gibbings and John Smith, of the Irregular Cavalry; of Herbert Gardner, Stuart Beatson, Lieutenant-Colonel Philip Goldney; Lieutenant Robert Stuart, Adjutant of the 6th Native Infantry; Major Banks, who fell in the performance of his arduous duties at Lucknow; and many other dear friends, it need simply be said, that they fell in the execution of their duty, victims to the incautious policy of rulers too weakly secure in their ideal empire of opinion, and too fully persuaded of their personal inviolability—of that "divinity" supposed to "hedge" the persons of the present race of Indian civilians in high office—to take the commonest precautions the trust delegated to them demanded, even when it was notorious that Mahomedan and other conspirators had for years been preaching a crusade against us, and the native press teemed with articles only too well calculated to produce disaffection and revolt. The English world will not fail to notice the heroic struggle made everywhere, and in the face of all difficulties, by the general body of officers, Queen's and Company's—all alike confident in the final result, even when most pressed upon and outnumbered; and we may be justly proud of bearing and conduct which has so gloriously upheld the national character.

If here and there imbecility or cowardice have been productive of great evils, as at Jullendur, Meerut, Dinapore, Allahabad, even at Calcutta,—where at least a sense of duty should have assumed the appearance of firmness,—it has been owing to that system under which mere negative merit, when backed by seniority, has been considered to possess a *claim* to fill situations of responsibility and importance. Under this system, which has been common to the Horse Guards equally with the Indian Government, old and infirm officers have been appointed to commands, to discharge the duties of which they were physically incapable; in a revolt such men were helpless, hence the Dinapore affair, for which however the Government is the *real* party to blame. In Calcutta,—and one cannot record it but with a feeling of shame,—at the very time when firmness, courage, and a good example were most required, it is mentioned in letters as a positive fact, that on the night of the 9th of that month, now popularly called "fright night," one member at least of the Supreme Council sent his wife, for safety, on board a vessel in the river, while the Military Secretary to the Supreme Government took his, under a similar plea, into Fort William. The scene of panic that would necessarily ensue, when the principal officers of Government set such a wretched example, may well be imagined; the only wonder is, that the native population were not incited by it to rise in revolt and insurrection; and if, seeing the causeless panic, they had done so, to whom but to these men could we impute the loss of the capital? It may be said, that it is easy to condemn others for want of firmness,—that if ourselves so circumstanced we might equally fail. That is true, in a general way, but we are to recollect that these persons are paid extravagantly for the *efficient* performance of their duties. The Councillor, whose timidity—the Military Secretary, whose "moral courage" induced him, at all hazards, to secure the safety of his "better half," receive, the former £10,000, the latter about £5,000 per annum of the public money. Surely, for such sums we ought to be able to ensure, at least, the respectable discharge of the duties entrusted to them? I may make such observations with the more confidence, because I never myself, while in office, shrank from incurring responsibility. On one occasion, even in a time of peace, I thought it my duty to point out to the Commander-in-Chief the inability, from age and other causes, of no less than three Brigadiers to perform their duties efficiently, and they were removed in consequence of such report from the command of their respective districts. On another occasion, I recommended the summary removal of an officer from the command of a station, who had demurred to obey the orders of His Excellency. And yet, with all these examples, no one, it seems, could be found to incur the responsibility of removing or suspending, at a most critical time, the officer commanding the Dinapore Division, when it should have been clear to any ordinary capacity, that the most sad results must almost necessarily ensue from his reluctance to disarm the native regiments there. At such a time energy and earnestness at the seat of Government were imperatively called for; and that the disasters in the Dinapore Division are imputable to the want of these qualities in those in supreme authority in Calcutta there can be no sort of doubt.

CHAPTER III.

It has often been asked, What are the precise causes which have led to this detestable display of the worst passions of human nature? Has love of country, or religious zeal and bigotry, or mere detestation of a foreign yoke, incited the native army to this revolt? To this I would reply, that fifty causes have combined to generate suspicion and jealousy and a general inimical feeling; but love of country or patriotism have no place in the catalogue. Our unhappy countrymen have been, in my deliberate opinion, the victims chiefly of the supine, unstatesmanlike, and weak, shallow views and proceedings of our rulers. It is painful to animadvert on the acts of men we have known and personally liked; and in speaking of Lord Dalhousie's administration I have no wish to say one word in unnecessary disparagement; but the truth is, that the rule of this nobleman has been most unduly extolled and over-estimated. He was young and of high birth, and the *protégé* and personal favourite of the Duke of Wellington, and he brought with him to India a reputation for quickness and ability scarcely exaggerated; but he had not the genius of the Marquis Wellesley, and his admirers (for he had many in India) were simply mistaken when they supposed him to possess a mind so gifted.

This is not the place to enter upon a general review of his Lordship's policy and acts, but I may observe, that much was no doubt effected by him worthy of praise and commendation, although, as a whole, his conceptions appear to have been destitute of originality. His thirst for "annexation" became a positive disease, and he was clearly not alive to the utter insecurity of our position, and was content, apparently, to believe with the herd, that the danger was distant, and the ultimate struggle for supremacy not to be looked for in our day; he seems to have shared, in fact, in that common feeling of common minds, who either do not really foresee danger, or else want the courage to look it steadily and manfully in the face. The annexation of Oude was one of the last important acts of his Government; that is a well-vexed question, and one on which excellent reasons may be adduced on both sides. It has been said that this act was urged on Lord Dalhousie from home; however that may be, my own conviction is, that it was as ungenerous, as ill-timed, and *wanting in good faith*, as it is now proved in its result to have been impolitic; for no one, save a mere partisan, can now hesitate to believe that this act of annexation, more perhaps than any other single cause, gave scope and enlarged compass to the revolt now raging. That act cemented into one inimical whole the Mohamedan population of Upper India: after that act there was no further demur; prince and nobleman and peasant were all of one mind,—to compass, if possible, our entire overthrow and extirpation! And now let us inquire how, after this boasted bloodless annexation, the noble Lord proceeded in that business. True, his unexpected occupation of the country was bloodless, that of course necessarily followed; when there was no preparation against, or anticipation of danger, there would be no immediate struggle. A wise statesman would have seen this, and would, even if he thought himself secure for the time, have proceeded to render "assurance doubly sure." The reverse of this happened; to the already overwhelming native troops of India, his Lordship added other yet more dangerous additions, in the shape of Oude levies, and it nowhere appears that consequent on this occupation he added a single European soldier to our military establishment! The just equipoise so absolutely essential to maintain our supremacy was forgotten, or only so weakly enforced as to be either overlooked or indefinitely postponed! Further words on this subject were useless. The revolt, the mutiny, gradually and slowly commenced; how it was met it is sad and humiliating to detail. The Commander-in-Chief did nothing; European regiments near at hand in the Himalayas were *not* called to the plains, where their presence would have overawed the disaffected; not a European soldier was sent to secure the safety of our depôts and magazines; Delhi, Cawnpore, and Allahabad were unregarded; General Anson finally betook himself to Simla! The Government was nearly as supine; in the beginning, the grave nature of the impending struggle with the Sepoys was ignored, and most valuable time was lost. If in the beginning the unmistakable magnitude of the danger had been bravely faced, much might have been done, and the Government here at home must have acted with decision and promptitude. Troops would at once have been sent, and by the nearest route; and the blood of hundreds of brave men and helpless women and children would have been saved. But in reference to the conduct of the Bengal authorities, I shall content myself with extracting from the 'Historical Narrative' of the mutiny the description therein given of the capacity and proceedings of the Military Secretary to the "Supreme Government of India!"

"*Colonel Birch.*—The Secretary to the Government of India in the Military Department was a man in every way unsuited for his position. Placed early in his career in the department of the Judge-Advocate-General, his confined understanding was exerted in mastering the quirks and quibbles of the law. His intellect being essentially shallow, he was unable to take a broad view of any question; but he would argue for hours, and exhaust all his ingenuity in combating some petty detail When Sir Charles Napier assumed the command of the Indian Army, Colonel Birch was Judge-Advocate. He was rather afraid of Sir Charles's downright character, and at their first interview exerted all his powers to please him. No amount of special pleading, however, would go down with the great Conqueror of Scinde.

"Sir Charles's bad opinion was, however, of this service to Colonel Birch, that it obtained for him Lord Dalhousie's patronage. That nobleman, eager to show his spite towards Sir C. Napier, took the opportunity of the first vacancy, to appoint Colonel Birch Secretary to the Government of India in the Military Department; thus placing him, *de facto*, at the head of the army in India—giving him a position, indeed, exactly analogous to that of the Minister of War in France.

"A worse appointment could not have been made. Colonel Birch was essentially a sycophant, always ready to give up his own opinion, if by so doing he could curry favour with his superior. He had tried this plan with Sir C. Napier, but Sir Charles found him out, and not only felt, but showed, contempt towards him in consequence; he found it an easier task to ingratiate himself with Lord Dalhousie and his successor.

"But he was also an ignoramus. He knew nothing of the Bengal Army. Many years had elapsed since he had even spoken to a Sepoy. He was ignorant of the composition of the army, as well as of its wants; whilst his previous training had so unfitted him for his post, that he could not even write an order without making it unintelligible by excessive quibbling."

So much for this functionary's characteristics, but that is not all: "Mr. —— had one recommendation: if he was narrow-minded and unscrupulous, he was honest; he could not 'smile and smile and be a villain;' he spoke his thoughts freely and honestly, and people, whilst they hated, could not help respecting him,—a sentiment never entertained towards his colleague in the military department."

And the colleague spoken of was Colonel Birch!

Again, the following, we are told, were his acts; and his antecedents quite prepare one for the detail:—

"Yet, in the face of these prejudices, of the order to respect them, and of the danger of the consequences which must result from their violation, no sooner had the Government of India resolved to introduce the Enfield rifle partially into the Indian army, than the Secretary to Government deliberately issued an order which, by violating the caste of the Hindoo, was alone sufficient to bring about a revolt. The Enfield rifle required a particular species of cartridge, and this cartridge, in England, was greased with lard made from the fat either of the hog or the ox. Without reflecting, or, if reflecting, ignoring the consequences of his act, Colonel Birch ordered that the cartridges for use in India should be made up similarly to the cartridges in use in England, and should be used by the native troops; that is to say, that Hindoo Sepoys should handle cartridges besmeared with the fat of their sacred animal, the cow. The knowledge of this fact was conveyed to the Hindoos in the most casual manner. These cartridges had been made up by Lascars—men of an inferior caste. It happened that one day a Lascar requested a Brahmin Sepoy to give him a drink of water from his lotah, or brass pot. The Sepoy refused, on the plea of his superior caste, and that the lotah would be defiled by the touch of the Lascar. The Lascar in reply taunted him for talking of defilement, when he every day touched cartridges besmeared with cows' fat. The Hindoo, horror-stricken, rushed to his comrades and told them the story; they inquired, and found it was true to the letter. Indignant, believing themselves deceived by the Government, they wrote an account to their comrades throughout India From that moment the work of the agents of the King of Oude was easy.

"For a man occupying the position of Military Secretary to the Government of India to make so gross a blunder, was unpardonable. Equally so, that, when the mistake was discovered, no disavowal was made by Government for four months, and then only in consequence of the outbreak at Meerut! Well aware that the idea had taken possession of the Sepoys' minds, Colonel Birch made no attempt to counteract it, gave no intimation that the manufacture of greased cartridges had been stopped. He calmly surveyed the mischief his acts had caused, and did—nothing. Yet this man, whose blundering incapacity caused the revolt, is still Secretary to the Government of India in the Military Department!"

Ex uno disce omnes! might almost be said of the Calcutta officials acting in this sad and disastrous crisis, though in fairness some of the civil secretaries should be excepted, and perhaps General Low. The civilians were necessarily ignorant of just military considerations, as connected with the mutiny. And it would be unjust wholly to condemn Lord Canning; he, no doubt, has done his utmost; he had not been long enough in India to acquire reliable knowledge and information; he was dependent, therefore, on the judgment and counsels of those who surrounded him. That they were altogether unequal to the crisis, few will deny. It is true, that after the revolt was full-blown, troops were sent for to Ceylon, Pegue, China, and other places, but time had been sadly wasted, and when, as I have before remarked, officers of experience were writing to me from the very seat of Government that we had now "*only to fight for it*," the Government was busy in ignoring the magnitude of the revolt, and in endeavouring to induce the belief that the excitement and danger was subsiding!

Again, long after the whole country was everywhere in open revolt or commotion; when scarcely a regular regiment was left; when, to the shallowest intellect, all reliance on the Native Infantry was shown to be simple delusion, what was the conduct of the Government? At Dinapore, a station only two days' post from Calcutta, where an infatuated old General between seventy and seventy-five years of age commanded, three native regiments were suffered to retain their arms. The General is to be tried, we hear, by court-martial. To what end? He *had been* a brave and able officer, and had the Government done its duty, his career would probably have ended in honour as it began. To trust the safety of Bengal at such a time to the discretion of an old worn-out man, whose sympathies naturally were with the troops he had served with for half a century, was unwise to a degree. He ought to have been *ordered peremptorily* to disarm the native regiments; the Military Secretary to Government should so have counselled the Governor-General; and if General Lloyd had demurred or hesitated, instant supersession should have followed. But mere omission was not the only fault of the authorities. The Calcutta community saw the imminent danger, and petitioned Lord Canning to avert it, by disarming the Dinapore Brigade. Even this solicitation, it seems, was unattended to, for official incapacity does not readily give ear to even the wisest counsel. The result of this culpable inaction is well known to the British public, and but for the able conduct of that gallant officer, Major Vincent Eyre, of the Bengal Artillery, more fatal consequences would have ensued.

I now approach, and with reluctance, the case of the Court of Directors of the East India Company. I am a retired officer of the Company; one of my nearest relatives, the late Henry St. George Tucker, was an honoured and a most influential member of the Court for many years, and I feel every disposition to speak of them in terms of respect. Nevertheless, I am constrained to state broadly my opinion that the delegated rule of the Directors is no longer beneficial to the State; its day for usefulness has apparently passed away; it no longer commands any real authority; its influence, from whatever cause, is weak, and its component parts do not present to the public view those elements of strength and wisdom adequate to the government of a mighty empire. In India, it is no longer regarded with respect or deference; even its old traditionary virtues are ignored; and when a Government has once ceased to command the confidence of the governed, the sooner it is made to give way, the better for all concerned. The Court has struggled on of late years in a sort of hand-to-mouth existence; and there can be little doubt that its speedy dissolution will follow on the re-establishment of peace. This recent revolt must show clearly to the blindest vision the hollowness of that boasted system the Company and its Governors-General have so long pursued. The temerity of that system; its anomalies and inconsistencies; its weak milk-and-water philanthropy, through which the natives have lost all salutary fear and awe of us; its incapacity or disinclination to protect its European servants when arbitrarily ill-treated and injured by the Indian authorities, will all form the subject doubtless of prolonged and grave inquiry. I will only here suggest one cause of its failure, and point to a single instance in elucidation. It appears, then, that the Court of Directors is composed generally of men too old or too long absent from India to be able to work effectively in its government, and too pedantically wedded in many cases to old opinions and ideas, forgetful that India has moved onwards, and is no longer the precise India of twenty-five or thirty years since, when, for the most part, those gentlemen left the country. We have, for instance, a distinguished member of the Court writing in the 'Times,' that, but for the trials of certain disaffected troopers at Meerut, the Bengal Army might have remained the "loyal Bengal Army" still! How little this venerable senior can know of that army I write a distasteful truth, but I do it deliberately, and I say now no more than I have often said before the late revolt, in confidential communications to friends and others interested, namely, that the Bengal Army never really has been, any time the last thirty years, a trustworthy or loyal army; by which I mean that it never has been a reliable, obedient, well-disposed body. We in our blindness have been pleased to assume that it possessed all sorts of virtues; we have ignored and even fostered its vices, and allowed ourselves to be flattered as individuals into the belief that we had won its love and devoted adherence; but a more vain, a more idle and impotent delusion I am confident never existed. In this I know I shall be opposed by many, by many whom I greatly esteem; but I speak after thirty-two years' experience and observation, and I unhesitatingly affirm, that even mere personal attachment on the part of the Sepoys to their European superiors has been isolated and rare; that the singular cunning and duplicity of their character has not been fathomed by us as a nation; that in their guile and craft they have invariably befooled and laughed us to scorn; and that, dispassionately regarded, a more mercenary, huxtering, really inglorious body of men never before were banded together! These will no doubt be considered extreme opinions; I am persuaded, nevertheless, that they are thoroughly well founded. The Bengal Sepoys for many years have been simple mercenaries, without an attempt at disguise, greedy, covetous, and exacting; in the beginning these characteristics may have been less marked, but since the siege of Bhurtpore, in 1826, from about which period my more intimate acquaintance with them first commenced, the peculiarities I have described have undoubtedly attached to them in an unmistakable manner. I shall be told that these Sepoys have fought bravely. Certainly, led by their European officers, they have done so at times; but how often has their conduct been the very reverse! how often dastardly to the last degree—pale, trembling, sneaking out of the ranks on one pretence or another! Many of their European officers in time of war have regretted that it was their fate to be connected with such men. And recently, in a letter from a distinguished staff-officer serving before Delhi, this sentence occurs:—"I never saw the Sepoys fight *half* so well for us as they now do against us." The writer had seen them in all the actions of the Sutledge and Punjaub campaigns. Will the present speak in proof? What, with their overwhelming numbers, and perfectly armed and disciplined, have they done? Except to murder their too trusting and confiding officers, and defenceless women and children, what have they done worthy of the struggle for supremacy they sought to maintain? No! these boasted mercenaries, however at times useful in upholding our dominion in the East, never were loyal, in the proper acceptation of that term; grasping self-interest has been all along their sole motive and consideration; they were thoroughly and entirely mercenary; and when they had become accustomed to consider themselves irresistible in numbers and discipline, they were ready at once to adopt any plea, such as that of the greased cartridges, for entering on that career of revolt and mutiny which, as they vainly hoped, would transfer to their own ranks and order the power and authority so supinely and unsuspiciously wielded by interloping foreigners. I maintain that for many years the Sepoy army was at heart disloyal to its very core, and all that was wanting to produce the blaze of mutiny we have witnessed, was just such a handle and opportunity as was so loosely and culpably offered to them. I cite the late Sir Charles Napier in corroboration of this opinion. He declared, on the occasion of his disbanding the 66th Native Infantry, in 1849–50, that no less than 40,000 Sepoys in the Punjaub were prepared to mutiny! Such was, we may now well believe, in reality the fact; and if the fortress of Govindghur had been seized by that regiment as attempted, the fearful revolt of 1857 would probably have been anticipated! But what did the Court of Directors know of this state of feeling? There was not a Bengal military officer a member of that body, to enjoin caution or inquiry, and all danger was denied and disallowed by the highest Indian authority in that famous controversy since made public. Sir Charles Napier was permitted to resign his office of Commander-in-Chief in India, and the unreflecting there and at home naturally followed in the belief which most administered to their own ease and quiet and to the gratification of their immediate superiors; so the dark cloud was suffered to grow and increase in density, hovering onwards till it broke in that overwhelming outpour which had so nearly uprooted us in our foundations. Whatever some of us in India might think and fear, there was clearly nothing to be said; all intimation of danger was authoritatively derided, and it requires more self-reliance than most men possess to persist in an opinion condemned and ridiculed by *all* around.

The 'Times' newspaper has said that those who accuse the Indian authorities of inertness and want of vigour, in not suppressing the revolt when it first appeared, and who say also that it was premeditated, and the result of previous conspiracy, are convicted of inconsistency in so speaking. The 'Times' is a great and weighty authority, and it is with deference I take leave to differ, and to state my opinion that this is only a *seeming contradiction.* For may not a conspiracy be crushed and overcome? And if at Meerut short, sharp, and decisive action had, on the massacre of their European officers, flooded the native lines with the blood of those miscreants, what more probable than that the outbreak would have been suppressed? Whereas impunity lent it strength. At Delhi there was nothing to oppose to it; no foresight had been exercised, no judicious arrangements made, no one single precaution appears indeed to have been taken by General Anson, whose practical inexperience and incapacity can never be effaced by that "charm of manner and demeanour" his friends dwell upon, and of which I am equally sensible; but until the flame had burst forth he did not move his European battalions from the hills to the plains, where their presence would have overawed the Sepoys, or put down forcibly their revolt; he neglected to secure with European troops our depôts and magazines; he did not organize a strong column for rapid movement in whatever direction the flame might break forth; he did not enjoin caution and vigilance on that incapable officer, General Hewitt; no commissariat carriage was made immediately available; in short, nothing was done in way of wise prevention, and so the flame burst forth in all its appalling intensity! That sooner or later our own fatal security, the Pretorian insolence of the Sepoys, and that Mohamedan intrigue and virulent hatred which has formed so principal an ingredient in the revolt, would assuredly have produced a similar result, few, I should imagine, will be prepared to doubt. From henceforth our rule will be stronger and sterner, and our hold upon the country much firmer, I trust, than it has ever yet been: it depends upon ourselves to render it so. And we need have no dread of missionary labours—these never have done the least harm. It has been our late greedy and grasping policy; our mismanagement of the Sepoys; our neglect to secure real power; our recent financial blunders, amounting, in appearance at least, to positive fraud; and, generally, the *too rapid* introduction, recently, of general schemes of education and changes in Hindoo laws and customs, which it would have been far wiser for a time to have postponed. These, at least, are my convictions.

I beg now to offer a few brief, general observations, such as in my judgment will be found most conducive to the future permanency and strength of our dominion in the East.

1. The abolition of the Court of Directors; and in substitution, a Secretary of State for India, with a staff of efficient under-secretaries in the various departments, civil, military, and political.

2. The entire abandonment of the narrow and exclusive system in the Indian Civil Service; men best qualified should be appointed, and open competition the test.

3. An entire reconstruction of the military system; no officer to be appointed a cadet before the age of seventeen or eighteen, and all to be required to pass through a military college, whether intended for the Line or for the Engineers and Artillery.

4. No natives to be enlisted who are Bramins, or who will not engage for general service anywhere; and the recruiting districts to be carefully laid down.

5. No officers to be taken from regiments for any merely civil situations, but only for military staff employ, in the strict sense of the term, and after undergoing an examination as to acquirements and aptitude for the particular department for which it is proposed to withdraw them.

6. A knowledge of the native languages to be a *sine quâ non* before any promotion or advancement can be allowed.

7. A strong, stern, but just system of government to be introduced, so that the same shall be viewed with awe and respect by the natives.

8. Europeans should not be subject to trial before natives; and the least outrage on any European, however humble his station, should be punished with severity.

9 The utter futility of the existing native pension establishment having been fully proved, should be carefully revised; and the forfeiture of all present pensions having been justly incurred by the revolt or apathy and tacit hostility of the pensioners, their stipends should be at once swept away, except in very special cases.

10. The natives of India within the British territories should be carefully disarmed, and watchfully kept so.

11. Respect for all Europeans, and for Her Majesty's Government, should be firmly and *persistently* enforced.

12. The native press in India should be kept under a strict censorship. It has been disseminating treason and sedition for years; and the recent classing of the European and native press together, was alike unjust and impolitic, robbing the State, at a critical period, of the zealous services of the former.

13. The discontinuance of the practice of bestowing upon Governors-General pensions of £5000 per annum. That system is of the "springes to catch woodcock" order; and but for the desire it has generated to conciliate the Court of Directors, a more just,

equitable, and generous policy would often have been pursued, while the community, native and European, might possibly not have been outraged by the recent five-per-cent. "swindle," whereby the credit of the Government has been injured, and our good faith called in question. A clear £30,000 a year, with all travelling and many other expenses paid besides, ought to be considered sufficient remuneration for any services.

14. The "blue-veined" aristocratic element should be more guardedly employed in responsible situations in the East. Mere men about town, however "charming in demeanour," should not be placed in command of the army; and known incapables should not be sent out as divisional commanders, merely to fill their empty pockets, or *to get rid of their importunities here.*

15. The military element in India, instead of being degraded socially, as hitherto, should be raised; a new and more just order of precedence should be introduced; and grey-headed officers should no longer be made to give place to boys in the civil service, whose chief merit often consists only in their very near affinity to the Directors in Leadenhall-street.

16. The native police employed in Bengal is now proved to be, as was generally suspected, utterly worthless; it should be carefully remodelled, and an effective and reliable intelligence department should be organized.

17. Battalions of Africans might with advantage be organized; there are many special duties in which they might with great advantage be employed, exposure to which would be injurious to the health of European troops—to aid, for instance, in garrisoning Fort William, and our various magazines, forts, and depôts.

18. The fortifications and public buildings at Delhi, Agra, and Lucknow, ought *not* to be destroyed; these may all be of great advantage to us in the future. At Delhi, the "Jumma Musjid," a commanding and excellent position, might be occupied for other than religious purposes, and all Mohamedan and Hindoo processions within the walls of that city may be strictly interdicted; a rule which, if strictly enforced, will sufficiently mark our re-assumption of power and authority.

19. A body of *efficient* light cavalry ought to be raised. An Inspector of Cavalry should be added to the establishment; the unwise parsimony which would not hitherto grant one has been, as foretold, productive of the worst results.

20. The enormous salaries of the Governors-General, Members of Council, and other high civil and military functionaries, should be

greatly reduced; and the "savings to the State" made by parsimonious clippings from the under-paid captains and subalterns of the army, and clerks and others in the uncovenanted service, should be abandoned. One uniform rate of pay should be given to officers everywhere; and finally, the long-standing absurdity of the half-batta system should be abolished.

CHAPTER IV.

In reference to the very inimical feeling with which the Mohamedan population, in my opinion, regard us, as recorded in the beginning of this Pamphlet, I wish to state that my observation on this point is confined to Bengal chiefly. It may possibly be otherwise in the Madras and Bombay Presidencies, and the feeling may be moderated in remote districts in Bengal; but I am confident, from personal observation, that at Delhi in particular, and in all our large Mussulman cities and bazaars, rooted dislike of us, as Christians and Europeans, is the invariable rule. Officers of the Army see much more of this than the civilians, because these last are in authority, and that with the Oriental generates more lip-service to an unbounded extent. With the military it is far otherwise; and no man of common observation could well ride through the streets of Delhi, or any large city or bazaar, without being struck with the malignant, fierce expression of countenance with which, on meeting their glances, one is so frequently regarded. The civilian on such occasions rides out with Sowars (armed horsemen) in attendance; and it is with bated breath and seeming respect and humility that these attributes of office cause him to be observed; but the whispered curse and smile of derision, which follow after, are as invariably a part of the performance. I was, as a young man, for three years in garrison at Delhi, and I know the place and its inhabitants well, and have often and often had occasion to marvel at their astonishing duplicity, effrontery, and low cunning,—characteristics common to the great mass of Mohamedans of the cities of Upper India, who, as a body, are as grossly ignorant, morally depraved, and fanatical as it is possible to imagine. I speak of *the mass;* for undoubtedly there are highly-respectable and upright men of this persuasion, but they are few and far between, and even these are fanatical to an uncommon degree. It may easily be imagined how injurious, with such people, has been our easy, unsuspicious, milk-and-water system. It has made them despise as well as dislike us; and the result we witness, in the fearful outrages and almost universal revolt of this class of our subjects, whenever there has appeared a chance of success against us. I think therefore that the greatest caution should be exercised in enlisting Mussulmans of the Upper Provinces. When, after the Sutledge campaign, so many Irregular cavalry regiments were raised, it was a common remark about Delhi, Meerut, and Seharumpore, that the effect had been to remove all the lowest scamps and vagabonds of the vicinity, who, in the zeal felt by officers to complete their corps, were far too easily entertained, without reference to character or connection. Fisher's Horse was thus unhappily organized, and its treacherous mutiny has cost us the lives of some of our best officers. For the future, or at least for some time to come, we should not, in my opinion, recruit in the Oude or Delhi territory, or in Rohilkund; the Punjaub and Cis-Sutledge states, together with our Hill Districts, will afford us a sufficient and much better field, and for this purpose the less we have to do with the disaffected districts the better.

Grave misapprehension has existed even in India as to the strength of Delhi and its means of defence. I have many correspondents now serving before those walls, and some details which I am confident may be relied upon, will be highly interesting at this anxious period. On reaching Delhi, General Barnard's force had to oppose a garrison consisting of the 11th, 20th, 38th, 54th, 74th Regiments of Native Infantry, the Hurrianah Light Infantry, portions of the 9th, 44th, and 67th and 5th Native Infantry, the majority of the 45th also, and 300 of the Sappers and Miners; of cavalry, a wing of the 4th Irregulars, the whole of the 3rd Light Cavalry, and detachments of the Oude and Gwalior regiments. In addition to these, it is known that the mutineers had a vast number of men who had gone on furlough to their homes. Of artillery, they had Captain De Teissier's battery complete, and four batteries of guns which were ready for issue from the magazine. From whence they obtained their artillery-men it is not difficult to guess; I have already explained that 100 per cent. of the infantry had been trained, under the auspices of Government, to the use of ordnance. The King of Delhi, moreover, had some artillery-men of his own, and there was a company of old pensioned artillery-men at the place.

That they had great numbers, and well-trained, there has been plenty of proof in the way they have served their guns, both from the batteries on the bastions and in the field; in fact their artillery has been the chief difficulty. In the Delhi magazine they found 114 pieces of heavy ordnance, with ammunition and stores in immense quantities; take for example the following items: 24-pounder round shot, no less than 37,700; of 18-pounders, 33,300; of 8-inch shells, 18,900; of powder, upwards of 14,000 barrels: these will show their means of defence. Besides this the enemy was joined by all the Customs' patrols, Burkundauze, and police, than whom no class of men are stated to have committed greater horrors and atrocities. All these trained men, added to the immense population of fanatical Mussulmans in and around Delhi, constitute a force and a power not to be treated contemptuously or encountered carelessly. It must be borne in mind, too, that the walls of Delhi are of considerable strength; there is a deep ditch also, and the place is at least seven miles in circumference; and as to cutting them off from communication with the Jumna and so investing the place, the idea is simply ridiculous, not to say preposterous. With 4,500 bayonets, of which the force originally consisted, that was not to be done, and on the whole the delay in storming the place has doubtless told to our advantage. One side of the city, which takes in the palace and the interior defences of Selimgurh, is washed by the Jumna, the bridge of boats across which we had been unable in the beginning to destroy, although the rise of the river must, when the rains commenced in full flood, have probably done that work for us, and thus one means of escape will, it is to be hoped, have been destroyed. Prematurely to have made the assault might have been eminently disastrous, and failure would have imperilled our authority throughout India. When the last letters left the Camp, on the 25th of August, the siege-train was within ten days' march; and we may, in my opinion, expect confidently to hear that by the 15th of September at latest the city was in our possession. Major-General Wilson is an officer of great ability and judgment, and every confidence may be reposed in him. With the re-occupation of Delhi, the revolt *in our old possessions in the Upper Provinces* will cease, and we shall have simply to resume our control and authority; with Oude it will probably be found more difficult to deal.

And now, before committing these brief pages to the press, I cannot do better than record my humble testimony in favour of the English in India,—of those men who are now so heroically fighting for their country's honour and supremacy, and with whom I can only wish that it was my good fortune to be serving at such a crisis. It may be all very well for those who, in the pursuit of mammon or notoriety, indite exaggerated stories in novels, or for those who desire to shine at the expense of their comrades, to indulge in the ideal description of imputed laxity and immorality in India. The fact is otherwise; simply I may affirm that *it is not so*, and for this sufficient reason, that there are neither means nor appliances available to the European officer for indulgence in vice. We all know what sort of conduct may be "sugared over" in London or Paris, but nowhere in India is the European able thus to pass unnoticed and unknown; the result is, that living openly, and as it were in the face of the community, vice is the marked exception, and decorum and decency are the natural and usual results of our position. The English public at large will not think the worse of Indian officers for being free comparatively from the *pretence* and *affectation* of superior virtue and goodness. My own experience leads me to the broad conclusion, that nowhere are men brought up to be bolder, and more free from all the subservient vices; more honest, sincere, and trustworthy, than they are in India. Our class, by which I mean the middle class, is well represented; there, no one need blush for them; and I will venture to predict that, when the causes of these tragical mutinies come to be hereafter sifted and ascertained, it will be found, that in no one instance were men incited to join in them by indignation or disgust at European vice or immorality. No! lust of dominion and of mammon, lured on these brigands to their fate. It may sound inflated, but theirs has been a struggle for empire; they have sought to "push us from our stools" and to rule in our place; they are now fatally undeceived. Their unexpected battalions burst irresistibly upon our defenceless out-posts, but their superiority has been short-lived; and it is to be hoped, that no puling miserable weakness will be suffered to interfere with the stern, just retribution which is due to the memory and fate of our slaughtered countrymen. If the Calcutta Government is too weak to deal with the mutineers and murderers, who have outraged human nature in the infamous atrocities they have perpetrated on our women and children; if, as reported, meekness, tenderness, and lenity are now being enjoined, by the Indian Government, on those who have endeavoured manfully to uphold our supremacy; if, as stated, the civilians who, at Patna and Monghir, acted with courage, promptitude, and decision, have been removed from their appointments under the displeasure of their rulers, a Royal Commission, to examine into and condemn the guilty who have taken part in this infamous revolt, should be at once sent out to India, and should be composed of men who know how to uphold the honour of our country, protect and avenge the innocent, and to punish the guilty. If a man escapes of those who have outraged humanity, in this fearful revolt, we shall ill have performed our part or our duty to those who have fallen.

In conclusion, I am aware that I shall be blamed by some for so openly expressing my opinion of the incapacity of the Indian Government, and of some of its more prominent subordinates; I shall be blamed for speaking as I have done of the Sepoys, for the delusion connected with these men is yet strong upon many; I shall be blamed, possibly, for presuming to censure some of the acts of the Marquis of Dalhousie. To all this I have but one simple reply, namely, that under ordinary circumstances I should have held my peace, for I have no further connection with public business, or desire to re-engage in it; but I consider that this, if ever there was one, is a time to speak out, and to make known boldly the truth and facts to the best of my knowledge and ability. In the inquiries which I presume will follow on the re-establishment of peace, it is desirable that the conduct of those who govern India should be rightly understood and thoroughly sifted; if it be then found that I have "set down aught in malice," I am content to abide the condemnation of my fellows. I need make no further apology for the open expression of my opinions; and I will only add, that the details I have given in connection with our position before Delhi have been added since the arrival of the Mail from thence of the 25th of August, and since the first part of the MS. was placed in the printer's hands.

Newport House, near Exeter,

October 16th, 1857.